Nine Steps to Well-Being

A Spiritual Guide for
Disconnected Christians and
Other Questioning Journeyers

WHISPERING TREE

Nine Steps to Well-Being

A Spiritual Guide for Disconnected Christians and Other Questioning Journeyers

Steven R. Smith

WHISPERING TREE

© Copyright Steven R. Smith 2014

NINE STEPS TO WELL-BEING

All rights reserved.

The right of Steven R. Smith to be identified as the author of this work has been asserted in accordance the Copyright, Designs and Patents Act 1988. No part of this publication may be reproduced, stored in a retrieval system, or transmitted, in any form or by any means, electronic, mechanical, photocopying, recording or otherwise, nor translated into a machine language, without the written permission of the publisher.

Condition of sale
This book is sold subject to the condition that it shall not, by way of trade or otherwise, be lent, re-sold, hired out or otherwise circulated in any form of binding or cover other than that in which it is published and without a similar condition including this condition being imposed on the subsequent purchaser.

Unless otherwise, marked scripture quotations are taken from the
HOLY BIBLE, NEWS INTERNATIONAL VERSION.
Copyright © 1973, 1978, 1984 by Hodder and Stoughton
Used by permission of the copyright owner
All rights reserved

Whispering Tree Original Books
http://www.whisperingtreeoriginalbooks.com

ISBN: 978-0-9927363-0-9

Printed in the United Kingdom
Book Design: M^2 Media Marek Mularczyk - Soul Travel Lodge

Contents

Preface		i
Chapter One	Conversion	1
Chapter Two	Faith	16
Chapter Three	Christ	28
Chapter Four	Prayer	42
Chapter Five	Forgiveness	55
Chapter Six	Scripture	70
Chapter Seven	Church	85
Chapter Eight	Growth	98
Chapter Nine	Victory	120
Acknowledgements		133

'It's not often you read something that is so honest and disarming as to make enjoyable the very necessary exercise of periodically subjecting fondly held Christian ideas to critical scrutiny. Professor Smith manages to make you laugh while also engaging both your interest and critical faculties – and in a way that breathes some much appreciated new life into the tried and tested good news of the Christian gospel, faith, and Kingdom of God.'
Reverend Canon Dr Ian Davies,
Director of Ministry, Diocese of Swansea & Brecon (Church in Wales).

'This is a seriously good book! Anyone, from the fresh-faced explorer to the weather-beaten Christian, will find inspiration in these pages. The reader gets to benefit from decades of Professor Smith's experience, reflection and learning. He draws on the often intensely personal to take us through key aspects of the Christian faith, skillfully demonstrating why, after two millennia, the gospel of Jesus is still alive and kicking. Both personally and professionally, this book is a winner!'
Reverend Ruth A. Bierbaum,
Mental Healthcare Chaplain, Kent Health Authority.

'This book captures the *zeitgeist* and speaks to our times. By its observation, intuition and deep and honest reflection it has arrived at a place where many "post-evangelicals" or emerging Christians are arriving, but is shared in a unique and original way. The book grows and develops very organically, with a mix of personal stories and insightful theological reflection. Professor Smith explores his faith with honesty and has the courage to address difficult issues. There are many parts of the book that touched me deeply, intrigued me and made me laugh, such as the swearing prayer in France – this being a "modern parable" in its own right. It is also well edited and accessible.'

Reverend Ernesto Lozada-Uzuriaga Steele,
Minister of the Church of Christ The Cornerstone,
Milton Keynes.

For Lyn, Georgia and Luke,
and to the memory of Monty

'Arise, my darling, my beautiful one, and come with me.
See! The winter is past; the rains are over and gone.
Flowers appear on the earth; the season of singing has come,
the cooing of doves is heard in our land.
The fig-tree forms its early fruit; the blossoming vines spread
their fragrance.
Arise, come, my darling, my beautiful one, come with me.'
(Song of Songs, 2:10-13).

Preface

Overall, my Christian life has been shaped by a sense of wonder at the mysteriousness of God's work and it has been transformed by the radical and far-reaching message and power of love, joy, and forgiveness in Jesus Christ's life, teaching, death, and resurrection. However, I have also been very affected by that part of me which feels disconnected from the church in its numerous denominational guises. What I mean is that, despite being continually called back to the life of the church and its people, I have often found it difficult to benefit from and be comfortable with its culture and social habits – its rituals, norms, and even its values. This is not to say that the church has not had a lot to offer many people, including myself; it has frequently challenged and opposed various forms of social oppression and exploitation; and it has a long history of finding expression for personal spiritual struggles and growth which has been deeply instructive and inspirational for countless people over many generations. But the church also has a much darker history; of supporting and perpetuating oppressive and exploitative practices and of stifling the spiritually of its members. Consequently, as a Christian, I have often been more comfortable with my life in the world beyond the church, and what this life has to offer in its variety and richness – including the many significant people I have known, loved, respected, learnt from and cherished, who would certainly not describe themselves as Christians.

However, it is also important to acknowledge that the source of this disconnection I describe is not, for me, straightforward. It is derived primarily from a restlessness within me which continually asks questions about who I am as a Christian, *and* the wider world I inhabit. So, although I enjoy the world beyond the church and have learnt so much of what it and its inhabitants have to offer, whether trivial or profound, I also know that this world is not enough. Indeed, at its worst, it can be small-minded, cruel, and hostile to the message of love and forgiveness promised in Christ. Therefore, I experience a personal struggle; while being a church member can make me feel not quite myself, as I commune with other Christians and live out the culture expected of us, I have also been caught up by an all-powerful and all-loving force that frequently seems nonsensical to the world I live in. I have embraced this struggle for sure, seeing it as a part of the disconnection which is integral to my growth in God's love, but it has created a tension in me as I also hanker after God's promises of belonging, peace and stillness which most of us, I guess, yearn for and seek.

Given this disconnection the book is, in part, a confession; namely, of my continual questioning, restlessness and inability to fully belong in the church and the wider world, so making me feel as if I am on the outside, looking in. I have therefore set-out to explore issues which will resonate with people who may often feel similar; but those who, like me, may attend church regularly and have been active participators within it.

Some Christians – for example, 'post-evangelicals' from

PREFACE

what has been called 'the emergent' or 'emerging' church movement – would recognise, and even strongly identify with the disconnection I describe, as reflecting our postmodern era. Briefly, the postmodernist claim is that previous certainties and answers – whether related to reason, science, morality, religion, or 'progress' – have been fundamentally questioned in our time. The resulting postmodern uncertainty is therefore the source of disconnection referred to here, and is expressed in numerous forms of contemporary culture, art, music, literature, philosophy, personal life-histories, and so on. According to the emergent church movement, the central task of the church and individual Christians is to meet this uncertainty and disconnection head-on as a new and contemporary postmodern phenomenon; this requires us to engage with Jesus Christ and the world, often in radically different ways to those that have been practised in the past.

Clearly, I have sympathies with this movement for reasons I have begun to outline here and which I will explore throughout the book. I am also strongly motivated to translate what God has to offer us in the here-and-now, so that this offering can be understood and accepted anew by our generation. However, I believe the premise that the disconnection referred to is peculiar to the postmodern era is incorrect and which, if committed to, risks skewing our present-day approaches and attitudes to both the church and the wider world. I assert that *every* generation has experienced this disconnection, as I have called it – albeit in different social, cultural, religious and non-religious contexts. For sure, many deny this disconnection exists and spend time attending to numerous distractions from it. So, it is, indeed, the central task of the church to help us face it and deal with it in ways which relate to us all, in the here-and-now. However, understanding the disconnection as a new, never-experienced-before postmodern phenomenon, for me, misrepresents the issue. By assuming that 'now' is very different to 'then', we risk throwing the baby out with the bath water, as the past (whether related to religious or secular culture) is mistakenly seen as irrelevant to our contemporary disconnected experiences.

My alternative starting point is that the disconnection, which I describe in a Christian context, is widely reflected in the human condition. I believe the experience of disconnection has *always* been with us – in the pre-modern, modern and postmodern eras – as many have critically examined the world and our lives in it, and then have asked these searching questions. Therefore, the postmodern premise of questioning certainties and answers runs much deeper within the human condition than is suggested by postmodern proponents. Moreover, it is a premise which is a central part of our journeying with God, and the love, liberation, joy and peace he has promised for us, as a result of wrestling with *him* during this process.

Therefore, despite the implicit reference to 'answers' in the title of the book and the steps that might be taken to well-being (or liberation, joy, and peace), I have, in the end, no complete or once-and-for-all answers to this disconnection. Instead, this questioning state, as the origin of disconnection, reflects who we are as journeying human beings. But if you, as a Christian, recognise the same experience – whatever movement, denomination or tradition you associate with – you will at least be able to identify with my struggle and restlessness as yours. You will also, hopefully, learn a little from my account of the steps to well-being made in this book, if only that you are not alone in trying to take them. My main

PREFACE

recommendation is that there must be a tension held between, on the one hand, questioning and disconnection and, on the other, believing and resting in the promise of God's belonging, peace and stillness. Maintaining this tension, with the ultimate goal of more fully accepting God's love and joy in your life, is essential, I contend, when taking the nine steps to well-being explored here.

The steps themselves are unsurprising; the chapters follow conventional themes in Christian meditation – conversion, faith, Christ, prayer, forgiveness, scripture, church, growth, and victory. However, through telling some of my own stories – mostly, but not exclusively, as a young Christian taking my first steps – these themes are also intended to capture the mystery and wonder of our many struggles with trying to apprehend and trust an all-powerful, loving God and the rewards of engaging with a God who became one of us in Christ Jesus. I firmly believe that only because of the incarnation – God made one of us – can God address our experience of disconnection directly and wholly empathically, demonstrating his love for us by stepping into our history and living in a particular time and place.

Indeed, his last searching question while dying on the cross is, in many ways, the most fundamental expression of disconnection. Being directed at God his father, Jesus shouts out his most dreadful question, as reported in Matthew 27:46: 'My God, my God, why have you forsaken me?' The Son of Man, as Jesus called himself, was, it could be said, the son of disconnection – feeling abandoned by God in this moment, as well as, paradoxically, being the son of God. We, living in and through this paradox too, are, by God's grace and love, able to share this title as Christ's siblings. That is, based on the forgiveness offered us by Christ's sacrifice and resurrection, we are able to also journey with him and experience his love and promise of joy and well-being first-hand. He lives in us and accompanies us *through* our disconnected lives.

Finally, if the disconnection of which I speak is derived from a more general human sense of displacement and restlessness – between our place in the church and the wider world, and what is promised by an all-powerful, loving God as an alternative – then, hopefully, the themes explored here will resonate with many, whether Christian or not. To this end, the book, although primarily targeting the Christian community (the church), it can hopefully cast its net more widely – namely, to those who recognise this disconnection, and are also committed to asking questions in their search for and journeying towards well-being, liberation, joy, peace, and love.

Chapter One
Conversion

I am sharing an account of my own conversion, not because I think it is special, but because it is mine. It is the only one I know fully and so, for me, is the best one to tell. I will certainly leave a lot out; personal accounts of significant events, however truthful, are always drastically edited. So, I would have needed much more than a small book, let alone a chapter of a small book, to tell my entire conversion story. The task, though, in telling some of my story is to have enough to explain the wider points I want to make about the experience of conversion in general and about my conversion to Christianity in particular.

I was like the blind man in Mark 8:22-25, who needed two healing events before he could see properly; my conversion was dramatic and happened in two stages. This is not to say that these stages were all there was to it. As will be explored towards the end of this chapter, it is important that conversion should be viewed as on-going and permanent; it is never a once-off event – or twice-off, in my case. However, dramatic aspects of conversion often are, by their nature, very revealing and for this reason, I think are worth exploring.

The first most dramatic stage of my conversion happened

when I was nearly nineteen and I was with friends, listening to an album created by Frank Zappa (and his band 'The mothers of invention'), called, *We are only in it for the money*. Bizarre as this might seem, there are a few lines in one of the songs which incredibly, suddenly and overwhelmingly, made me see the world differently. In their deliberately simple expression, they promise something radically different to the world as it is by suggesting that living a life of love and generosity of spirit which does not judge or condemn, is the only real response *to* our lives. The lines go:

> There will come a time when everybody
> who is lonely will be free
> to sing and dance and love.
> There will come a time when every evil
> that we know will be an evil that we can rise above.
>
> Who cares if hair is long or short or sprayed or partly grayed, we know that hair ain't where it's at.
> There will come a time when you won't even be ashamed if you are fat!

Of course, the words of the song, heard with a poetic ear, are naive and even crass, but for me (and I am sure for Frank Zappa and his band), this is precisely their charm and power. The childlikeness of the rhyme and the message of the words disarm a supposedly more profound understanding of the world by expressing the very simple yearning we all have for unconditional love and liberation. One of the friends with whom I was listening to the song was very over-weight. I knew he'd endured years of being teased at school and consequently had very low self-esteem, which inevitably meant that he could do nothing about his weight-problem. When the song ended, I glanced at him and it was as though my head had been suddenly swung around so that I could see the world completely differently from the way I had seen it before.

First, I saw afresh the importance and immovable characteristic of reaching out to others and being held by others in love and, more especially, in our pain and vulnerability. Second, this kind of love is the basis for experiencing a joyful and free life. Third, and most surprisingly to me at the time, I saw that this was also the message of Jesus Christ. Up until then, I had more or less rejected his message; this was my response to my earlier experiences of what, to me, were boring and irrelevant Sunday school lessons and what I believed were the fairy tales of Jesus' birth, life, death and resurrection I had heard during church services, school religious assemblies, and the like.

But, what were to me, the worn-out Christian moral recommendations which I had listened to repeatedly through my childhood – love your neighbour, love your enemies, do to others what you would have them do to you, do not judge others, do good to those who harm you, and so on – in this moment of conversion, were no longer devoid of meaning or relevance. Instead, remarkably to me, they were alive and meaningful and, indeed, *more* alive and meaningful than anything I had known or felt before. After this experience, I spent the whole of that first night awake, unable to switch off what was, to me, this startling revelation. More or less the only thing I could say to my baffled friends at the time was, 'I think I have seen the light!' Probably none of them would have described themselves as Christians or even as religious. Like me, they would likely have considered the Christian message they had heard at school and in other contexts, to be irrelevant fairy tales. So for me to have 'seen the light' would have sounded ridiculous to many of them and, for some, even evidence – without exaggeration – that I had probably gone mad.

The second stage of my conversion came about three or four weeks after the first and, although not quite as intense, was at least as important because it established my connection, not just with the message of Jesus Christ, but with Jesus himself and what he did for me, and us all, on the cross. I had just finished watching the harrowing, but deeply thoughtful film, *Apocalypse Now*, which was directed and produced by Francis Ford Coppola and was loosely based on Joseph Conrad's novel, *Heart of Darkness*. The film explores, via the US intervention in Vietnam, the very dark side of human nature and how humans are capable of all kinds of appalling deceits, hypocrisies and cruelties.

One of the main themes of the film is that these kinds of actions are not confined to 'monsters' but are to be found in the nature of people like you and me. Consequently, we cannot judge or condemn those who are brutally cruel but only recognise these qualities, albeit often in less significant forms, in ourselves. They derive from our shared 'hearts of darkness', however much these motivations might be buried, petty, or shrouded in self-deception. Bleak stuff for sure, but after watching the film, I was again struck by what seemed to me to be a clear insight – that for all this talk and promise of love and the importance of responding to others' pain and vulnerability, we so often think and behave in ways which fall drastically short of these aspirations.

CONVERSION

In other words, despite what we are told in the Beatles' song, love is not all we need if this means trusting in our own capabilities of exercising love, as this trust assumes an unflawed human nature that has not been corrupted. Certainly, humans are capable of amazing sacrificial acts, even for strangers, but as I saw it then (and still see it) we are also capable, of being either spectacularly cruel, or mundanely hurtful to others. Our personal and social histories testify to this and we would do well to own up to it. Consequently, the film made me realise that, as well as Jesus Christ's message of love, I also needed forgiveness. Moreover, I started to see that somehow – although I wasn't sure exactly how – this forgiveness was promised through Jesus Christ's death on the cross. Also, I needed God's help in overcoming my weaknesses, promised in Jesus Christ's resurrection. When I came out with this revelation to my friends, many of them no doubt would have concluded that I had *definitely* gone mad!

However, to backtrack a little and in their defence, any reporting of my 'madness' would not have been so surprising to those of my friends who were used to my wilder speculations concerning the world and our understanding of it. For most of my adolescence – to some extent encouraged by discussions with my father – I had been struggling with two disarmingly simple questions which seemed to have no clear answers: 'What is truth?' and 'How can it be verified?' I have since discovered that these questions, and similar ones beside, are a central part of traditional philosophical enquiry, and have troubled many over the years. However, at the time, my father and I were unaware that others, especially philosophers, had posed and pondered these questions too, and had even written countless books trying to address them.

In any event, I was very disturbed by the notion that 'truth' was elusive and the search for it uncertain; and this had been increasingly affecting my life.

About six months prior to my conversion experience, I was travelling in Spain with a group of friends after we had spent about six or seven weeks working on the vineyards in France picking grapes. We were mainly travelling through the south of Spain, moving from place to place, spending the money we had earned, taking in the sights, relaxing, reading, drinking beer and smoking dope when we could get hold of it. However, although I enjoyed this experience (I have never had *that* much of a problem enjoying life), I was also becoming increasingly affected – assisted by the dope-smoking no doubt – by the profound sense of uncertainty concerning the nature of truth and reality. So much so, that my friends – and especially my best friend, Monty – were becoming worried about my state of mind. After a particularly intense period which included, albeit very briefly and not all that seriously, my contemplating suicide, I left our apartment and walked to the end of a promenade overlooking the sea. Mentally and emotionally exhausted, I just lay down on an empty plinth and, looking up to the night sky, shouted, 'Help!', over and over. I didn't know who I was shouting to or what I was shouting at, and I wasn't thinking of God particularly, but I felt a need to shout it, regardless. What I did know was that I had had enough of the state I was in and that things needed to change radically.

Looking back, this cry, I believe, was my first heartfelt prayer. Although at the time it did not feel as though God had responded, what happened six months later revealed a response from him which was overwhelmingly real and utterly life-changing. In retrospect then, he heard my cry for

CONVERSION

help – as he does with all such pleas – and reached out to me. In my desperate state, I recognised that I had nothing to offer; only a shout for help. I believe that without realising it, in that moment I was effectively asking God and Christ into my life. This request God honoured, leading me to places of joy, hope and love I could never have anticipated.

It is also important to acknowledge that I certainly still ask questions and I realise that answers to questions about 'truth' are provisional and often beyond our grasp. Indeed, God has even turned this asking into a profession for me. In my role as a university professor, God has taught me that questioning is a healthy part of growth and development as we expose ourselves to new ways of seeing and experiencing our lives and the world. Consequently, I have found, and I am still finding that those things that most people consider to be unquestionably true are *very* questionable; questions concerning what we know and what we can explain, who we are and what we do; the world we view and inhabit. On all of these subjects we have beliefs and opinions for sure. But, I have also learnt that we do well when we meditate on these matters and do not take these beliefs and opinions for granted. We can also anticipate that it is in precisely these moments that God can find a way into our lives. With his love and liberation he challenges us with alternatives to the world as we presently see and experience it, by unsettling our 'certainties' in our beliefs and opinions, and offering us something new.

Of course, one response to my questioning and truth-seeking would have been to abandon it. But at the time, this did not feel like an option, and still doesn't. I believe this to be an essential part of the human condition; namely, a basic need to ask these questions, to enquire about ourselves, our understanding of the world we live in and our role in it, regardless of whether there is ever a true finished product or a stopping point, where all is revealed and explained. However, what I have learnt, during this process, is that, via our questioning and truth-seeking, we can become more open to God's love and the many ways he can enhance our well-being through simply accepting his love, and not expecting to understand everything.

My conversion experience, then, as described here, should be seen in this wider context. I recognise that the need to ask searching and fundamental questions is integral to who I am, and how I view the world, and at the same time, acknowledge the permanent and profound limits of my knowledge and understanding. However, the love of God is the rock we must stand on – not that this rock will provide answers to everything (or even anything), but it is a permanent place of questioning which is also steady and sure as we grow *into* the love of God and love's many manifestations.

But, what does this brief account of my conversion story tell us more generally about the nature of conversion, and more particularly about the character of Christian conversion? What are the wider lessons we might learn about how God reaches out to us, and how might we be open to the responses he makes to us?

****

First, as already said, my conversion has not altered my need to ask questions, nor should it. While asking questions tends to lead to more questions than answers, it is a necessary part of being open to further change and conversion. My conversion, then, has not meant that I have rejected my

CONVERSION

assumptions about the inevitable opaqueness of what we can 'truly' explain and understand. We see but a 'poor reflection'[1] in the mirror, as Paul put it in 1 Corinthians 13:12.

Second, what my conversion has also shown me is that full explanations and understanding ultimately cannot deliver what I actually was after, and still am after – a life that is faithful to God the creator, as distinct from a life which is faithful to my own answers.[2] I recognise too that this creating cause is also love, because God *is* love, according to 1 John 4:8. It is a love which, even in prayer, is beyond our explanation and understanding, yet, if believed and fully embraced, promises a life of joy, liberation, and well-being (also see Philippians 4:7).

Third, seeking after proof or 'the truth' to justify my belief, therefore, misses the point about faith (as I will explore further in the next chapter). I have also found that my conversion, even if it did not shift my questions about the nature of the world and my understanding of it, did fundamentally alter my basic orientation to the world I live in and to the people who I live alongside – that is, even though I

---

[1] All bible quotations throughout the book are taken from the New International Version (NIV).

[2] It is pertinent to note that many contemporary philosophers, following Ludwig Wittgenstein's work in the early part of the twentieth century, have also defended elaborate arguments recommending we abandon the quest for answers in philosophy – or at least the quest for answers to traditional questions posed by philosophers over the centuries, such as those just outlined. In short, they recommend saying goodbye to philosophy – as it has sometimes been put – and instead concentrate on describing how language is used, rather than what answers to 'truth' can be discovered. This strategy in turn has been the main plank of much postmodern philosophy as it developed in the latter part of the twentieth century.

am bound to continually ask these searching questions.

Fourth, while a conversion experience can be a sudden event or a gradual one, it has to drastically change the way you view the world and experience it; so much so that you feel things will never again be the same. Importantly, then, conversion means, to use Jesus' words in John 3:3, being 'born again' – starting afresh in how you see the world and live in and experience the world.

Fifth, there are many types of conversion and they need not be Christian, but in order to be converted, you must be open to being radically changed. Without this openness, it is unlikely to occur. Certainly, there have been reluctant converts; people who resist being changed. To some extent, we all belong to this group – but those who are ripe for conversion are open to new possibilities, despite this resistance.

Where precisely this openness comes from is also hard to pin down as people's lives and stories are very different, so their accounts concerning the causes of conversion are also varied and disparate. For some, it is an openness prompted by their circumstances which may be beyond their control; for others, like me, it is more about the way they think or understand themselves or others; for some it is found in what they do or don't do; for others, in a more general sense of confusion, disappointment or bewilderment they might have about their lives – for still others it may be any combination of these factors, and more besides. The point is that for every convert there is a common theme to our past lives or stories; that, as with the prodigal son in Luke 15:11-32, we are in some way deeply dissatisfied with how things are – life is somehow not right– which prompts us to recognise that it is time for change.

CONVERSION

Certainly, timing is complicated too in matters relating to conversion; as we are often immersed in the moment, we are not always fully aware of our sense of the need for change. Sometimes we are very distracted, whether through work, play, or other preoccupations and barely see it as a need at all. At other times, we feel so oppressed by the condition of our lives we think there is no possibility for change. But then there are those times when we open ourselves up and expose ourselves to what else there might be, to new possibilities which promise something different – and it is these moments which are the most precious; where we have little or nothing to offer only that we ask, even shout, for help. If we don't cherish and harness these moments, we might spend all our lives in a state of limbo; neither feeling right nor fully seeing the possibility for exposure and change toward those things new – and ultimately exposure to the love and liberation of God himself.

Sixth, the secular or non-Christian sources of my conversion may seem strange to some and may even lead to a certain scepticism concerning the genuineness of my conversion. I ask you please don't go there; otherwise you are in danger of limiting God to what *you* see as conventional or 'proper' experiences of conversion.

For me, at the start of my Christian journey, there was no preacher, no one 'leading me to Christ', no church family helping me in troubled times; just me shouting for help and God using Frank Zappa and *Apocalypse Now* to turn me towards him. Certainly, he used other things leading up to this conversion experience, including the love and concern of my friends which touched me deeply. I also had brief encounters with Christians at the college I attended when I was between sixteen and eighteen years old, and even in Spain which, although I dismissed at the time, in hindsight I have no doubt was God working 'behind the scenes' for me. However, the conversion experience itself was as I have described and so can be viewed as profoundly secular and non-Christian in its sources, and should be acknowledged on these terms. Otherwise, as I say, we risk confining God to more conventional Christian channels of communication and change, and so limit his love and power.

I have certainly made many close Christian friends since then and as I have grown in my Christian life, I have discovered that Christian friendship and communion are crucial to my well-being and development as a Christian. However, what my conversion showed me, too, wonderfully and starkly, is that if God is seeking us out and we are open to change, then he will use every means possible to reach us. Rest assured, if the church doesn't do it for us at the time, then he knows what else to do, and where else to go. So, as Jesus explains in Luke 15:4, the shepherd will leave the flock and look for the lost sheep, wherever he should go. During this process, I believe God can and does use much of secular culture – its art, literature, music, philosophy, media, and so on – as well as our significant relationships with others, whether Christian or not, to reveal his love to us in its many different forms.[3]

Consequently, if we are open to learning from others who may be very different from us, with different beliefs, attitudes

---

[3] We might also question whether indeed there is a rigid secular/sacred divide in these matters. I would argue, from my experience – that there probably isn't. The point here, though, is that these sources are often *perceived* as being secular and so not sacred – both by Christians and non-Christians alike. I am grateful to Reverend Canon Dr Ian Davies for raising this issue in his reading of an earlier draft.

and lifestyles, God can teach us and show us important aspects of himself (as a God who *is* love), as well as the reality of who we are. As Paul instructs the Philippians in 4:8:

> ...whatever is true, whatever is noble, whatever is right, whatever is pure, whatever is lovely, whatever is admirable – if anything is excellent or praiseworthy – think about such things.[4]

Therefore, we had better have our ears, minds, hearts and souls open to what God has to say from all parts of the world around us, in its rich variety and wide range of colours. Otherwise, we risk missing possibilities for change and so miss the opportunity of returning to and replenishing our conversion experience in our everyday lives.

Seventh, given these possibilities, we also have to learn to be humble and listen attentively to God's voice as it is often heard in the most unexpected places. We will find that it is precisely in these places where we learn most profoundly about ourselves and the world we live in. However, if we approach our relationships with others, especially those who are not Christian, with the attitude that we only have something to teach 'them' because of our conversion, then we will not only come across as being proud, self-righteous, unable to listen, and patronising, but we will also ignore the richness of God's word and love for us, from its many different sources.

These various places are where we learn about God's love

---

[4] I will return to this passage of scripture a number of times throughout this book, as it points so clearly to the various manifestations of God's love in his world to which we should always be open.

and where, I believe, healthy questioning can occur. The openness, so described, requires us to first reflect critically upon our lives and ask questions of it and the world we inhabit. These questions, as I have said, often express our deep sense that life is not right and it is time for change. However, I have also claimed that change does not necessarily provide answers, if by answers we mean a neat, once-and-for-all set of responses to our questions which would fully explain the world and its workings.

Therefore, conversion does not mean finding a manual which will give ready-made solutions to the unfathomable, rich and unpredictable aspects of life. Rather, conversion means changing our view and experience of the very unfathomable character of life. Indeed, I would go as far as to say that seeking answers to all things is a phoney form of conversion – a kind of magic-wand variety, which gives the appearance that the meaning of life can be fully understood and grasped, but only as trickery. Those always seeking answers as solutions to the hard and difficult-to-grasp aspects of life trick us into thinking that conversion is about explaining all, and that it is for all times and all people. This deception effectively dethrones God's authority and, contrary to scripture (Philippians 4:7), places his peace within reach of *our* understanding, distracting us from our main task of being open to change through him and his love for all of us. As it also says in Proverbs 3:5-6:

> Trust in the Lord with all your heart and lean *not* on your own understanding; in all your ways acknowledge him, and he will make your paths

CONVERSION

straight.[5] (Emphasis added).

Finally, one other common magic-wand solution that a phoney conversion offers is expecting it to change the past – this is plainly impossible and symptomatic, not of faith in a loving God, but of hopeless, wishful thinking. The fact that the world is not right cannot be solved by a changing of what has already happened – this even God cannot do. But what can happen is that those things in the past which cannot be changed – most notably those which oppress, hurt and scar – can be experienced differently in the here-and-now. For all of us, the past remains the same but the events can be interpreted and viewed differently as we, for example, are able to forgive and be forgiven, and can love and be loved by others. It is these abilities which indicate a genuine conversion, as we see and experience the world and our lives, continually afresh, and as we grow further into the love and joy that, ultimately, God offers us all.

---

[5] I will return to this passage of scripture throughout the book, as it shows so well how our understanding is not a platform for trusting God, but rather the more concrete acceptance and acknowledgement of his loving presence in our lives.

Chapter Two

Faith

The world often seems to be against us. This perception can make it difficult for us to believe in an all-powerful God who loves us, is kind and has our best interests at heart. Belief in a loving God requires faith which is exercised by understanding the basic separation between what happens to us in the world (which can feel hard and very difficult) and the belief that God's love is real and protects and supports us. For me then, one of the big faith questions (perhaps *the* biggest question) is whether we see the world and God as being against us or whether we are prepared, through faith, to believe in a loving God who is all-powerful and with us or beside us when we inevitably struggle?

I will now tell a story from my life which will, hopefully, show that if we don't make this separation, it is likely that the very idea of an all-powerful loving God will appear as a cruel joke; given our everyday, normal experiences often feel hard and very difficult. The main reason I tell this particular story is because I think it offers a good metaphor for life in general and can be applied to many people's circumstances. It is also an example of me hearing, with no ambiguity, God speaking to me. At the time, this lack of ambiguity came as a complete

FAITH

surprise. Mostly, I hear God's voice subtly and at a low volume, within the nooks and crannies of everyday experiences. However, at that time, it was one of the relatively rare occasions when God spoke to me loudly and clearly and where the voice was unmistakably his – that is, with a well-formed sentence addressed to me in the second person (you), from him in the first person (I or me). Of course, it is this kind of clarity and unambiguousness which made it surprising. It felt, unusually, like a voice from the outside 'coming in', so not part of the conversations or dialogue we often commonly have with ourselves.

****

I was in my late twenties, in South America. Our party of four was prepared to walk one of the Inca trails. We had enough provisions for the two or, maximum, three days the walk was supposed to take. We were carrying the appropriate camping equipment and were ready to follow the trail and enjoy the history of the country and continent, as well as the beautiful mountain scenery.

However, because of our inability to speak Spanish properly and without us being aware of the confusion, we were taken to the wrong end of the trail. This meant that instead of the walk starting with a day, at the most, of a hard steep climb and followed by walking downhill for the rest of the journey, we landed-up walking uphill for over three days, finishing with about half a day downhill.

Even at that relatively young age, my body was not used to physical challenges and I had never been the type to welcome them, so this whole affair was a shock to my system, to say the least. Plus, the packs we carried were very heavy and the rain beat down most of the time. By the end, we had run out of food. Ironically, despite the rain, water was also hard to come by, and so we were reliant on the occasional stream we came across for replenishing our water bottles.

In these circumstances, when you are walking upwards, wet through to the skin, hungry, thirsty and unsure about how long this experience would last, but knowing that there was no option but to carry on, you have to 'dig deep', as they say. You stop speaking to the other members of the party and they stop speaking to you. You just trudge forward one step after the other, relentlessly, and lost in your own thoughts. And this was when God's words came to me, out of the blue, as clear as a bell ringing in my head, and with him addressing me in the second person, from him in the first person. It was only one sentence, but in the form of a disarmingly simple question: "Why do you think I am against you?"

Even now, more than twenty years on, I still laugh when I hear this question. My humour is often sardonic, liking comedy which comes from a place of doubt and even despair. Sardonic humour, for me, reflects an attitude of triumph over adversity and so often strikes me as quite wonderful. So, with the humour I enjoy, the situation I found myself in made this question from God all the more pertinent. The question sounded funny to me because it seemed, on the surface, so obvious why I would think God was against me. My response to him, as a result, could have easily been with another question – and then a rant:

> Why do you think? I've been walking upwards for three days. I am tired, hungry, thirsty, and wet and you ask me why I think you are against me! You are

FAITH

supposed to be an all-powerful God who loves me and I end up, through no real fault of my own, in these barely tolerable circumstances which feel so difficult.

I *could* have responded to him in this way, but, thankfully, I didn't. Instead, as soon as I heard his question, I saw exactly what God was trying to tell me – that to have faith in him, I must differentiate between what happens to me in the world and the difficulties which life inevitably brings, and what God does for me every day, every moment, in the here-and-now. In other words, I must believe and have faith and trust that he is always there for me, supporting me, loving me, *whatever* happens.

The flip-side to this, though, is that if I did not make this differentiation, I would assume that what life brings directly reflects whether I am loved and supported by God. Because life is often difficult, I am bound to lose faith in an all-powerful God who loves me and cares for me. This is because my 'faith' here is effectively being built on the sand of worldly circumstances. As Jesus said to his disciples in Matthew 7:24-27, when the winds come, the rains fall, and the floods rise, the house built on sand will inevitably fall down. Therefore, the sands of worldly circumstances can never be a rock to stand on, for, to use a contemporary expression: 'life comes with no guarantees.'

Having this insight at the time, I could now laugh in my own circumstances for two reasons. First, without this separation between worldly circumstances and what God offers us, the very idea of a loving God becomes like a cruel joke, as life is often hard. Second, having made the differentiation, I am no longer defeated by circumstances, and so, knowing God's love and support is always with me (even after my death where I will be in a blissful place with him and my loved ones forever), I can still face the world and what it throws at me, however difficult or grim.

This is not to trivialise the terrible pain, loss, and even horror many people have to live through. Nevertheless, because our faith in a loving God is based on this differentiation, it helps generate an attitude of praise and thanksgiving, regardless of what happens, which produces, I would say, a divine kind of laughter. Divinity is apparent when what happens to us does not determine our response to these circumstances. We are caught up in this other-worldly power which equips us with the ability to overcome such circumstances – and so to be joyful, loving and triumphant despite what is happening. The laughter is therefore born from knowing that nothing can touch us *so* much that we are *wholly* defeated.

The point concerning my own story is that once I saw God's joke and did, in fact, laugh out loud in response, my load suddenly felt lighter, my body did not ache so much and my discomforts felt very temporary.[6] Moreover, I was able to

---

[6] Following what has been examined so far, in many Christian circles laughter is, I believe, a profoundly underestimated quality of God (and his desire for us to experience his well-being, joy, and love). Laughter does not always reflect this quality, for sure, but when it does, the power of it is releasing and liberating and a very visible witness to God's presence in our lives, despite what may be happening to us. As the Psalmist states in Psalm 126:2 – "Our mouths were filled with laughter, and our tongues with songs of joy. Then it was said among the nations 'The Lord has done great things for them.'" The notion of 'divine laughter' (as I have called it here) is also used and recommended by Herman Hesse in his novel, *Steppenwolf* – where he explores a man's persistent search for meaning and purpose, in the face of what often appears in life as absurd and unfathomable. This book had an important influence on me in the months leading-up to my

FAITH

look up and appreciate the view, the ancient workmanship of the trail and even give other members of the party some words of encouragement. Although later I did get tired again and the original elation left me a little, the power of God's word and the promise of his love for me pushed me on. Remembering that moment has been an inspiration to me ever since.

****

The metaphor for life is obvious from this story, as we so often feel like we are trudging upwards with heavy loads, alone, and unsure of where we are going. However, the lesson for me was clear – be assured that God's love, despite our circumstances, is for us and not against us and that he wants us to be in a place of rest, peace and joy (well-being in other words), where the burden is light, as promised by Jesus in Matthew 11:30. That place cannot be found in the world, but it can be found inside *us*. Jesus also declared in Luke 17:21,

'...the Kingdom of God is within you'. So we are able to connect with, accept, and *trust* the love of an all-powerful God, as a love which is always, without fail, for us, and not against us. What else does this story tell us about faith?

First, we all live in a world which is very unpredictable, where life does not often go the way we plan and can be profoundly disappointing, where, even if we ask God to do something, it doesn't always come about and where very bad

---

Christian conversion, outlined in Chapter One. In Chapter Four, I also give a personal account of how God's laughter (it being filled with his love for us and the promise of our salvation in Christ), can even be a first response to our prayers, and which we would do well, then, to listen for.

things can happen to very good people, for no apparent reason. Of course, there may be many responses from the faithful to this counter-evidence of a loving God, and some are important to hear and learn from. For example, what we want or desire is not necessarily in our or other people's long-term interests. Consequently, what looks like an unanswered prayer may, in fact, be God protecting us from our own short-sightedness, foolishness, shallowness, and so on (this response from God will be explored further in Chapter Four on prayer). In addition, while we might not want to walk the trail the 'wrong' way, God will have a lot to teach us about his love and trusting him if we do, and moreover, we would not be able to learn from him if we refused the journey.

Second, what seems like wholly bad and unredeemable circumstances may prompt a response which digs deep and allows you to be more open to God's word, and love. Growth, in other words, must include some level of pain and hardship (this theme will also be explored further in Chapter Eight on growth). Although a life of constant struggle and hardship is neither, what we should want nor is what God would want for us; his loving promise and faithful response to us is not that we should be masochistic. However, if we have faith in an all-powerful, loving God who is always for us and never against us, then we can take pain and pleasure in fairly equal measure,[7] seeing both as potential avenues for his blessing and nurturing.

Third, however, we need to be very careful that we don't see the above kind of responses to pain and hardship as his

---

[7] This is reminiscent of a turn-of-phrase used by Friedrich Nietzsche (he recommends suffering and joy being taken this way). Albeit, Nietzsche was a notorious atheist and anti-Christian, and so would have certainly poured scorn on my bringing God into it all, especially as a Christian.

FAITH

last word, as there may be other reasons which we cannot see that have no bearing at all on these possibilities. Beware, then, of becoming Job's comforters, giving reasons for pain and suffering which, although they may seem plausible, are often just plain mistaken (see also Job 42:7-8). Indeed, our best response to pain and the difficulties and hardships of life is often to resist explaining or providing answers and reasons of any kind. Instead, God's call is for us to just be empathic and exercise kindness and love to the person who is bearing pain, whether ourselves or others. Faith, in this context, is about coming alongside those who are suffering in what is often an unknown, frightening and disappointing world. That is, relying again on making the clear separation between worldly circumstances, which often seem hard and against us, and God's love which is always supportive and for us.

Fourth, and following the themes explored in Chapter One, it might be said, then, that faith is exercised when someone still believes, even though there is no conclusive evidence for this belief from the *world* we live in and experience. This characterisation of faith may perhaps sound extreme as we often seem to rely on a certain kind of evidence to justify our faith based on reasons; for example, he has changed my life; I know he looks after me; I felt his comforting presence; he did this for me, and so on. However, although these reasons are important to hold on to and remember, relying *solely* on these reasons for 'faith', based on worldly circumstances, misses the point of a faith that believes in any case.

Fifth, we therefore believe in an all-powerful loving God, not because there is conclusive and unquestionable proof via what happens to us, but simply because God asks this of us, and this benefits us deeply, regardless of what happens. To

23

believe otherwise and count on all-conclusive evidence for believing is, ultimately, foolishness. While it may look as though we are defending a loving God, there are bound to be counter-reasons why this evidence, although coherent and plausible, is not the last answer to all what happens in our lives. Reasons for an all-powerful loving God's existence, therefore, although are often coherent and plausible are never reasons which defeat all other alternative explanations.

Sixth, faith then follows conversion, as explored in Chapter One. Faith is the lived-out expression of the radical change in how we look at and live in the world through asking the all-powerful loving God and Christ into our lives. As result, we experience the world profoundly differently. Faith, according to Jesus (Matthew 17:20), can move mountains, and so can and will change the landscape we find ourselves walking in, so shifting the shape of the world around us. Therefore, faith should always hope and expect change, as God in his love for us, wants good things for us, including change in our circumstances. But, mountains come in many shapes and sizes, and the change delivered might not be to do with the facts of our circumstances, but rather our attitude and view of them. After faith in a loving God is exercised, what may have initially looked like a mountain, may resemble more of a hill; not because what is faced or what we must do has changed in any way but because the mountain, once perceived, now looks less onerous and foreboding, and even a place of deep and unexpected blessing and joy.

****

FAITH

Finally, developing these themes of faith, Soren Kierkegaard, the nineteenth century Danish theologian and preacher, examined the character of faith and obedience in a deeply insightful book, *Fear and Trembling*, first published in 1843. He dissected the bible story of Abraham and Isaac in Genesis 22, where Abraham, being the paragon of faithfulness in the Jewish and Christian traditions, is commanded by God to climb a mountain over three days walk from his home and sacrifice his son, Isaac. This command is clearly against God's own moral code, is contrary to a father's natural inclination to protect and love his off-spring, and is commanding Abraham to destroy his gift from God that he and his wife, Sarah, had waited so long for.

As Kierkegaard highlights, God's instruction seems to be a completely insane and utterly unloving command with no good reason for performing it. Recognising this, though, is precisely where Abraham's obedience and faith begins for Kierkegaard. As we know from the story, of course, at the last minute God retracts his command, revealing that he was testing Abraham's obedience and faith in God. But, of course, Abraham while climbing the mountain could not see this eventual outcome. Faith and obedience in a loving God, then, is exercised by Abraham, not only without good reason, but also without any benefit of hindsight.

We are rarely, if at all, put in this kind of position by God, but there may be times when, like Abraham, we feel we are being asked to do or face things that are too difficult for us. This is why the lesson of Abraham is so instructive. Life often feels unbearably difficult; we are full of fear and trembling; we are unclear about where a loving God is in it all. Like Abraham, we often don't have the benefit of hindsight and, being immersed in particular circumstances, we have no guarantee of a positive outcome. However, this is where faith in a loving God comes into its own, as we take a step of belief into the unknown and unfathomable. Although there are no guarantees for our circumstances, we can believe and trust in the love of an all-powerful God regardless of what happens to us. Only when we believe in this way, can we be truly liberated from the world. We can step into this new and unworldly place of hope, trust, willingness and openness, so being held by God, whatever terrible circumstances our lives may bring.

But where else does this kind of faith take us, given what has just been explored? First, we become blessed for sure, as our lives and our view of the world can centre, not on ourselves and what we experience, but rather on the divine 'back-drop' and to that which shapes our responses to what circumstance throws at us. We respond, therefore, to what God wants of us and not to the world of circumstance. Certainly, we have a duty to act lovingly. Faith without loving deeds, as James' letter testifies in 2:26, is dead. But the action itself arises from an underlying belief, which we choose to make, that the circumstances of the world are never wholly defeating – that these circumstances can never completely overcome or overwhelm us, and our faith in an all-powerful loving God. Consequently, we declare in that decision of faith, a love for God which is then translated into hope-filled, loving actions, whether these are small acts of kindness and consideration which we are able to receive or give, or larger acts of sacrifice and cost. Either way, a life of faith *becomes* a life of love.

Second, what is promised in the exercise of this action-based faith is, paradoxically, a profound stillness. However, this is not a stillness delivered through refusing to act or

FAITH

engage with the world, or a stillness derived from answering, once-and-for-all, every question about what has happened in our lives. Faith is exercised in response to our living in the world, and through accepting the unknown and unfathomable character of God and his creation. Consequently, it is a stillness and peace generated through resting in a loving God, in his place of dwelling and belonging, even if the world seems chaotic and threatening. As Jesus calms the storm in Mark 4:35-41, it is also a place of silence and quiet – where there is nothing left to say, no reasons to find, no evidence to collect and decipher, no circumstances to rile against, no expectations to live up to – only you and him.

Chapter Three

Christ

There are so many reasons why believing in Jesus Christ is utterly strange and incomprehensible, it's difficult to know where to start. Putting aside the Western cultural baggage which associates Christianity with respectability and social conformity, Christianity asks us to believe in someone who, if thought about reasonably or rationally, is very difficult to make any sense of. Whatever part of the New Testament you read, sooner or later, some stupendous claim will be made about Jesus, regarding who he is and what he has done for us. The problem is that, in the soap and froth of selling the Jesus story at Christmas, Easter, in school assemblies, church, and the like, we have all become culturally desensitised to these claims. Subsequently, we have also become desensitised to the most radical and far-reaching implications of them that, as well as being a man called Jesus, he is also Christ our saviour.[8]

However, assuming their truth *for me*, my story as a

---

[8] I am grateful to Reverend Ernesto Lozada-Uzuriaga Steele for highlighting this distinction between the name Jesus and the title Christ, in his reading of an earlier draft.

CHRIST

Christian has meant a repeated return to these stupendous claims in an effort to embrace and accept them more profoundly. Surprisingly perhaps, when I do this, my life makes more sense. I have found, paradoxically, that the more I fully recognise the nonsensical and bizarre quality of these claims, the more I can feel comfortable with the uniqueness of Jesus' love and my relationship with him. This chapter explores three main claims central to Christian belief – that Jesus is God manifested as a human; that, in his death on the cross, he assumes the blame for our wrongdoing; and that to demonstrate his power and love for us, after his death, he rose from the dead.[9] All of these claims, I will argue, underpin my relationship with him as Christ.

****

When I first became a Christian, acknowledging the relationship between Jesus and me was in some ways hard to do. The first, and probably silliest, obstacle was that I found myself wincing – and confess I still do – at Christians who announce very publicly and proudly that they have 'a friend in Jesus'. Whether this is proclaimed on car-stickers, badges, street corners, or very randomly in conversations about football, I am basically embarrassed by these proclamations. I am sure that some of this embarrassment reflects my own insecurities about being a Christian, and for this I am at fault. I also know that those who use these methods of communication and make these proclamations don't mean

---

[9] In Chapter Eight I also explore a fourth stupendous claim; that the Holy Spirit is the spiritual manifestation of Christ's love living in our lives today.

any harm by them. They think they are promoting some good, in 'spreading the word'. Nevertheless, I also know that, even if some good is done through them, they often just irritate, and so put a lot of people very off Christianity.

Regarding the latter group, I am especially concerned about those questioning friends of mine who would not describe themselves as Christians, but think about life's issues seriously and resist, quite rightly, these issues being addressed through what they see as trite proclamations and slogans. Even from a Christian perspective, the type of 'I have a friend in Jesus' sloganising, can have the effect of trivialising or ignoring the deep and often bewildering aspects of the Christian faith. In short, the badges and the slogan, despite good intentions, seem to render shallow my own belief in Christ's love for me.

Of course, one can get too touchy about these things and end up not focussing on what is important about being a Christian. Moreover, I *do* have a friend in Jesus and, contrary to expectations maybe, fully recognise that the faith of those Christians who display this slogan is likely genuine and similar to my own. Nevertheless, what these proclamations notably miss out is that any friendship with Jesus is built on a foundation that cannot easily or readily be understood.

To start with, and as I will explore below, a friendship with Jesus offends, or at least turns upside down, what we usually count as the basis for being friends with another person. To compound the problem, the difficulty of having a friend in Jesus can only begin to be addressed if we also accept some of the stupendous claims, referred to earlier, about the character of Jesus as Christ, and what he has done for us, and because he loved us first. We, therefore, have to get to grips with some extremely perplexing and puzzling issues and commit to some bizarre suppositions before we can make any sense of our friendship with him.

First, being friends with someone usually assumes a position of equality between the persons involved – indeed, it has to, if the friendship is to survive. That's why, for example, being good friends with your boss often doesn't work. This is because your boss is in a position of power over you, as he or she is your paymaster and can fire you. Despite attempts to forget this when making friends with your boss, this power inequality will not go away and so will likely, at one time or another, skew your friendship with him or her.

Second, being friends with someone also assumes some kind of on-going mutual exchange; a relationship of give-and-take. Often friends take it in turns to give and receive with the expectation that what the other has to offer is valuable, and that it will be returned in kind. The mutuality therefore enriches and nourishes the friendship as both parties benefit from this loving exchange.

Third, friends are living in the world presently and therefore are able to engage in such exchanges. So, people have to be alive and able to enrich each other for healthy friendships to be fostered. When you have a friend who dies there is a time of deep grief and mourning as the friendship has had to end, at least for now in this world.

However, these various characteristics of a loving friendship are not straightforward when applied to the friendship we might have with Jesus. If Jesus is who Christians say he is – the incarnation of God – then how do we have a loving relationship with him, given that friendships imply some sort of equality between persons? Any relationship with him is surely the epitome of inequality – namely, a relationship between the creator and the created, or, more abstractly, between what is 'above' and 'below'. Moreover, if we grant that Jesus is the incarnation of God, however improbable this might seem, what on earth can we give *him* in this loving exchange? If friendship involves some kind of reciprocity or mutual exchange, what's 'in it' for Jesus if we become friends with him? Surely, there is nothing I can give him to enrich his life, if he is God. In any case, if we were to give something to him of value in his eyes, such as loving life, or an attitude of thankfulness for the life given to us, we are still left with a troubling issue, explored in Chapter One – namely, that what we do, think and are disposed to, often fall very short of these loving aspirations. Not only do we have little, if nothing, to offer the incarnate God but even the things we do have to give, are flawed and tarnished.

However, let's assume we can negotiate the above uneven and strange terrain. It still does not make sense to be friends with Jesus if we don't also assume Jesus is now alive. Otherwise, it would be impossible to maintain a loving relationship with him. The claim that he is alive now, certainly, is as stupendous as he is God made a person, but if we are to be friends with him, his being alive also has to be accepted otherwise we are trying to have a loving relationship with a dead person, and this is not possible in this world. In other words, 'doing this relationship thing' with Jesus exposes how unique he is for sure – and so completely unlike any other religious leader. However, this unique relationship can only make sense if it is also based on these stupendous claims about his status as Christ our *living* saviour, and what he has done for us.

****

CHRIST

Turning in more detail then to the incarnation, or God being made a person, it is useful to look at John's gospel, 1:1-14. In the first part of the passage, John explains that in the beginning was the Word and the Word was with God, and the Word was God, and that through him all things were made. So far so good, we might say. If we believe in God, then this seems to be a pretty standard account of how God created everything through a command; the Word, which brings into existence things that were not there at the start. We therefore have the Judeo-Christian version of creation which separates the creator from the created and gives sole authorship and authority to a non-created God (the Word which commands things into existence); a God who is the source of all creation.

However, John gets to verse 14 and hits us with a bombshell and overturns, or completely reshapes this standard account. John claims that the Word has become flesh, in the person of Jesus, and has even lived amongst us. Why is this claim so outrageous? Well, it is one thing to say that a creator reflects himself in what he creates. This notion is relatively easy to understand. So, an artist reflects her personality in her paintings, or a mother reflects her love for her child in the birthday cake she makes for him – both the artist and the mother are producing something different and external to themselves, but which represents or reflects something of who they are and how they relate to others. However, John's claim about the Word becoming flesh is much more radical and difficult to comprehend. Analogously, the artist literally becomes the painting while remaining the artist; or, the mother literally becomes the cake while remaining the parent of the child.

Consequently, according to John, the separation originally established between the loving creator and the created, has been ruptured as God is *also* a person, while still maintaining his sole and sovereign authorship and authority over creation. In other words, God, the non-created, is both himself and is one of us, or one of the created. He therefore is not just *reflecting* his image in us, as stated in Genesis 1:27, he also *becomes* one of us in Jesus Christ. The latter is a fundamental Christian claim that, when put starkly, sounds bizarre and stupendous.

So why do people, including me, believe it? One very plausible answer is that we are completely deluded. If we are to believe in a loving God at all, it might be argued that we should commit to a much more sensible and manageable faith. Consequently, we can plausibly have faith in a leader, Jesus, who may reflect God for sure and even reflect God's love, as we see it, in a unique way, but we should steer well clear of claiming that he is God. Indeed, as C.S. Lewis explores in his essay, 'What are we to make of Jesus Christ?'[10], the latter claim is deeply problematic for religious ears, as it puts a mere person, even a person who uniquely reflects God, on the same level as God. In most religious circles, this claim is at best ridiculous; or, at worst, profoundly offensive, as it seems to undermine God's unique authority and status as a non-created creator.

However, aside from being completely deluded, a more generous response is that, despite the odds, we might be right, and therefore we should explore the implications of the utterly strange character of these claims, if only to see what might happen. If God did become a person, then maybe all sorts of positive and beneficial possibilities arise concerning our relationship with a loving God, which previously would

---

[10] From C.S. Lewis (1971) *God in the Dock* (London: Geoffrey Bles).

have been unthinkable.

For example, returning to the principles of friendship outlined earlier, God, in becoming one of us, has in one important way assumed an equal relationship with us by sharing our humanity. He has become our brother or sister, as stated, for example, in Paul's letter to the Hebrews 2:10-18; moreover, using Jesus' own preferred title of himself, he has therefore become the Son of Man (for example, see Mark, 13:26; 14:62). But, isn't it better for us, and certainly more respectful and reverential, to refuse a friendship with him even if he has shared our humanity, precisely because *we* cannot assume equality with Jesus? Isn't it right that we keep even Jesus' humanity at a distance, a bit like the more healthy relationship with our boss, suggested previously?

The answer to both these questions, from Christians at least, is a resounding, 'No!' First, having God as a friend, by implication, allows us to enter a place of profound blessing, well-being and enrichment, born out of the intimacy and connection promised in his loving character *as* a human being. Second, he wants us to be his friends in order that, through his love for us, he can give us good things, and where refusing his offer of friendship is therefore a kind of snub to his love. For sure, because of his love, he has blessed many others who have not allowed themselves this privilege, and so in this way at least, all is not lost. But, for Christians, to openly accept Jesus as a friend and as God made a person makes the access to his love and blessing more direct and potentially powerful, *for us*. In any case, given this choice, Christians ask back: wouldn't we prefer thinking of a loving God as a friend or ally, literally living alongside us, enriching us, and making us feel valuable through the things we give him, however meagre?

Developing the last point, it also seems that if we are friends with him, he lives alongside us and we are able to give to God as well as receive from him. Consequently, we engage in mutual loving exchanges, as friends do, and as we facilitate a relationship of give-and-take with God. We are, therefore, able to find ultimate and everlasting value in what we do and become in the various loving acts, however big or small, we perform.

Again, this claim sounds bizarre, as, to repeat, humans surely cannot give anything of value to God as he is the source of all love, with all value coming from him. Moreover, as I highlighted previously here and in Chapter One, part of what Christians also acknowledge is that we, as human beings, often fall short of even our very limited understandings and capacities of how we should love others.

Nevertheless, recognising fully the latter problem gets us to the second stupendous claim concerning what Jesus has done for us as Christ our saviour. By serving us and sacrificing himself, because of his love for us, he identifies with and even *becomes* our flawed selves, as he takes onto himself the burden of human imperfection through his death on the cross. Paul states in 2 Corinthians, 5:21:

God made him who had no sin to *be* sin for us, so that in him we might become the righteousness of God. (Emphasis added).

Put another way, God becomes a person and then assumes the blame for what we have done wrong, making it his fault and not ours, and so making us right with God.[11] Of course,

---

[11] The phrase, '*it is all my fault!*', expressing what Christ did for us on

CHRIST

there is no justification in heaven or earth for this misplaced blame but, for Christians, this proclamation is God's loving response to our flawed natures and the most extreme and radical version of his love toward us. As a result, Jesus, as he was dying on the cross, experienced the ultimate rupture and disconnection with the God he calls father and so becomes completely abandoned and alone, crying out: 'My God, my God, why have you forsaken me?' (Matthew 27:46)

As I explored in Chapter Two, we often experience the feeling of being forsaken by God. The circumstances of our lives frequently seem to bear witness to us being abandoned. On one level then, Jesus as a man making this cry is not unusual or incomprehensible, even given the terrible circumstances of being tortured to death while nailed to a cross. What is unusual and much harder to comprehend, is the implications of this cry, given the previous claim that the Word had become flesh, in the person of Jesus, which means that he *is* God.

What follows though is that God, by loving us first, has wilfully torn himself apart in order for us to be reconciled with him. He has, through assuming the blame for our wrongdoing, become disconnected from himself, in order to deal with the disconnection between our flawed selves and his perfection as a loving God. When he makes it his fault, and not ours, he also makes us, unjustifiably, perfect in the

---

the cross by assuming blame for our flawed characters, was used by Dr. Reverend Tony Campolo in his now famous address to the 'Spring Harvest' event in 1982. Over thirty years later, this is still one of the best sermons I have heard concerning the character of Christ's love, his blessings for us, and the radical implications for our lives if we have a relationship with him. I will further explore this theme of blame and fault and where these are placed, in Chapter Five on forgiveness.

37

process and so wholly and completely reconciled to him. This reconciliation occurs, not because we deserve it, but because he loves us so much that he is prepared to take the blame, and sacrifice himself for us – in other words, in this act of love, Jesus is able to also assume the title of Christ our saviour. Our salvation occurs, then, because the love and grace we have received from Christ's sacrifice *releases* us. So, it liberates us from the Old Testament covenant or agreement made with God (leading to our attempts at following God's law but resulting in his judgement, as we inevitably break it). This being replaced by the New Testament covenant or agreement made with God, based on us accepting his forgiveness and mercy, as *he* takes the blame for our wrongdoing and so diverting the blame from us *to* him (also see Paul's letter to the Romans, 7; and Chapter Six here).

But where is the victory in all this, given what has happened on the cross? So, God has demonstrated his love and forgiveness for us by dying for us, but where does it leave us, other than with an all-powerful God unjustifiably blaming and demeaning himself in this way? These questions get us to the third and final stupendous claim about Christ, to be explored in this chapter at least – that despite his very public death, he rose again, and showed himself to be alive and victorious, even over death itself.

****

The resurrection story is very familiar – too familiar in many respects. Also, there is no need to quote chapter and verse, as it is easy to find in all four gospels. Just go to the end of Matthew, Mark, Luke and John, and the same basic story is told in different ways. It is also variously discussed and testified to in the reports and letters of the early Christians in the last parts of the New Testament. The point here, though, is that the story, of Jesus rising from the dead, escaping his tomb, and revealing himself physically to various people on numerous occasions afterwards, is *so* outrageous and stupendous that if it didn't happen, then, I conjecture, no one would have invented it, through fear of being completely ridiculed. For sure, the disciples would have been deeply disappointed in an outcome that ended in the death of their leader. But many causes have been 'resurrected' through leaders who have become martyrs. The disciples could have relatively easily increased their following by celebrating his life and death, and presented him as an example, even the ultimate example, of a Godly life which all should follow. However, they did not do this. Instead they propagated the more preposterous claim that he died a slow, painful death on a cross, his body was entombed, and then he came back to life again, escaped the tomb, and variously revealed himself to others in his physical form!

My question then, as a Christian, is why would the disciples tell this story, if it wasn't true? Collective madness might be an explanation but this looks odd to say the least, when characters such as Thomas were around, doubting at every turn and insisting on believing in the resurrection, if, and only if, he could touch an alive Jesus and see and feel his wounds (John 20:24-29). Moreover, others following in the wake of Jesus' death and resurrection, such as Paul for example, were staking their lives and high reputations on this claim. Paul's entire faith, repeatedly articulated, was based on what he saw, at least, as the fact of Jesus' resurrection.

Of course, all of it could be made up and Paul and other Christians could just be mistaken, being duped by the original disciples. But if this is the case, how do we account for the other historical evidence that Jesus died, for sure, but his body was apparently missing? The disciples could have snatched the body, which is an explanation the religious authorities were keen to spread. But then we are back to the question, why would Jesus' disciples do this, when other much more credible claims could have been made to generate a following, celebrating the life and death of their leader?

It might be that the disciples were just plain stupid, and got their tactics very wrong by telling lies. But this response, too, seems implausible. It would have been such a bizarre lie that if the disciples were so stupid, it seems difficult to believe they could imagine such an inventive and fanciful story. In any case, would all of the disciples have continued to support this claim if they had known it was a lie? However dull someone is, a person usually doesn't allow himself or herself to be ridiculed, persecuted, and even killed, based on something he or she knows is made-up. One person, or a few people, may perhaps do this if they were psychologically damaged in some way. But we are talking about a relatively large number of people who, before Jesus rose again, seemed very able and keen to protect themselves from persecution, given what had just happened to their leader. Even one of those closest to him, Simon Peter, was prepared to deny three times even knowing him (see Mark 14:66-72).

Finally, it might be argued that these were strange times – or certainly strange from our twenty-first century perspective – and so people then, believed in all sorts of bizarre ideas and notions, so why not this one? However, as can be seen from the gospel accounts and from the rest of the New Testament, even if this fact about their culture is granted, it also struck people at the time as completely incredible that a man could be tortured to death, his body put in a tomb for three days, only for him to come back to life, escape from the tomb, and then reveal himself physically. Consequently, the bizarre character and strangeness of distant cultures extends so far, but not enough to accommodate this story. From any cultural perspective, when you're dead, you're dead, and particularly when considering the manner in which Jesus died and what happened to his body afterwards, there is, and was, no room for ambiguity. So, according to the gospels, it seemed just as crazy to them as it does to us now, that he came back to life and then did what he did.

No doubt, there are other objections to his resurrection and, as I explored in Chapter Two, the Christian faith, in any event, does not, and *should* not, depend on all-conclusive evidence. However, if we concede that these arguments for the resurrection are, despite the odds, plausible, albeit not all-conclusive, we can finish this chapter by clarifying one last claim – that a loving friendship with God is made possible with Jesus, because, not only has God become one of us and so can live alongside us; and, not only has God assumed the blame for our own flawed characters and so we can give perfectly good things to him even though we don't deserve it; but equally bizarrely, despite Jesus being slowly tortured to death, he rose from the dead, and so overcame death and is still alive today!

Chapter Four

Prayer

In its simplest form, prayer is, quite rightly, about having a conversation with God – you talking to God and, in the process, being open to what he is saying to you. Prayer, though, becomes more difficult when we recognise that it is also in other ways very unlike the conversations we have with people. I suggest that we should acknowledge these difficulties and meditate on their consequences, before we start talking with God, otherwise we may get on the wrong footing with him from the start.

First, we are told in scripture that he already knows what we will say when we express our deepest thoughts, even before we say them. As the psalmist in Psalm 139:4 puts it: 'Before a word is on my tongue you know it completely – O Lord'. Therefore, he anticipates our deepest thoughts way before we are consciously aware of them and so is already responding to them before we articulate them in prayerful words. Sometimes a person can anticipate what another might say, if she knows him or her well enough, but most of the time this doesn't, and cannot, happen between people. Indeed, good conversation often involves enquiring after another's thoughts, precisely *because* we don't know them.

PRAYER

Second, God is also privy to our deepest desires, motivations and the many machinations of our emotions. Again, according to the psalmist in Psalm 38:9: 'All my longings lie open before you, O Lord: my sighing is not hidden from you.' He knows us, then, much better than even we know ourselves – our emotions as well as our minds, and all the way to the bottom of who we are. This also doesn't happen in our ordinary conversations with people. Some people may think otherwise; it is often believed that psychologists and counsellors can read people's minds and emotions, but this is a misconception – they can only, at best, partially and dimly perceive a person's deeper yearnings and longings.

Thirdly, while God has access to everything about us, we know barely anything at all about him. Certainly, we know various aspects of his character, as illustrated in the life of Jesus, and the many other bible stories we are told in both the Old and New Testaments. We also can discover through our own lives what he is like, as well as witness his work through others who are Christian, otherwise religious, or neither. However, we are told repeatedly in scripture that we must never assume to know him fully. That his secrets, unlike ours, are completely unfathomable – that his work and plans are often mysterious and indecipherable. For example, in Romans 11:33 Paul proclaims:

> Oh, the depth of the riches of the wisdom and knowledge of God! How unsearchable his judgements, and his paths beyond tracing out!

Then in verse 34, Paul cites the Old Testament prophet, Isaiah 40:13, to reinforce his point further: 'Who has known the mind of the Lord? Or who has been his counsellor?' Again, this utter one-sidedness in our conversations with God – where he knows all of us, but we know little of him – is not a feature of our ordinary conversations with people. A good conversation is usually based on recognising a degree, at least, of mutual ignorance, where we find out about each other as we go along – and so take turns in giving each other information as to who we are, what we do, feel, and think.

Fourth, given the above, we also cannot ever deceive God, or hide ourselves from him. We might, deliberately or inadvertently, deceive or hide from ourselves, but God sees right through any deception and any attempts to cover ourselves with things which we are not. As God asks rhetorically in Jeremiah 23:24:

> '"Can anyone hide in secret places so that I cannot see him?" declares the Lord. "Do not I fill heaven and earth?"'

Certainly, poor conversation frequently encourages a high level of deception and hiding from others, so the quality of exchange may never get past superficial niceties, or even bare-faced lies, as a result. However, all conversations, including deeper exchanges between people, involve a degree of hiding, and often for good reason. For sure, often hidden things are better out in the open, but if we were to say out loud everything we thought and felt to the people we encounter, including those closest to us, we would be very insensitive and unloving. Good conversations between people, then, necessitate making wise judgements between what should and shouldn't be said, and so what should or shouldn't be disclosed. However, this possibility is not an option with God, as there is no place to hide, and nor should we try.

Finally, and perhaps the most obvious difference between conversations with people and with God, is that with people we are very aware of being in a particular place and time and that we can either, see, hear, or touch a person we are talking with. With God, none of these characteristics apply as he transcends time and place. He is not encountered as a physical entity appearing before us. As we explored in Chapter Three, Christians do believe that God became a person, in Christ Jesus (I will return to this theme in Chapter Eight when I explore the character of the Holy Spirit in this context). But even accepting this incarnation of God, it does not mean we can go to God in the same way as we might go to a person, and begin a conversation. So Paul, in 1 Timothy 6:15b-16, declares:

> …God, the blessed and only Ruler, the King of kings and Lord of lords, who alone is immortal and who lives in unapproachable light, whom no one has seen or can see.

Consequently, when we speak to God out loud it can seem as though we are speaking to air or speaking to ourselves. Conversations with people can also seem a bit like this too, if the person you are speaking to is not listening to what you are saying. But this, we are told, is not happening with God, because if we come to him in humility and reverence, he always listens to us. In Anglican services, during intercessions the congregation is invited to say: 'Lord, in your mercy, hear our prayer'. Consequently, as believers, we expect him to hear us, as an expression of his love and mercy and who he is. Yet, it can still *feel* as if he is not there even though we may *believe* he is – unlike the person who listens well to what you are saying, and so feels very much to be immediately with you without us having to also believe it.

In summary then, God knows already what we will say in prayer; he also knows our deepest desires and motivations; while he knows all about us we know relatively little about him; we cannot deceive or hide from him; but no one can see him or touch him. Given these features, our conversations with an all-powerful, loving God are in many ways very different to the conversations we have with people. For sure, both involve words and both involve speaking out and listening to the other. Both also commit to the other by the very act of conversation and so are committed to forming a relationship. But aside from these characteristics, the similarities pretty much stop there. So, where do these observations lead us, when it comes to understanding the practical business of prayer?

****

If God knows what we are going to say, before we say it, a reasonable question would be: what's the point at all of saying anything? In one way I think this is a good question, but in another it is not. It is good because what we should do in any conversation with God is first remain silent. There is no need to rush in with lots of words, as if he doesn't know what we are already going to say – as he does. But also, more subtly, there is no need, in the first place at least, to listen attentively to what God might say to us, in some kind of nervous or heightened sense of expectation. After all, he may choose not to speak to us, given his ways are also often deeply mysterious and unknown.

The main reason then we must first remain silent, as instructed by God in Psalm 46:10, is that we can 'be still, and know that [he is] God'. It has taken me a long time on my Christian journey – indeed, far too long – to understand the profundity of this wonderfully brief command – and even now, I feel I have only scratched the surface of what I should and can learn. However, prompted by a Christian friend of mine, Ruth, to meditate on this verse nearly twenty or so years ago, I have returned to it repeatedly, feeding from what I experience as its unfathomable depths.

Being still and yielding to the knowledge that God is God, where nothing is said or heard but only this fact is accepted, inevitably brings an experience of calmness and peace. It is an act of trust and surrender to him and his loving character, slowing down, and eventually stopping, the many words buzzing around my head, and settling my fears and anxieties as these seem to slowly turn from mountains to hills, and then even to plains. Only at this point, might I be ready to speak, and hear his love and word for me, and even this is not yet guaranteed. As I am writing this passage I realise that, while I am learning to be still, I never am still enough and that I am always too anxious to speak and hear. The onus is on me, therefore, to *keep* being still, and not, in the first place at least, expect to say or hear anything.

However, as previously stated, saying nothing to God can also be a bad response to him. It can be symptomatic of our giving up on God and his love for us, rather than giving in to him. This giving-up type silence is, then, a kind of sulk, as we refuse to engage or even believe in an all-powerful God who cares about us and what we think, desire, hope and fear. It may be, of course, that we have been very disappointed by

God; that he seemingly hasn't listened or answered our prayers. As I explored in Chapter Two, it could also be that our circumstances are such that we find it difficult to separate the world being against us from an all-powerful loving God being for us. Consequently, we can be overwhelmed by what life throws at us and find it hard, even impossible, to have faith in a God who loves us. But if we are not to be wholly defeated by what happens in our lives, then we must, at some point, speak to God. For sure, being still turns our fears and anxieties from onerous mountains to terrains which are much more passable, but we still need to journey through life and act as persons with particular desires, aspirations, fears and hopes. We cannot stop this journey and so cannot put on hold these particulars about ourselves. Moreover, I would argue that even if we tried to, we would deny our own humanity and the various and rich experiences of life, given to us by the love of God our creator.

Therefore, the next question is: what do we say to him when we are ready to speak? The short answer is anything and everything. There is no place to hide from God, as he has already seen you uncovered, but this implies, then, that all truthful utterances are permissible. To stop saying something truthful about who we are to God, however unattractive or ugly, would again be trying to deceive him, which is impossible. As the Old Testament repeatedly testifies, even the angriest, most twisted, and bitter cries to God, if honestly delivered, are honoured by him if, *in the end*, you are willing to engage with and trust him. He may not answer your prayers the way you want, but he will always honour your honesty and willingness to relate to him in this way, wherever your motivation comes from and whatever is said, and as he responds to you with grace and mercy, because he loves you.

PRAYER

What God will not honour, and will even turn his face from, is any attempt to use prayer to deceive yourself, or others, or especially to exalt yourself over others. Jesus declared in Matthew 6:5 that we should not be like the religious hypocrites, and pray to show-off and impress. In other words, God wants to hear us, warts and all, in a private space where we can speak to and engage and relate with him honestly, without regard for our public image.

****

My first big lesson in the importance of honestly engaging with God in the way just described, came when I was nineteen years old, hitch-hiking through France two or three months after my conversion. It is a story I'd like to tell in some detail, given the many things it taught me.

I had been living in a squat in the south of France with a bunch of unemployed and homeless people. In a fit of generosity and putting my trust in God to supply my needs, I decided to give all the money I had to the squatters and other beggars on the streets of Avignon where I was staying. I then decided, on what I thought was also God's instruction, to hitch-hike back to Paris to reconcile with my French girlfriend, with whom I had broken up a week or so previously.

What I didn't reckon on was the interminably slow progress I would make on the road to Paris. Three days after I started, I think I had only travelled about forty kilometres of the nearly 600-kilometre journey. In retrospect, it perhaps was not that surprising. I was very unkempt, to say the least, and having been living in a squat and sleeping rough, I would not have been very appealing as a passenger to even the most sympathetic motorist. So, towards the end of the third day, I was on the side of the road, praying like mad for a lift. Every car that came toward me I shouted to the heavens: 'Please make them stop!' but, when I stuck my thumb out, nothing happened.

By this time I also hadn't eaten for about twenty four hours at least. In the first day or so I came across other hitch-hikers, who shared some of their food with me, but they had long departed. By the third day, I was by myself with no money, no food and, of course, desperate for a lift. Remember too, this was 1980, before mobile phones were commonly available and there were no internet cafes to Skype or e-mail home for help. As you can imagine, as time went on, my prayers became increasingly desperate, frustrated and angry, but not so much with the car drivers as with God. I started to feel outraged at his apparent neglect of me. I had given practically all my worldly possessions to 'the poor and needy', in trust and expectation that, in his love, he would supply my needs – and, I was supposedly following his instructions to return to my girlfriend in Paris. The problem was I had nothing to show for it, except an empty stomach, and being hundreds of kilometres from my destination.

By the end of the third day, and after seeing the dome of a church in the distance with a cross on top, I started to shout at God, not just in my mind but, as I was alone, out loud. My prayer, at this near breaking-point, went like this:

> Right, I am going to ask you to give me a lift – give me a lift! (car shoots by). Right, I am going to ask you again to give me a lift – give me a lift! (car shoots by, and so on).

PRAYER

After God knows how many cars shot by, I started another more extreme rant which, although still shouting at God, also proclaimed his non-existence. I had already prepared this rant in my mind, assuming a lift was not forthcoming. My prayer, at this final breaking-point, and as the sun started to go down on the third day, went like this:

> The reason why you are not giving me a lift is because you don't f*****g exist! Look see! Give me a lift! (another car shoots by) – you don't f*****g exist!

Then, what I can only describe as a miracle happened. No, I didn't get a lift, but a series of events occurred that, in my eyes were, and are, much more remarkable. After I had repeated the last prayer a number of times, I started to get my anger out of my system and so calmed down a little. And, it was in these quieter moments I heard, what I felt then and still recognise now, God laughing at me. Not screaming at me, as I had just done to him, but chuckling, completely unfazed by my shaking my fists and cursing. I experienced this laughter as being very loving and knowing … well, he had seen it all before – countless people across the generations ranting against him like this. But also I sensed, in the nooks and crannies of my experience, that in his love for me, he was telling me something about what would happen. And his telling went like this:

> Look, my son, I am not giving you a lift tonight, but because I love you, what I will do is fill you with good things which will make it unimportant to you that you are staying here for now.

And these good things he duly did give to me, for I turned and looked across the road, and saw the beginnings of one of the most beautiful sunsets I had ever seen in my life. I crossed the road, walked about three or four hundred metres to the Rhône river and sat by its bank, appreciating the view, the wildlife, and the glorious changing colours of the sky. About half an hour later I felt spiritually filled and completely new and was able to laugh with God at my previous ranting and raving. Then, I said another prayer, which went like this:

> Sorry God for being like I was, and thank you so much for all this beauty in your creation, and for the fact that I am now spiritually full.

And then I added these lines:

> But I am still very hungry. I don't mind that much not eating, given what has just happened to me, and in any case, we seem to be in the middle of nowhere. But if you can find some food for me, I would really like some now please.

I waited for a bit, and nothing appeared to happen, but this time I didn't care that much. So, I wandered off, not really sure where I was going but vaguely looking for a place to sleep, as it was dusk by now. About five or ten minutes later, at the most, I had walked through a small clump of trees adjacent to the river, and came to a clearing.

To my complete surprise, the clearing opened-up onto a rugby pitch with a small pre-fabricated-type building which was presumably the rugby club house. By the building were about a dozen or so people standing around a table full of

PRAYER

food. I knew I didn't have to ask for any as the food was already earmarked for me! And sure enough, a French woman, after seeing me come through the trees, walked toward me with both arms full of baguettes and cheeses, insisting that I take them, otherwise, she said in broken English, they would go to waste. Apparently, the rugby club had come to the end of a function and the food was left over. I thanked the woman, took the food and walked back among the trees to find a place to sleep, now feeling bowled over by the wonderful presence of God in my life. The next morning, after about a twenty minute wait, I was given a lift all the way to Paris.

What does this story teach us about prayer? First, I can rant and rave at God – in fact I believe he *wants* me to rant and rave if that is what I truly feel, otherwise we are in danger of vainly trying to deceive him. God already knows my deepest angers and frustrations and that at least some of these emotions get directed towards him. Therefore, nothing will be a shock to God and I can't take him by surprise by what I have to say to him. In addition, as stated earlier, any pretence is ignored by God as he sees through us to our deepest emotions even if we try to hide them from ourselves (I will also return to this theme in Chapter Eight on growth).

Second, however, when I ask or demand in anger that he does things for me, they are unlikely to be done. This is not so much because God refuses to give in to what is, in effect, a very stroppy child; but more because what we want in these moments is often far from what we actually need. Being honestly angry with God, certainly, is the best and only place to start when we begin to speak to God, if that is what we genuinely feel, but it is not where we should finish. My speaking to God must also come with an openness to engage with him and listen to him as he responds to my anger in love, by turning his face to me and honouring my honesty. Once this openness to listen and to receive his love occurs, though, I start to become more ready to accept what is happening in my life (even if this feels very hard and unfair) and acknowledge his authority over me, despite life not going the way I want it to.

Third, I must again move into an arena which is quiet and still; to that place I must at all times claim before I first speak and listen to him. But once I have entered this place, I can then experience his love first-hand. I can say sorry for where I was previously and believe and trust in his love and forgiveness, as he prepares me to receive things much richer and more beneficial than meeting my mere wants. Finally, it is only in this place that I can give deep-felt thanks for all his blessings to me and can dare to live out Jesus' promise to his disciples (John 14:13) that I may ask for *anything* in his name.

Chapter Five
Forgiveness

As an opening to this chapter, I will explain why I do not include stories about forgiveness from my own life. Trivially, the preceding chapter contained a fairly long personal anecdote as a way of illustrating more general points about prayer. There is only so much you can take, probably, on the personal front, and certainly there is only so much I can divulge about myself at any one time.

More seriously, there is a personal story I could have told in this chapter concerning forgiveness, but I have decided to save it until Chapter Eight where I explore the character of growth. The story concerns the break-up with my first wife who had met someone else, a woman, who – after a two-and-a-half year or so on-off affair – she preferred to be with. Before the affair started, we had been married for just under twenty years, had two children and we were both active members of a local Baptist church. In matters concerning hurt and forgiveness, this was by far the most intense and challenging experience I have ever had to work through in my life. Why do I not include this story in this chapter then?

First, while at the time the break-up was obviously extremely painful and heart-breaking, I have since met and remarried a wonderful woman, Lyn, who has enriched my life hugely. My relationships with my children and my wife are thriving and I am looking forward with excitement and anticipation to the future. I have therefore 'moved on' – as they say – and the event of my break-up with my first wife is well and truly behind me. For this reason, the story is probably better placed in the chapter on growth as it allows me to explore issues in addition to forgiveness, including how pain, God's unexpected blessings, and our unpredictable journeying with Jesus Christ can contribute so profoundly to our well-being, personal growth and development.

Second, and most importantly, I recognise that although my experience of marriage break-up was no doubt the most challenging for me, in the grand scheme of things, this story is still fairly small beer for a lot of people regarding the meaning and importance of forgiveness. On the whole, my life has been reasonably well protected from serious hurt from others. I have loving parents and was never neglected, abandoned, or abused by them. I have never had to endure the hurt of oppression and exploitation of social, economic or political systems which millions of people in many parts of the world have to deal with on a daily basis. My workplaces, on the whole, have not been a source of hurt; rather I have experienced very supportive and enriching relationships with colleagues. I have also been blessed, over the years, with many loyal and loving friends and the families I have belonged to, in both my marriages, have been relaxed, fun to be with and, generally, very loving. Consequently, in matters relating to forgiveness I think I have had it relatively easy, and, aware that some readers would have experienced hurts much deeper and longer lasting than mine, I thought it better to not talk too much about forgiveness in my personal life.

FORGIVENESS

Recognising this, though, does not mean that the issue of forgiveness does not touch all of us very deeply, and on a daily basis. Regardless of what kind of life we might have led, everyone needs and has to learn about how to forgive and be forgiven for wrongdoing committed – however small, large, long- or short-lasting. Moreover, if we don't meet these needs to forgive and receive forgiveness and learn from these experiences, life will not be good – even if, like me, you have been relatively spared from hurt. Bearing this in mind, I will now explore, in more detail, what forgiveness means.

****

To get our terminology correct from the start, it is very important to make a clear distinction between forgiving and excusing – these are not the same things at all. The Lord forgives our sins or wrongdoings (for example, Mark 11:26) – but he doesn't excuse them, and so does not assume we are without blame. Likewise, when you forgive someone, you are not excusing the person for a wrong done to you, so making him or her blameless. If there was no blame, then there would be no need for forgiveness. Instead, forgiveness involves acknowledging that you have been wronged by the person and it was his or her fault, but you have chosen not to keep score of the wrong.

Forgiveness is, therefore, something very personal where not keeping a record of the wrongs committed against you means that you no longer feel a need to punish or hurt the wrongdoer for his or her wrongdoing. This does not mean that for other reasons we might think it right that the wrongdoer is punished (as will be explored below); it may even be, in some extreme cases, the perpetrator has to be punished first, in order for you to then forgive. However, the litmus test of forgiveness is that *your* need to punish and keep a record of the wrong has gone; you are able to 'let it go'.

It is possible for a person to cause a wrong against you without it being his or her fault, but according to the distinction just made this would be because there was an excuse. Here, the wrongdoer would have had no control over the circumstances leading to the wrong and so could not be blamed. This possibility raises all sorts of complex, sociological, psychological, political and philosophical questions about the degree of control people have over their lives, which are very open to debate and have no definite answers.

However, there are some cut-and-dried cases; take someone who, by accident, has driven into the back of your car because of an unavoidable brake failure in his vehicle. He has damaged your property, for sure, and so has wronged you (and so something has to be put right), but he is not morally culpable. The driver takes responsibility, via his insurance company, to make good the wrong, because his vehicle caused the damage – but he is not held morally responsible for the damage, as he wasn't to blame. Therefore, it would not be appropriate to say to this person 'I forgive you' as there is nothing to forgive.

Having made this distinction, when we hear someone say, 'I have no reason to forgive that person because there are no excuses for his (or her) behaviour' a basic mistake is being made concerning the meaning of forgiveness, as forgiveness requires acknowledging that the person you forgive has wronged you and that there are no excuses. The point is that this acknowledgement is precisely the reason why forgiveness is called for.

FORGIVENESS

However, once the meaning of forgiveness is disentangled from excusing in this way, we immediately realise how extremely difficult it is to forgive. It requires, on the one hand, that you make no excuses for someone who has wronged you and, on the other hand, you write-off the wrong and not hold it against the offender; there is no need for you to punish or keep a score of the wrong, even though it might be right for the offender to be punished. This is very hard and, indeed, for many of us, it is *the* hardest thing to do – especially when the wrong committed is deep and lasting.

It should be no surprise, then, that Christians put forgiveness at the heart of faith – so nurturing healthy and loving relationships between people, and between people and God. For example, the Christian claim; the claim from which all other Christian claims could be said to derive – is that just as we accept Christ's love and forgiveness for our own wrongdoing, so we also need to forgive others for the wrongs done to us. In Matthew 18:21-22, Jesus instructs Peter that we must forgive those who wrong us repeatedly; there is no end to it. And, as in the parable that follows of the unmerciful servant, it is only when we are prepared to forgive others that we are in a position to accept God's love and forgiveness for our own wrongdoing. Consequently, the central issue for practical living from a Christian perspective is that forgiveness, while extremely difficult to exercise, is what we all must do. The consequences of not doing so are that our lives will be made worse, so undermining our well-being. Why though, will we make it worse for ourselves if we don't forgive?

****

First, our hurts become magnified because not only have we, and maybe others around us, been hurt, but we also find it harder to have our hurts, caused by wrongdoing, to be healed by God – either to be healed by him directly or through others around us – if we don't forgive others. This is not because a loving God does not want to heal us if we are wronged by a culpable wrongdoer. Indeed, one of God's names in Hebrew, as identified in Exodus 15:26, is 'The Healer' (or *Jehovah-Rophe*). The problem is that when we maintain a need to punish the wrongdoer in some way and so keep a score of the wrong, we always remind ourselves of the wrong committed, thereby keeping the wound open and sore.

To become engaged in the healing process when we have been hurt is, therefore, a two-way affair. We need to first bring our wounds to God with the expectation these will be healed as a response to our own forgiveness of others, and of God's love for us. Healing, though, is multilayered and involves us being open to receiving health from the many places of love God can make for us in our lives – in friendships, family, the kindness of strangers; in music, art, books, scripture; in joy, laughter, beauty (natural or human-made), and so on. These multiple places of healing also involve us looking for opportunities to give love, however small or large, recognising Jesus' promise as reported in Acts 20:35, that: '…it is more blessed to give than to receive.' In short, the act of giving love makes us more able to receive the love and healing of God.

To become engaged in this two-way process of healing, then, we must ask for the love of God to come into our lives in his many manifestations, acknowledging that we are being healed by the source of all love and joy – indeed, the source of all creation. So our wounds are closed by an all-powerful, loving God. This divine 'closure' – using the terminology from popular psychology – while it does not make the hurt disappear, allows scars to be formed, closing off and letting go of our need to punish the wrongdoer and keep a record of the wrongs committed. Moreover, as with physical scars to the body, the wound is then healed by God's love and joy which knits us together with more strength than before – so leaving completely any outstanding issues of justice or judgement to God. As the psalmist in Psalm 103:3-6 asks:

> Who forgives all your sins and heals all your diseases, who redeems your life from the pit and crowns you with love and compassion, who satisfies your desires with good things so that your youth is renewed like the eagle's? The Lord works righteousness and justice for all the oppressed.

Second, it is harder for us to receive forgiveness from others and God for our own wrongdoing, if we don't forgive others, as we are less able to receive the blessings of forgiveness when we are reluctant to give them. Therefore, we must take the initiative and be the first to forgive, so stimulating the blessing. Also, it is incumbent upon each one of us to forgive, assuming, as John did in his first letter (1:8) that: 'If we claim to be without sin, we deceive ourselves and the truth is not in us'. In other words, the shoe is bound to end up on the other foot when we, too, need forgiveness. From whatever side then, it seems that it is bad news for us all if we don't forgive. But, before we examine more closely the role of Christ's love in forgiveness, it is important first to deal with some natural enough objections to what has been said so far.

Someone who refuses to forgive, or who cannot forgive even if they want to, often claims that in not writing-off the wrongs done to her, she might protect her, and others, better. The worry being, that if she does not count the wrong against the wrongdoer, then he will more likely commit the wrong again as he is not being punished. Therefore, contrary to what Christians claim, not forgiving makes the problem of wrongdoing better not worse.

However, this conclusion is derived from another basic error of not properly distinguishing between exercising punishment for good reasons, and forgiveness, which is a very personal act of letting go of *your* need to punish and keep a record of the wrongs. For example, it is reasonable for a woman to report her physically abusive husband to the police and decide to never have him back in her home. She needs to avoid further abuse of her and/or others close to her – but at the same time, embark on what will no doubt be a long personal journey of forgiving him. Forgiving this person does not imply that the wrongdoer should not be punished; justice must take its course in this case. It does imply that his wrongdoing should not be held against him *by her*. Indeed, sometimes, the hurt is so deep that a person can only forgive and 'let go' if the wrongdoer is first punished by the appropriate authorities which can only then clear the ground for the person relinquishing her need to punish and keep a score of the wrongs. Again, this is a good non-personal reason to punish the wrongdoer which certainly does not exclude forgiveness, but rather facilitates it.[12]

---

[12] Recently, listening to the radio, I heard a harrowing account from a victim of war crimes who felt she could only move on and 'let go' of her experience and what was done to her family, after the wrongdoer had been punished by a war-crimes court. This seems to me entirely

FORGIVENESS

However, even if the above is granted, it could also be said that the whole point about keeping scores, and not writing-off wrongs, is so that the wrong is not forgotten. It might be argued that if we forgot the wrongs committed, we throw away our moral compass, as it would be unclear how we determine what is just, or what is right. To address the latter issue I will look more closely at precisely how we might write-off wrongs, and so forgive in love.

****

In one way, forgiving is about forgetting but in another way, it is not. When a person is truly repentant – and deeply regrets his wrongdoing – the person who forgives, often invites the wrongdoer in love to 'forget it', as the expression goes – so allowing the wrongdoer to let go of his or her burden of wrongdoing, his regret and remorse, and move on.

This type of 'forgetfulness' is illustrated very well in Jesus' parable of the prodigal or lost son, found in Luke 15:11-32. The younger son, after squandering his father's inheritance, is filled with regret and remorse – so much so he returns home with no expectation that his status as son will be restored – this lack of restoration being his rightful punishment. However, his father, in seeing him from a distance, is filled with compassion. The father's loving response is to run toward him, to forgive him for everything he has done, and to restore his status as son, by killing the

---

consistent with facilitating forgiveness via punishment, exercised by the appropriate authorities. If it is not possible to mete out justice, though, it is still better, in my view, and as will be argued below, for the person who has been wronged to forgive, again for her sake and for her well-being.

63

fatted calf and celebrating his son's return with his household.

It seems that in this way, the wrongdoing of the son has been forgotten, allowing the son to start afresh as if his transgressions had never happened. Indeed, at the end of the story, the elder son, who had remained at home and always been loyal to the father, complained bitterly, precisely because it appeared as though the father had forgotten both what the younger son had done to his father and the commitment of the elder son. The response of the father was to remind the elder son that he had always been blessed in his father's house and that it was right to celebrate his brother's return, simply because the younger son had come home. He was lost but now he had been found, so it was time to celebrate his return and not remember his wrongdoing.

However, in another way forgiving isn't about forgetting at all because, while no score is kept of the wrongdoing and the need to punish has been dropped, what shouldn't be forgotten, in the parable and in all our lives, is the pain and hurt caused by wrongdoing. To illustrate this, I ask you to imagine a world where we could all immediately and completely forget the pain caused to us, and by us – where the pain leaves no trace in anyone, and we have no other recollection of the wrongdoing. Clearly, in this very fanciful world – as in the world where there are always excuses – there would be no need for forgiveness, as there is no pain caused of any lasting significance.

But we don't live in this world and I, for one, am very glad of it, as we *would* lose our moral compass. There would be no need to worry about how we act toward others, for example, as our collective amnesia would mean we could do what the hell we liked. In our world though, we do remember both the hurt we have caused and have had inflicted on us, however small or large, which then, thankfully, gives us our bearings concerning what we should and shouldn't do to each other in the future. The lost son, for example, would never have returned repenting of his wrongdoing if he had had no recollection of the pain he had caused his father and family, as a result of his behaviour. Likewise, the father would have had no reason to celebrate if he had had no recollection of the pain of his son being lost. Feeling pain then, as will be explored further in Chapter Eight, is a necessary feature of our growth and love for others – of developing loving relationships with others, and of developing a loving relationship with God, *our* father, in heaven.

This gets us, though, to the harder case; that of the unrepentant wrongdoer, who may have little or no insight of the pain caused and so has few or no regrets. Or who is aware of the pain he has inflicted, but has few or no regrets because he doesn't think what he has done is wrong. Probably the worst case is where he is aware of the pain he has inflicted, but has few or no regrets, even though he acknowledges he has done wrong. Should we also forgive these people? And if so, what good will it do? I will answer the last question first, as I believe it offers an incentive to forgive even the unrepentant.

Forgiving an unrepentant wrongdoer does him no good, as there is no burden of regret or remorse to be lifted. From his perspective, if you forgive, things stay the same. There is no comfort or blessing for him by you not wanting to punish him or keep a score of his wrongs, as he has no regrets about the hurt he has caused. Forgiving also though, you might say, does no harm to him either, as you are no longer *holding* the wrongs against him; and for this reason alone is problematic for those who are contemplating forgiveness. As the Old

Testament repeatedly testifies, we naturally want and expect the unrepentant wrongdoer to experience at least some level of harm for his wrongdoing as a matter of justice. It does not seem fair if this is not the case. If the harm to him also prevents him from committing more wrongdoing, or even provides a clear path for your forgiveness, then this is all to the good.

However, as I stated previously, he may be punished for his wrongdoing, and punished all the more perhaps for being unrepentant, but this is a very separate issue to him being forgiven by those he has wronged. Also, punishment can come in many guises, from very explicit forms of punishment administered by the authorities to more subtle, and perhaps worse, forms, where the life led by the wrongdoer is more impoverished than it otherwise would have been. It is relatively easy to point to examples of both, as well as to examples of those who have been punished needlessly or excessively. The point here is that whether you forgive or not, punishment will be 'rolled-out' to the wrongdoer separately. So, it is quite possible to forgive someone who is in jail for committing a wrong against you and for you to think it is right for him to stay there. Alternatively, you might find it hard to forgive someone who has wronged you, but still could admit (reluctantly no doubt, given the personal nature of forgiveness), that it is time for his punishment to stop. For sure, the second example is rarer than the first, but the point here is that issues concerning punishment are different to those concerning forgiveness and so should be kept separate. If these are not separated, the already difficult task of forgiving is made more problematic but for very mistaken reasons.

Of course, there are examples of people who, although

they commit many wrongs, seem to thrive in their lives and are not punished in any form at all. This state of affairs, when witnessed, will be extremely frustrating for sure, but the general rule, even in these cases, is still to leave the punishment and judgement to God; *you* still have the responsibility for forgiving the wrongdoer.

So, our task is to love our neighbour and, more problematically if we are to do as Christ instructed in Luke 6:35, to do good to those who hate us and so want to hurt us without regret. In Paul's letter to the Romans (12:19, citing Deuteronomy 32:35), he explains that it is God's job to be angry. Moreover, in verse 21 he tells us that we should 'not be overcome by evil, but overcome evil with good.' Hard messages, for sure, but crucial to hear and take on board if we are to receive the full blessings of forgiveness. Therefore, the long and short of it is: focussing on what good is done by forgiving the unrepentant wrongdoer leads us no further than the forgiver herself, and leaving the rest to God. But how is this good manifested exactly and how are benefits and blessings accrued?

****

The main claim from Christians, as highlighted previously, is that as we forgive others and as the harm and pain caused by the wrongdoer is presented to a loving God for healing, we receive blessings from him. In this process of forgiving (which can be long and arduous), and as explored previously, the pain and harm is repeatedly handed over to God to deal with. He then uses the multilayered expressions of his love to make us whole and healthy again, as far as we become open to receiving the strength and blessing of his healing love. As a result, the forgiver relinquishes her rightful power of punishment over the wrongdoer by writing-off the wrongs against him, and instead puts the pains and hurts caused on God's loving shoulders instead. But how does this transfer of pain and hurt happen exactly?

I explored in Chapter Three, how the burden of wrongdoing is handed over to the person of Jesus Christ, who demonstrates his love for us by taking on the sin and wrongdoing of the world by dying on the cross – and so, as Paul puts it in 2 Corinthians 5:21, 'God made him who had no sin, to *be* sin for us' (Emphasis added). Consequently, Jesus is able to declare, contrary to any principle of justice and what is right, that it's all his fault. But, given this declaration, we are able to transfer all wrongdoing to his shoulders, including the wrongs done to those close to us, which we also find hard to forgive. We have a place, subsequently, where we can, in prayer, unburden all the pains and hurts we have witnessed and which have touched us – and this place is at the foot of the cross.

Therefore, despite the apparent difficulty of the command for us to forgive repeatedly and for every transgression, we have no better option than to forgive others the wrong they do us even if they are unrepentant – given that the God who loves us, has forgiven us all our wrongs in exactly the same way. It may be that our wrongdoing has not been directed to those who have wronged us and that it is not nearly as deep and far-reaching, but all of us still act wrongly to differing degrees. In Colossians 3:13 Paul says, 'Bear with each other and forgive whatever grievances you may have against one another. Forgive as the Lord forgave you.' Similarly, the Lord's Prayer implores us to seek forgiveness from God the father for our trespasses, but with the condition that we

FORGIVENESS

forgive those who also trespass against us.

Finally, in becoming sin for our sakes, and by taking the blame onto his shoulders, Jesus proves not only his love for us, but also his authority to forgive sins – not just those wrongs done to him, but all wrongdoing – demonstrated through his healing power. This is vividly illustrated in the story of the paralytic man in Mark 2:1-12, who is brought to Jesus for healing by his friends. Jesus declared that the man's sins were forgiven and instructed him to get up and walk. This declaration shocked the crowd and outraged the religious leaders present, but the point of his proclamation and action was to demonstrate, through the fact the man did walk, that Jesus Christ does indeed have the authority to forgive sins.

Again, as I explored in Chapter Three, understanding how and why this authority is bestowed upon him, is only made clear after we accept the equally stupendous claim of God's incarnation – that a loving, all-powerful God became a person in Christ Jesus.[13] Nevertheless, it is an authority we need to take seriously, if we are to accept his love and forgiveness, so facilitating our forgiving of others – acknowledging he took the blame for our wrongdoing and those who wrong us on his shoulders, by dying on the cross for us all.

---

[13] If we don't accept this foundation for his authority, then according to C.S. Lewis in 'What are we to make of Jesus?' (see *God in the Dock* first published in 1971 by Geoffrey Bles), we are left with the proclamations of an ego-maniac madman who is utterly deluded about his own status and ability. Therefore, we have a stark choice, according to Lewis – either, accept Jesus' divinity as God made man, or condemn him as a deluded fool. What we can't choose, even though many try, is the belief that he was not divine in this way, and also believe he was sane and wise.

Chapter Six

Scripture

As a result of my initial conversion experience leading up to my nineteenth birthday, and as explored in Chapter One, I was completely overwhelmed by a sense that love, and Christ's message of love, met all our needs, and addressed our most fundamental questions concerning what our lives should be based on. While I didn't get any sleep that night, as I was so taken aback by this experience, the morning after, I was still a little nervous about my conversion. Being concerned about its validity, and thinking it might be a flash-in-the-pan, I thought that I had better test it out, and find out what was said in the bible. As we didn't possess a bible in my family home, early that morning I walked to the nearest bookshop and bought one.

I wasn't totally unfamiliar with bible stories, and the bible's sayings and moral recommendations. Up until the age of eleven, I had attended Sunday school and experienced there, and at regular school, the kind of sugar-sweet version of Christianity often taught to children. I even studied Mark's gospel for my school exams at sixteen and was intrigued by some of the religious debates and issues raised in class. Despite this, my knowledge of the bible was sketchy and I

SCRIPTURE

was curious to find out whether reading it again would have any resonance with my experience the previous day.

I was very aware, especially through my late-teens, that my overall experience of church, and many things connected with Christian culture, had become increasingly irrelevant and disconnected from my life. Consequently, I had more or less rejected Christianity as being, at best, superficial and, at worst, hypocritical and deluded. Buying the bible, then, with a view to reading it post-conversion, was a big test as there was the danger that the dissatisfactions I had with Christianity would surface. Therefore, reading the bible I risked either confirming my conversion, or possibly rejecting it.

So, I walked to town which was about a mile away, and purchased my first copy of the 'Good News' bible. Eager to begin looking at its contents, I thumbed through it, especially the New Testament, on my way back home and was utterly and completely startled by the impact it had on me. Certainly, some of it seemed strange and didn't make much sense, but a lot of its contents jumped out from the page and connected with me like electricity in a main circuit wire. The words had a very new kind of meaning for me and were now alive and relevant. From that moment, I realised the bible was a very special book, and that I would need to grapple with it, if I was to nurture my new-born faith.

****

Although having this very positive experience at the start of my Christian faith, I have never found the bible an easy book to read and meditate on. Over the years, it has challenged, even scared me at times; it has also been deeply comforting, and inspiring, and has offered me much hope and insight.

While it provokes me and 'rattles my cage' of my taken-for-granted beliefs and opinions, it points to a God who is wonderful and awe-inspiring, but who is also fiercely uncompromising. His anger, especially as seen in the Old Testament, often appears greater than his love and underpins many accounts of violence, destruction, and the punishment of various wrong-doers, whether this punishment is derived from natural or human sources. The bible also appears to present as fact much which is unbelievable and bizarre. This latter characteristic of the bible can be deeply troubling for those (like me) who believe that the bible is, in some fundamental way, true. It can lead to either a paralysis of thinking as disbelief is suspended and ignored, and where the reader only focuses on the more plausible sections of the text; or, to a dogmatic assertion of bible 'facts' which seem to fly in the face of scientific and other evidence, to the contrary. In both cases, these responses, I believe, can distract us from the profundity of what the bible and a loving God teaches us about *his* truth through scripture, which, as I will explore below, is often beyond our understanding of 'truths' and 'facts' however these are presented (also see Proverbs 3:5-6 and Chapter Two here on faith).

To add to the above problems, the bible also doesn't often pay attention to rules of clarity and logic, of the kind I have got used to in my career as university professor anyway, given that so many of the themes and issues explored appear contradictory, or are in tension, at least. For example, from the story of Adam and Eve onwards, the exercise of freedom and individual choice is repeatedly championed in scripture as a hallmark of our godliness and indicates how we must take responsibility for our actions and more generally, our lives. Conversely, if we assume we are not free and responsible

SCRIPTURE

then we cannot be held accountable for what we do and who we are. Moreover, this would contradict much of the dialogue and encounters between God and humanity, as illustrated throughout scripture. The assumptions of individual freedom and responsibility are found in the original fall from grace, when Adam and Eve first chose to eat from the tree of the knowledge of good and evil and are held responsible for this act (Genesis 3); in the recurring disobedience to God throughout human history as told through much of the Old Testament; and in the free gift of God which we can either choose to accept or reject, concerning his love and forgiveness, and reflected in the life and sacrifice of God's son, Jesus Christ (for example, see Romans 6:23, and see Chapter Three here).

Nevertheless, in many other parts of the bible we are also told of how we can become motivated by forces completely outside of our control, because of circumstances and experiences which seem just to happen without our choosing (such as conversion or other forms of miraculous intervention); or, from more direct and specific motivational changes of a person which are set in train by God himself to illustrate his power. Regarding the latter, for example, in Exodus 9:12, it states that God hardened Pharaoh's heart which then lay the foundation for the story of the Jews miraculously escaping slavery from Egypt against Pharaoh's will. In Romans 9:18, Paul repeats this theme in recounting the Exodus story, and asserts that, 'Therefore, God has mercy on whom he wants to have mercy, and he hardens whom he wants to harden.'

Of course, it is possible, and even likely perhaps, that the up-shot of all this is that we only exercise freedom, choice and responsibility as a matter of degree, and this is indeed what the bible, read as a whole, points us toward. But this response, although it contains important insights about the limitations of our freedoms – recognising that while we are free in certain domains of our lives, we also lack ultimate control as human beings – it too conveniently sidesteps the more difficult issue; that at different times in the bible, strong cases are made both for *and* against individual freedoms, so exposing, quite plainly, contradictory elements within the text. The bible, in other words, often does not seem to promote degrees of things, this being a subtler strategy, but rather everything or nothing, and that these promotions often pull in opposite directions and so are *in tension* with each other.

However, despite all these difficulties in reading the bible, and more beside, I have found that its stories and exploration of God's character, ancient Jewish history and its people, Christ's life and his message, and the thoughts and experiences of the early Christians, are full of a passion and energy which is hard-hitting and engaging. The bible when read in a certain way, has a fairy-tale quality to it, but when you look past this reading, it becomes a very real force which can penetrate our lives; in short, it draws us closer to the deeply mysterious, all-powerful, loving God. For these reasons, it is centrally important to explore what kind of attitude we should have to the scriptures, so as to develop and nurture our faith better. Psalm 119:16 tells us to delight in his decrees and not neglect his word. Given this instruction, how exactly then are we to approach the scriptures?

****

SCRIPTURE

Following what has been said so far, probably the most important lesson I have learnt about approaching the bible is that we should not see it as akin to a car manual for life. What I mean by this is that we should not expect to find in the bible neat-and-tidy, once-for-all answers to problems, presented in a clearly defined order, explaining, without ambiguity, how life works and how God operates. Certainly, we will receive many answers from the bible – if we approach it right – but these are necessarily provisional or, what we might call, 'a work-in-progress'. In other words, as we engage with the bible – expecting that it will challenge and deepen our faith – any answers are likely to lead to further questions concerning the character of God's love for us and our relationship with him, which then stimulate deeper reflections, so nurturing our faith further, and so on.

The problem is that many Christians, both now and in the past, have approached the bible as if it is a car manual and have nurtured all sorts of ridiculous beliefs and attitudes. They have, for example, insisted in answering everything 'in one go' as if there is a once-for-all explanation, and/or mistakenly assumed that any deeper questions asked of the text is somehow betraying God's word. Consequently, so-called 'truth' is read as if it can be tidily expressed in formulaic terms, ironically missing the point often made by the same group of Christians, that the bible is 'living' and so is an organic and moving force. The point is that if it is living, then, by analogy, it is precisely not suited to being permanently fixed and having one correct, once-and-for-all, interpretation. Rather, as stated previously, the living text would actively engage with God's people such that the words stimulate an on-going *relationship* with God that allows for further questioning, reflections and development of faith.

In contrast, the rigid and inflexible dogma generated from the car-manual approach to the bible, has led to bitter divisions in the church over many years, often based on very trivial matters of 'correct' interpretation. As Christ declared scathingly to the religious leaders of his time, in Matthew 23:24: 'You blind guides! You strain out a gnat and swallow a camel.' In the clamour for the correct, once-and-for-all interpretation of scripture, priorities can become grossly distorted, and the much more important and *fundamental* messages of justice, mercy, love and faithfulness end up being lost. As a result, leaders of churches have often become appallingly oppressive and exclusive, imposing their understanding of the bible on others, even to the point, in the worst cases, of torture and death if this imposition is not submitted to.

In summary, then, the car-manual approach to reading the bible I believe seriously diminishes our capacity to love God with our minds, because our God-given ability to question and wonder are effectively dispensed with. It also diminishes our capacity to receive his love and to love others, as anyone who happens to disagree with the supposed 'true' interpretation of the bible is condemned as being unsound, an unbeliever, the mouthpiece of Satan, and the like. Consequently, the car-manual approach to the bible encourages men, and sometimes women, to sound and appear as God. They often slander and condemn others who are not like them and don't think and believe like them, declaring that they, instead, are both right and justified in doing this.

****

SCRIPTURE

How then should we approach the bible, given what we should not do? If we expect scripture to challenge us and stimulate questions about our faith, but at the same time not deliver once-and-for-all neat solutions or answers, then our approach should be, in the first place, deeply humble, so suspending the expectation that we will be able to fully understand and take meaning from everything God says to us in scripture. We, therefore, must not assume our wisdom is sufficient to decipher everything from the text, what is pertinent or suggestive. Rather, scripture points to meanings which are often opaque, riddled with conflict and tension, and where the meaning God gives us, is frequently illusive, despite religious and philosophical pretensions to the contrary. We should also recognise that these pretensions are, indeed, precisely what the bible warns us against, lest we end up trusting our own understanding of God, rather than God himself.

For example, the opening lines of Ecclesiastes 1:1-2 states: "'Meaningless! Meaningless!" says the teacher. "Utterly meaningless! Everything is meaningless.'" This theme concerning the impossibility of full explanation and meaning being delivered in our lives is relentlessly pursued throughout this Old Testament book. The contemporary (even postmodern) tone of its passages is staggering – given the age of the text – resonating with current views, including my own, that access to *any* meaning and explanation to life's experiences is so limited. Moreover, Ecclesiastes is not a one-off either, and so the vain hope of full meaning and explanation for our lives being delivered through religious and philosophical reflection is quashed in other parts of scripture too.

In the book of Job, for example, God never told Job the

reasons for his suffering, even though the reader is privy to the mysterious deal made between God and Satan at the beginning of the story, which sets the scene for Job's awful testing. Instead, toward the end of the account, when Job confronts God with enraged questions of why he should suffer this way when he has done nothing wrong, God does not directly answer the questions but proclaims his own authority as the Lord of all things and creator of the universe. Job's response, at the end of the drama, (in 42:3), is to submit to God's authority and concede to God's refusal to give answers or any meaning and explanation for his suffering. Paradoxically, then, the answer for Job is that there is no answer, because God's ways are beyond his understanding, which Job finally realises and accepts: 'Surely I spoke of things I did not understand, things too wonderful for me to know.' In the epilogue (42:7-17), God, in his love, rewards and blesses Job for this insight and humility for the remainder of his life – while God also chastises Job's comforters who, earlier in the story, tried foolishly and in vain to explain Job's suffering in human and religious terms that they could understand.

Even when meaning is gleaned from scripture, there are, as explored previously, basic tensions and conflicts that often emerge at various significant points in the bible. For example, the tension between God's untouchable holiness or justness and the extreme demands he makes on his people for all-or-nothing devotion and obedience, seems often to pull in opposite directions to God's grace and forgiveness, which reaches out with generosity and mercy to those who are weak and flawed. Moreover, this is not just a division *between* the Old and New Testaments. For sure, and very importantly, the love and grace we have received from Christ's sacrifice is, in

SCRIPTURE

many ways, the hinge upon which the Old and New Testament's turns and so divides these texts. That is, as the old covenant made with God, leading to law and judgement, is replaced by the new covenant made with God, leading to forgiveness and mercy (also see Paul's letter to the Romans, 7; and Chapter Three here for a further exploration of how Jesus Christ has taken the blame for our wrongdoing, so making us right with God, and thereby avoiding God's judgement). However, this conflict and tension concerning the character of both God's judgement and mercy, and how he subsequently relates to us, is also exhibited *within* the Old and New Testaments, and is revealed, most starkly perhaps, in the life and teachings of Jesus himself.

The gospels show Jesus as being compassionate and forgiving to a desperate and lost people, but also as utterly uncompromising and demanding when it comes to faith and discipleship. The former voice shows how Jesus is tolerant and inclusive and without judgement, as reflected in John 3:17: 'For God did not send his Son into the world to condemn the world, but to save the world through him.' Whereas, the latter voice of Jesus seems to both divide and judge. So in Luke 12:51, Jesus asks rhetorically: 'Do you think I came to bring peace on earth? No, I tell you, but division.' And, in Matthew 7:13-14, Jesus proclaims that many people will enter through the wide gate which leads to destruction, while only a few will enter the narrow gate and what he calls, 'the road that leads to life.'

For sure, Jesus' judgement and the division promised was often reserved for the religious leadership at the time who were, it seems, oppressive, arrogant and enjoying the status generated from being members of self-serving and powerful religious institutions. However, many other groups, too, were in the firing-line – the rich (for example, Matthew 19:24), the self-important (for example, Luke 14:7-11), the cowardly (for example, Matthew 25:24-30), the unprepared (for example, Matthew 25:1-13), the faithless (for example, Mark 4:35-40), and the racist (for example, Luke 10:25-37) (plus other groups beside). So, when I read the gospels I often feel uncomfortable that I am, in more than a few ways, part of these other groups and, like the religious leaders and hypocrites, also should beware.

However, in my own fallibility, I am also deeply encouraged by the other voice of Jesus which promises me forgiveness and support – especially when I recognise my own weaknesses. This deeply empathic and non-judgemental response to frailty is epitomised in the opening line of the Sermon on the Mount, in Matthew 5:3: 'Blessed are the poor in spirit, for theirs is the kingdom of heaven.' Jesus makes it clear, then, that it is not the holy or righteous who are the recipients of the promised enrichment, but those who are broken or weak and so who have little or nothing to offer. For this promise, I am both glad and relieved, recognising that I, too, am often poor spiritually and so in need of his blessing and replenishment.

Developing this theme of humility in our approach to scripture, it is important to also be open and ready for change. The instruction from Jesus in Mark 2:22 is that we should be like new wine in new wineskins and so not assume that our old selves can hold or contain his new message of love. Most of us have a relatively fixed mind-set or entrenched attitudes about what is right, pure and holy. This fixedness often leads us to conveniently bury those parts of scripture which go against our more cherished beliefs. Of course, as already said, the bible is likely to reflect a range of mind-sets and attitudes,

SCRIPTURE

so generating various conflicts and tensions. However, what we shouldn't do in response is try to solve these conflicts and tensions by highlighting or stressing what we like in scripture and ignoring what we find more difficult. If we exercise this kind of bias, then we are effectively using old skins for new wine which, as we are told by Jesus, cannot mix with any useful result.

We should first acknowledge those passages which go against our grain and then, openly and honestly, grapple with them, recognising that some, perhaps many, of our cherished beliefs may have to be sacrificed, or at least adapted, as a result. However, being open to change is not an emptying of our minds and a dispensing of these cherished beliefs and attitudes. This can lead to a vulnerability to manipulation often associated with religious cults. The emptying of our minds is self-deceit – a denial of who we are and what God has made us. Being open to change is, instead, predicated by our grappling and wrestling with deeper truths and understandings concerning how we ourselves, including our most cherished beliefs, authentically relate to God's word and the different and various narratives expressed and told throughout the bible.

As scripture is approached with an attitude of humility and openness to change, we also must acknowledge that scripture tells us that we will, in the process, struggle with God and who we are, in order to receive his blessing and love. For example, there is a very strange story in Genesis 32:22-32 which tells of Jacob spending the night physically wrestling with a man who turns-out to be God, leading to God's blessing and Jacob being re-named 'Israel' (meaning: 'he struggles with God'). Consequently, we too should expect and welcome this deep and intimate struggle with God as a mark

81

of our being chosen and blessed by him. Far too often, wrestling with God and his word, is seen in Christian circles as a mark of weakness and a lack of faith, when more often than not, the opposite is true. This struggle, instead, indicates the committed engagement of someone who is critically reflective in her relationship with God. She is not prepared to submit to quick 'solutions' to conflict which merely ape submission to God, but rather persists at wrestling with him, knowing that this ultimately brings her in closer contact with God and the many manifestations of his love with which he wants to bless her.

However, as with Jacob, we should also expect, at the end of this struggle, to be incapacitated or silenced by God, if only temporarily. Therefore, at some point, we should say, *with* God, 'enough is enough'. So, we must also acknowledge the importance of resting with God as well, to receive his blessing without resistance and struggle. If we don't recognise and foster this fundamental tension between struggle and resting in the love of God, I believe we are left with one of two bad outcomes, undermining our well-being – either a perpetual and unceasing conflict which threatens the peace and stillness with God and his blessing of belonging; or a complacent 'faith' denying the deep connectedness with God derived from struggling with his often opaque and impenetrable character. Instead, when holding the tension between wrestling and resting with God, we should expect scripture to take root in our lives and to enhance our well-being. Scripture should subsequently deeply connect and grow *through* us, shaping and engaging with how we think, feel, and experience our lives and the world we inhabit, with the ultimate goal in mind of more fully accepting God's love and joy in our lives as we increasingly obey and trust him.

SCRIPTURE

Finally, while recognising the uniqueness of scripture and how we can relate to it in these ways, we should also see that his word does not, by any means, finish there – as if fossilised in a museum cabinet labelled 'The Bible'. Scripture reveals, for sure, the epic history of God's engagement with humanity, and its continuing power is found in how scripture can enliven and enrich people's lives today. However, the bible is not the *last* word from God – of who he is and what he wants to say to us. If we use the bible as the foundation of our understanding of him through the written word, as a place where we always *start* in our journeying with him – then we can also hear his word and experience his healing love in many other places too, both religious and secular. As Paul instructs the Philippians in 4:8:

> ... whatever is true, whatever is noble, whatever is right, whatever is pure, whatever is lovely, whatever is admirable – if anything is excellent or praiseworthy – think about such things.

Throughout history and in all cultures, God speaks to us of his love and the strength to be found in embracing and submitting to this ultimate, all-powerful, life-giving force. He points us to the importance of forgiveness and redemption in our lives and the capacity for courage and faithfulness in the overcoming of our weaknesses, but also of our frailty and flawed characters which undermine our ability to love well, or even at all.

God also says many things to us about his love that heals through the beauty of his creation and our continued discovery of it, and through the love we give and receive from others – as well as through our attempts to express this beauty, joy, and love in numerous forms of art, music, writing, and so on. Moreover, even as we strain to honestly express our frustrations, pains, anger, and fears in our lives, we also hear God's voice and his response, which honours our honesty and listens with compassion and mercy to our frequent sense of being lost and abandoned. So, God's voice of love is found in all the nooks and crannies of our experience, and this – if we care to look closely enough – is precisely what the bible teaches us too.

Chapter Seven
Church

A church leader once said to me: 'If you find a perfect church, for goodness sake don't join, as you are bound to spoil it.' Contrary to Groucho Marx's witty comment: 'I wouldn't join a club that would have me for a member', the church is filled to the brim with flawed characters, like you and me. Also, when I attend church I meet people with whom I often have little in common, other than that we go to church and we are Christians. The latter commonality counts for a lot, certainly, given that our core beliefs are similar. But the important human connections I might make with fellow church-goers otherwise – through common interests, compatible personalities, shared senses of humour, mutual likes and dislikes, and so on – often seem tenuous.

Given this arena of human frailty and lack of human connection, it is no surprise, then, that members of a church can feel disconnected from each other, let alone from those outside. Moreover, as the hilarious sit-com, *Father Ted* depicts so well, in the church there can be mutual irritations, back-biting, and other divisions, which (in Western culture at least) are thinly disguised by the niceties of Christian politeness. At worst, these divisions fester and become deep fissures. The result of these divisions has been that numerous church denominations have formed, and there has even been much violence and war.

To add to these woes, the church also has a long history of rubbing shoulders with, and even being at the apex of the most powerful groups and institutions in society, to the detriment of those less powerful groups the church is supposed to represent. There have been many times, for sure, when the church has championed the cause of the exploited and downtrodden, and sided with justice and what is right. But, the church has often pointedly not stood against oppression and exploitation, and even supported its perpetrators, both within and outside its ranks – either to protect its own interests, or from an exaggerated and distorted commitment to obeying 'the governing authorities' (as recommended by Paul in Romans 13:1-7).

However, if this passage is examined more closely, Paul recommends this obedience on the assumption that these authorities are doing what is good for its citizens (Romans 13:4) and for this reason, quite rightly, we should obey them – pay our taxes, keep the law, etc. But Paul's far-reaching qualification to his instruction means our obedience, while generally expected, is nevertheless conditional. Consequently, we might legitimately ask: what if the authorities are *not* doing what is good for you, and are, say, systematically exploiting and oppressing its people? Of course, no government is perfect, but this is beside the point, as presumably there is a line which can be crossed – between some degree of tolerable imperfection, and explicit and systematic abuse – over which we are no longer obliged to obey government.

CHURCH

Where exactly this line is to be drawn is controversial. However, that a line can, in principle, be drawn is plain,[14] even according to Paul's own arguments. It can most notably be drawn for those authorities who by their very character or constitution, abuse and oppress their people. The church has no reason to support these types of regimes yet it often has, and, in the process, has flimsily used Romans 13 as an excuse to avoid its responsibilities to defend those who are downtrodden.

In addition, as well as exhibiting political cowardice and timidity in the face of oppressive regimes, many elements of the church have accumulated large amounts of wealth and private property – so much so, that for a lot of people, church means the physical buildings and assets belonging to it. All this is for a God who, according to Stephen in Acts 7:48-50, and citing Old Testament scripture, 'does not live in houses made by men'. Therefore, the church as well as being allies with, and part of, the powerful who have frequently exploited and oppressed people, it has also been allies with and members of the richest classes. Consequently, the history of the church – whether this is the world-wide church or local churches where people meet – concerning the wider promotion of justice and liberation, is very chequered, to say the least. Given these deep-seated problems within the

---

[14] The United Nations 1948 Declaration of Human Rights is probably the best attempt to date at having an agreed line over which, if Governments step, are condemned by the international community as being systematically abusive. Of course, the precise interpretation of these rights is still disputable, as is the enforcement of these rights. But this declaration shows the possibility, at least, of establishing universal rules for government behaviour which are both definable and practicable.

church, why don't we just abandon the project of church altogether and get on with nurturing our faiths individually? Why do we need Christian communion at all, and what is in it for us who are members, and for those outside? More bluntly, what is the point of the church?

****

Importantly, human flaws and imperfections, both within and outside the church, are never entirely movable or avoidable, and so getting rid of, or ignoring the church, would not alleviate this basic human problem. On the flip-side, if we commune with other Christians, we at least have to face this fact together, as part of the universal church (or the Body of Christ, as will be explored below).[15] Therefore, honestly recognising that this imperfection exists within its midst can also be the church's greatest strength. It is important, therefore, to acknowledge that we are bound to take with us, to the physical place of church our personal weaknesses, imperfections, and hurts – our heavy burdens, or our 'personal baggage' as it is called nowadays. However, this is precisely what the universal church invites us to do – to openly and honestly unburden ourselves, recognising that for all sorts of reasons, some our fault and some not, we are fundamentally flawed and imperfect and so need to be part of the Body of Christ.

As also explored in Chapters Two and Three, our Christian faith is hallmarked by us first acknowledging our

---

[15] I am grateful to my copy-editor, Clodagh Springer, for highlighting the distinction between the universal church, the world-wide church, and local churches where groups of believers meet.

own weaknesses, imperfections and burdens, which are then directly dealt with by the loving forgiveness and healing of Christ. As Jesus proclaimed in Matthew 11:28:

> Come to me, all you who are weary and burdened, and I will give you rest. Take my yoke upon you and learn from me, for I am gentle and humble in heart, and you will find rest for your souls. For my yoke is easy and my burden is light.

So, Christ offers us a place to unburden ourselves, and, if the universal church is the human manifestation of his love and our common baptism into the one body (1 Corinthians 12:12-13), then it too should be a place where we let go of our frailties and weaknesses and rest with him, in his body, in joy and in love.

The problem, though, is that the church in the world (whether globally or locally), by it often supporting a culture of politeness and social and political conformity, frequently encourages us to merely hide these weaknesses and burdens and not allow members to express them honestly and openly. As a result, personal issues are buried in the churchyard, before we even walk through the doors, to be dug-up and carried on our backs again when we leave. Moreover, this hiddenness further reinforces the disconnection between its members, and between the church and those outside. Many, subsequently, whether church-goers or not, engage superficially with the church – either attending only when convention tells us to – for weddings, funerals, and the like – or, if, attending more regularly, go through the motions of 'the service' but without properly engaging with the message and healing power of the Body of Christ. Our job then, as

Christians within the church, is to allow ourselves to say and be what we are – warts and all and with all our hang-ups and questions– and cultivate the universal church as a place where we can be truthful and authentic, and so not be false and mannered. It is only within this latter context, I believe, that the love and lightness of Christ's yoke can be fully experienced, and true rest and well-being can be found for our souls.

In addition, this lack of truthfulness and authenticity can also be reinforced by a lack of human connection with church members – concerning, for example, common interests, compatible personalities, shared senses of humour, mutual likes and dislikes, and so on. As stated earlier, in one way this lack of connection is only superficial, compared with our common faith and baptism which is shared, but in another way it can be a significant obstacle to developing our faith. It is important in human contact to find people we can identify with and so enjoy and relate to; otherwise life can feel very lonely and isolated. Similarly, in church-life it is important to engage in relationships which are connected, so allowing for the full expression of ourselves in the Body of Christ, and reflecting the wide range of personal characteristics which we all possess (also see 1 Corinthians, 12:12-31).

****

When I first became a Christian, I found this human connection with other Christians very difficult to achieve, as I didn't relate or identify with many of the Christians I encountered; in church, in student Christian unions, on street corners, etc. For want of a better word, their lifestyles were not my own and so I was unable to connect with their personalities, interests, humour, likes and dislikes. However, there were exceptions to this, for sure, which proved vital to my growth and development as a Christian.

Soon after my conversion, a punk-rocker friend I had known from college when I was between the ages of sixteen and eighteen, heard through the grapevine that I had 'found religion' and become a Christian. He contacted me to explain that he'd gone through a similar experience a couple of months previously. He had joined up with a small bunch of Christians in his hometown about ten or so miles from my own, but had not relinquished – thank God – his previous personality (which was warm, witty and disarmingly honest), or his punk attire which, for me, was wonderfully outrageous and bold.

Meeting up with Mick again, at this early stage after my conversion, was crucial to me developing and nurturing my faith, especially given that I, like him, felt very disconnected from regular church. His authenticity and openness in expressing his new-found faith was a lifeline to me, as, without this, I think I probably would have floundered and become unsure of myself and my conversion. Mick made me realise that people like us – the punks and the misfits – could also make sense of what Jesus' love can mean in our lives, and, at the same time, not feel as if we had to apologise to the world and to the church about who we were and what we looked like.

What I also experienced, of course, was Jesus' love reaching out to everyone, and identifying, as he did in his life and is still doing now, with those who the world and established religion, often rejects. He consciously chose to associate with social outcasts and those who were at the lower end of the social stratum – lepers (for example, Mark 1:40-

41), prostitutes (for example, Luke 7:36-50), tax-collectors (for example, Matthew 21:31), despised foreigners (for example, Luke 10:25-37), adulterers (for example, John 8:1-11), common fishermen (for example, Mark 1:16-20) and many others besides, none of whom were highly respected or even respected at all. Jesus was severely criticised for his identification with these 'outsiders' and his mission was called into question by the religious authorities, as a result. This was despite the various and unexplainable miracles he regularly performed and the authority with which he seemed to speak which attracted, initially at least, a very large following (Luke 7:18-35).

In the end, as we know, Jesus was rejected by both the authorities and the people (see John 18:28-40), and he paid the ultimate price for this rejection, in his slow tortured death being nailed to a cross, as recorded in all the gospels. But what these stories of Jesus' life tell us is how little he was concerned with supporting and identifying with the conventional, the socially approved, respected or those with high status and standing. Instead, Jesus connected and identified with those outside 'the fold' and separate from the crowd, and often, in the process, he – alongside these outsiders – were despised, ridiculed, and persecuted.

Regarding my own experience (inevitably perhaps as I have grown older) in matters concerning dress-code and general demeanour, I have become more socially conventional and conforming, and, sadly, I have also lost touch with Mick. But, what this lesson taught me in my very early development as a Christian, and has since been repeatedly confirmed, is that I should never pretend to be someone I am not – either to God or members of the church. Pretence leads to a superficial engagement with God and others, and to loneliness, and self-deception. Consequently, if a particular church can't handle who you are, move on and avoid falling into the traps of these pretensions and deceptions. Be patient though, because eventually you will find, with God's help, Christians who you can genuinely connect with and be yourself – whoever or wherever you are. Remember, too, that while you wait, Jesus connects with and loves who you are now, and so you are already included in his universal church and Body regardless. In other words, he does not wait for you to become some different person who others, and even yourself perhaps, would prefer you to be, for you to become a member of *his* body.

As a result, since this earlier period of my conversion, I have been able to enjoy many deep and lasting Christian friendships and I have been able to connect with these friends humanly in the way just described – most notably in Oxford, where I lived for fifteen years, and was a member of a small Anglican church – but also in other places too. For example, about seven or eight months after my conversion, I went to live in Newcastle-upon-Tyne to study politics at the university based there. I tried a couple of churches in the area, but eventually settled, after a year or so, in a church which was part of 'The House Church Movement' in the UK. I found the worship painfully embarrassing, with a lot of dancing and prancing about; I used to watch but never joined in, but the preaching was good and, most importantly for me at the time, I was able to connect with the people there.

Certainly, the faith of its members was very genuine and alive, but I also noticed that there was friendly banter among them (which I have always enjoyed in any company), and they did other 'normal' things – such as go down the pub, watch football, go to the movies, hold parties, have conversations about who they fancied or didn't fancy, what kind of good or bad days they had, etc. Most importantly, perhaps, they also accepted and seemed to enjoy who I was too – partly as I liked doing these things with them, but also because they wanted to hear what I had to say and what I thought about my faith – even if this, to many of their ears, would have sounded sometimes strange and unconventional. Indeed, I remember one of the members, Jane, saying that I should write a book telling about my stories as a Christian and what I had learnt – and over thirty years later, here we are. Better late than never, I suppose![16]

I also found this same connection with the church members in Oxford, and as a leader there, I positively encouraged the kind of openness and honesty about who we are with each other, so we could deepen our faiths and our relationships together. Most of them have moved on now, including me, and many have become church leaders after training for ministry. I have managed to keep my friendships with a number of them though, and one very special friend, Ernesto, who is now a vicar, blessed my marriage to Lyn in 2010. His positive influence on me, what I have learnt from him and shared with him, has been huge, alongside the others from this group – such as Ruth, Nick, Kes, Debbie, Simon, and Anna, for example – but also the many more in this church (if I had to name them all the list would be too long), with whom I had the privilege to be friends with, during this

---

[16] As a footnote to this experience in Newcastle, Jane, I also discovered, and to both our amazement, knew Mick, even though Newcastle was almost 400 kilometres from where Mick lived. Jane was brought up in Mick's hometown and Mick was close friends with her brother. Is this coincidence or God's loving hand in everything? I know what I believe!

fifteen year period.

In summary, then, in various church-based contexts over the years, I have tried to express and reflect who I am – genuinely and authentically – and have encouraged others to do the same, in order that we, as Christians, might humanly connect with each other and, in the process, nurture our faith. However, despite this endeavour, and the many wonderful relationships which have ensued, I still feel a lack of connection with many other Christians which should also be acknowledged. This lack of connection, I believe, reflects the inevitable character of the worldwide church, with its many imperfections and flaws, but also, more positively reflects its variety and richness.

Following from the latter point, I have grown to understand how Christ has included in his one universal church a huge range of personalities and characters, each possessing many and varied gifts. Therefore, each of us has a special role to play in his body, where God can use our differences positively, and at the same time, unify us through our shared faith in Christ. Again, as Paul explains in 1 Corinthians 12:18-20:

> But in fact God has arranged the parts in the body, every one of them, just as he wanted them to be. If they were all one part, where would the body be? As it is, there are many parts, but one body.

In the making of this body, the universal church, I also know that Christ's love fully recognises who I am, and can uniquely use what I have to offer, and for this reason alone I can fit in any particular church regardless. Certainly, on a personal level, this might not always feel comfortable, but that's OK, as church is not essentially a social club, but a place where you can meet God whether or not you connect with others who are there on a personal level. But I also know that I will sooner or later meet Christians who I can humanly connect with; who I am able to relax and be myself with, and that out of these relationships will come healthy learning and a deepening of faith.

The more I grow in these places and the greater my experience of the liberation of being honest with myself and others then, paradoxically, and as Paul said in 1 Corinthians 9:19-23, I will be able to be all things to all people, in order to share and nurture our mutual blessings in Christ. As I have become less hung-up about where I fit, I find I can easily worship by singing modern choruses, traditional hymns, or following ancient liturgy. In any of these places I know God will be reflected and his voice is there to be heard if my ears are open to hear. I have also learnt how to speak with vicars, bishops and lay people, and anyone else besides, without presenting myself any differently and yet also discern what is appropriate to say, or not say in specific contexts, for our mutual benefit.

I am also comfortable doing the same with others outside the church and feel I can fit well into so-called 'secular' places too. I therefore try to adapt, in love and service, to the particular situations I find myself in, but remain at core the same person in each. I assume the view that I can, with God's guidance, learn from and share the blessings of God's love for us in any situation by coming alongside anyone who is willing to do so. I have found that life, experienced this way, becomes rich and unpredictable. As I commune and celebrate with church members and with others, I have no pre-conceptions or pre-conditions about where and how I will encounter the love of God and Christ.

Finally, this encounter is profound and long-lasting as it also defines and shapes what can be redeemed from the darker history of the world-wide church, described earlier. It provides a foundation for radically challenging the status quo, and what is presently viewed by the world as wise, strong, and respected – and to make room for a humble recognition of God's authority in our lives. Again, according to Paul in 1 Corinthians 1:27-29:

> But God chose the foolish things of the world to shame the wise: God chose the weak things of the world to shame the strong. He chose the lowly things of this world and the despised things – and the things that are not – to nullify the things that are, so that no one may boast before him.

Therefore, and to repeat Stephen's proclamation in Acts 7:48-50, our loving God does not live in houses made by human hands, but lives through his re-shaping of the world and turning it upside down. By setting aside what we vainly edify and exalt ourselves with, he asserts his loving power and glory through elevating those who, like his son Jesus Christ, are rejected and abandoned. Consequently, as Stephen also proclaims in the above passage (citing Isaiah 66:1-2), and just before he was stoned to death by the religious authorities himself, heaven is God's throne and earth is his footstool. So, his loving power – having made, and being in, all things – can be found, and will find you, anywhere.

Chapter Eight

Growth

Growth here relates, not to increasing the numbers of people attending church or converting to Christianity, but to the personal journeys Christians and others take – what we all learn about and incorporate into our lives that brings us closer to the love of God, and the peace and well-being which result, whether we are aware of God's presence or not. Given this clarification, I will address two questions here: how is growth best facilitated? And, what does growth more specifically entail? When addressing the first question I will not use personal anecdotes much, but instead will lay out my broader understanding of the Holy Spirit's character. In underpinning personal growth, the crucial role played by accepting Christ's love in the person of the Holy Spirit will be addressed. When addressing the second question I will use examples from my own life, drawing out general lessons about how we can utilise both our gifts and painful experiences for our personal growth and well-being.

Christians believe that personal growth – whatever this entails and which will differ between people – must, in all cases, be facilitated by the power of the Holy Spirit. This power is said to underpin growth, like soil underpins the growth of plants. Different plants thrive in different environments but all need soil to grow. This is the same for people, so the Christian account goes. Our talents or gifts are very different – as are our experiences – and we all require a particular nurturing environment for personal growth. However, despite these differences, what we all need in common to underpin this growth is God's Holy Spirit. Consequently, we must learn, and continually re-learn, the importance of depending on God's strength and power, and *not* our own. Recognising this commonality and dependency gets us though to the more difficult question: what is the Holy Spirit's character and how does this character relate to the love of God?

****

The first problem we encounter is the use of the term: 'Holy Spirit' often conjures up peculiar images. For example, when I went to church as a child, the Holy Spirit was often referred to as the Holy Ghost. This put in my mind the idea that God had created some kind of phantom thing, separate to himself, which wisped around spooking people. Of course, this is a childish response to the question of the Holy Spirit's character, but this does, I believe, reveal a deeper problem concerning how the Holy Spirit is viewed and understood.

We often think of the Holy Spirit as an 'it', rather than a 'he', and so, like the ghostly phantom, making him an object or thing which is either separate from God or, more plausibly, as a characteristic of God – 'it' being God's positive power, for example. However, although attributing this characteristic to God captures an important aspect of the Holy Spirit, as

Christians often, quite rightly, talk of the power of the Holy Spirit, it doesn't convey the full meaning and implications of the Holy Spirit's character reflected in scripture and in Christian doctrine. Jesus Christ makes it clear in John 14:15-31 that the Holy Spirit is a 'he' being the spiritual manifestation of himself, as distinct from his physical manifestation, and that he will be, as a result, with his disciples always.[17] In John 14:15-18, Jesus Christ declares:

> ... I will ask the Father, and he will give you another Counsellor to be with you for ever – the Spirit of Truth. The world cannot accept him, because it neither sees him nor knows him. But you know him, for he lives with you and will be in you. I will not leave you as orphans; I will come to you.

And then in John 14:23:

> If anyone loves me, he will obey my teaching. My father will love him, and we will come to him and make our home with him.

---

[17] It is important also to acknowledge, that the Hebrew for Spirit is Ruach which is feminine, so in the Old Testament, at least, the Spirit is a 'she'. I am grateful to Reverend Ruth Bierbaum for pointing this out in her reading of an earlier draft, highlighting the deeply mysterious character of the Holy Spirit and how an essentially un-gendered person of the Holy Spirit (and God) can be understood. I appreciate that my using the masculine form throughout the book to describe God and 'his' characteristics may be profoundly objected to by some readers. All I can say in response is that my intention, at least, has been to emphasise the personal character of God, and so the possibility of our subsequent relationship *with* God, and certainly not to imply any essentially masculanised form of this personhood.

GROWTH

It seems then the imagery of the Holy Spirit as an 'it', reflecting the power of God, for sure, is a more accurate representation than the Holy Spirit pictured as a phantom-like ghost – but this still doesn't capture the very personal character of the Holy Spirit. 'It' seemingly has no relationship with the personhood of God (*him* the father) or the personhood of Jesus (*him* the son) – as 'it' is relegated to an impersonal force or attribute of God, but not as a manifestation of God and Jesus Christ himself, and of his love for us.

However, by depersonalising the Holy Spirit we also avoid the much more difficult and mysterious notion of seeing God as both three persons, and one. Consequently, we avoid the stupendous claims made, and also explored in Chapter Three, concerning the trinity and the divine personhood of Jesus Christ – namely, claiming God as Father, and as Son, and as Holy Spirit. Nevertheless, the additional equally stupendous claim in this chapter is that if the Christian notion of the trinity is undermined or conveniently by-passed, this reinforces the divide between God and us. Consequently, if we do not acknowledge the Holy Spirit as the 'third layer' or spiritual manifestation of God and Jesus Christ, we end up missing out on how the grace and love of God is also living with us. As stated by Paul in 2 Corinthians 13:14, and repeated in church services worldwide:

> May the grace of the Lord Jesus Christ, and the love of God, and the fellowship of the Holy Spirit, be with you all.

But where does the divine personhood of the Holy Spirit come from? And, why is it so important to believe this last difficult claim, rather than the easier metaphorical image of the Holy Spirit as a de-personified characteristic of God's love or power?

I admit that I too have often found it difficult to understand the personhood of the Holy Spirit. Even after getting to grips with Christian doctrine concerning the personal divinity of God the Father and God the Son, it still can seem superfluous or unnecessary to understand the Holy Spirit in this way too. Isn't it enough to have God 'up there', as the almighty creator and loving father, and God 'down here' in the person of Jesus Christ, the son? Why do we also need the Holy Spirit?

I have meditated on and prayed about these questions over the years and the main lesson I have learnt is that the claim regarding the presence of the Holy Spirit is supposed to be difficult and mysterious. But when I acknowledge that the Holy Spirit as person is so impossible to grasp, I have discovered, strangely, that the feeling that he is superfluous starts to retreat too. But how does this happen exactly?

Again, as explored in Chapter Three, the notion of a loving God made incarnate, and so being made a person in Jesus Christ is hard enough to even begin to understand, as it seems to turn upside down the Judaic notion of God the creator, being separate to the created. Adding another 'layer', the Holy Spirit, appears then to compound the problem. However, what I want to suggest here is that, as Christians, we have no choice but to embrace the 'third layer', otherwise we can't properly deal with the implications of the two other stupendous claims, also explored in Chapter Three – that in demonstrating his love for us, Jesus Christ died for our sins and so became sin for our sakes, and then came back to life again. Without the Holy Spirit we would also find it difficult to believe in the power that Jesus himself exercised as demonstrated through his various miraculous interventions, and the subsequent importance of depending on God's power in our lives for personal growth, as *distinct* from our own power.

First, it is important to highlight a practical feature concerning how the disciples were said to receive the Holy Spirit. According to Acts 1:1-11, the disciples were instructed by Jesus Christ to wait for the Holy Spirit to come to them – that is, some days after they had experienced Jesus' resurrection as he appeared to them in his physical form on various occasions. So, we are told in Acts 1:4-5:

> On one occasion, while he was eating with them, he gave them this command: 'Do not leave Jerusalem, but wait for the gift my Father promised, which you have heard me speak about. For John baptised with water, but in a few days you will be baptised with the Holy Spirit.'[18]

Consistent with this command, we know for sure (whether Christian or not), that Jesus didn't stay with us in his physical form – even after, as Christians believe, his resurrection. Therefore, we might say that waiting for the Holy Spirit – as promised by Jesus Christ in this passage and elsewhere in the gospels – is a waiting for him in his spiritual form, given his physical form has certainly left the world.

But why has Jesus Christ, in this world, abandoned the

---

[18] It is also important to acknowledge that, according to the Gospels, Jesus himself was baptised by the Holy Spirit, by John. For example, see Mark 1:9-13, which again demonstrates that these questions are indeed impenetrable and mysterious.

physical form for the spiritual? If the claim about the resurrection is true – that he came back to life three days after being put to death – then why doesn't he keep his resurrected physical form for all time, here with us? If he did this, there would be no argument from anyone, about whether he had come back to life or not. We could point to his physical body as a living person and say 'look, there he is; the one who came back to life again over two thousand years ago' and so have clear, incontrovertible evidence that his resurrection actually happened. He would look the same, he wouldn't die again, would be able to tell stories about his life across many generations, and so on. No one would have any choice but to believe in the authority of Christ, given this stupendous and utterly unique feat, proving without any possibility of doubt, his divinity.

However, the most straightforward and immediate answer to the question of why he did not maintain his physical form is already contained in the proceeding sentence. If there is no choice but to believe, then this, as I explored in Chapter Two, undermines the meaning and purpose of faith which is a step of trust into what is not known, or not incontrovertibly proven. Having no choice but to believe also undermines having any kind of loving relationship with God which, by necessity, must be freely engaged in, as with all loving relationships. Love, in other words, necessarily entails freedom of choice. Without the latter no sense can be made of the former, as no one (not even God) can force someone to love another. Being presented, then, with his undeniable physical body and life, which no one could dispute, would be tantamount to bullying us into submission, which fundamentally betrays the quality of the loving relationship God is fostering between us and him.

GROWTH

Moreover, and just as importantly, having a spiritual form, unlike the physical, means that Jesus Christ's love can transcend time and place, and so bizarrely, for our ears at least, he can be in two places at once. Maintaining his physical body here would for sure limit him, and would limit us too, given physicality constrains anyone, even God, to time and place. Transcending time and place through the spiritual form is crucial then, if Christ is to love and support all of us, all the time. Therefore, the spiritual manifestation of Christ in the Holy Spirit, allows us to understand his resurrection as something which is empowering for everyone, including you and me, even though we were not alive at the particular time and place of Jesus' life, death, and resurrection. Without the Holy Spirit, the resurrection becomes nothing more than, to use the words of a previous bishop of Durham, David Jenkins, "a conjuring trick with bones". It would have no direct relevance to us, as we could not live out the implications of Christ's love for us – even given his resurrection overcame death – as his Spirit would not be living in us, in the here-and-now. Consequently, we could not participate in what Paul promised to the Romans in 8:11:

> And if the Spirit of him who raised Jesus from the dead is living in you, he who raised Christ from the dead will also give life to your mortal bodies through his Spirit, who lives in you.

Following Paul's observation we can also conclude that, waiting for the Holy Spirit (Christ's spiritual manifestation of himself), helps us to see that it is not enough to know and believe that Jesus Christ came back to life, and even that his death on the cross is the route to human salvation and peace with God. We also must be empowered by his grace and love to overcome the world, by us allowing Jesus into our lives, via the Holy Spirit. This last move is the nub of the issue, but is even more difficult to comprehend because it brings to the fore, not only that Jesus died for our sins, and died and rose from the dead, but that he and his love can also, *literally*, be alive in us today. And this, as just said, he can only do through his spiritual personhood as manifested in the Holy Spirit who transcends time and place. Once we acknowledge and accept this reality though, we are then able to depend on God and Christ and not our own power.

In summary then, the Holy Spirit is a 'he/person' and not an 'it', because Jesus was and is a person, who now lives in us through the Holy Spirit. However, I must stress again that Jesus Christ – in his intention to cultivate a free and loving relationship with us – will not invade our personhood or take us over and dominate us.[19] Again, according to Paul in 2 Corinthians 3:17: 'Now the Lord is the Spirit, and where the Spirit of the Lord is, there is freedom.' Therefore, he will keep your personhood completely intact in his living through you in the Holy Spirit – your personality, voice, personal attributes, and so on. But he provides a different place or arena for you to *be* you and to be more fully and completely the you God intended for you to be – so fundamentally

---

[19] This commitment to us will still be maintained when Christ returns to us in his physical form in the 'second coming', as Christians also believe. However, there is considerable controversy amongst Christians concerning the precise character of his return, which I will not explore here. Nevertheless, my main contention following from the above is that, however and whenever he returns, he will still respect our freedoms and choices in the ways just described.

changing and transforming how you experience and respond to the world, but only for the better. His power, in other words, lives in you such that you are able to depend on his power without fear of being dominated, which in turn serves your best interests and enhances your well-being.

But there is a flip-side to this understanding of the Holy Spirit living through us but not dominating us – namely, that given he will not invade or possess us as this would undermine our freedom, it is very possible for us to either ignore his presence in our lives, or confine him to certain areas, and exclude him from others. Therefore, it is crucial to cultivate our on-going relationship with the Holy Spirit, as the spiritual manifestation of Jesus Christ living in us. We should not take this relationship for granted, otherwise there is the danger that our growth will be stalled and our continued transformation will be undermined. As Paul makes clear in 2 Corinthians 3:18:

> And we, who with unveiled faces all reflect the Lord's glory, are being transformed into his likeness with ever-increasing glory, which comes from the Lord, who is the Spirit.

Acknowledging this on-going relationship with him gets us to the last question: why is the Holy Spirit so important to our growth? The obvious answer from what has been said so far is that, without this spiritual manifestation, Jesus Christ cannot live in us and so we cannot fully experience his power in our lives – that is, his love, healing, and the taking of our burdens upon himself.

This does not mean, though, that those who are not Christians cannot, or do not, experience the power of God and

Christ in their lives. They often do. The Holy Spirit, acting throughout the world, as the spiritual manifestation and love of Jesus Christ, is found in many places outside the confines of Christian circles. Paul instructs the Philippians in 4:8:

> Whatever is true, whatever is noble, whatever is right, whatever is pure, whatever is lovely, whatever is admirable – if anything is excellent or praiseworthy – think about such things.

Moreover, we must also recognise that, given the choice we all have concerning our relationship with Jesus Christ and the Holy Spirit there are many who, as a result, exhibit the loving qualities of Jesus Christ much better than Christians – and this is something Christians also would do well owning up to. To repeat Jesus' words in John 14:23, the stress, in the first instance at least, is on those who obey his teaching, rather than believing in certain dogmas. Indeed, for Jesus in this verse, obeying his teaching is even a condition of our love for him, and of receiving his Holy Spirit:

> If anyone loves me, he will obey my teaching. My father will love him, and we will come to him and make our home with him.

Therefore, what allows us to receive the Holy Spirit is not belief as such – remembering, too, that according to James 2:19, 'even the demons believe.' Rather, our actions and behaviour become conduits for Jesus Christ's love and his spiritual manifestation found within the Holy Spirit, living in us and through us.

However, as a Christian, I also assert that regardless of

GROWTH

whether the relative loving qualities of different people – Christian or not – are better or worse, acknowledging the presence of the Holy Spirit in your life (as the spiritual manifestation of Christ), is very directly connecting with the supreme all-loving force of the universe. This is a force which has overcome death and reconciled God to us, and so it is always better to accept God and engage with him directly, *for your sake*. Conversely, without acknowledging his presence in this very immediate way, through the Holy Spirit, we risk becoming radically disempowered as we end-up depending on our own powers to deliver good outcomes – and, like turning off the main switch in an electricity generator, we then risk drastically reducing our capacity to fully enjoy God's blessings and love in our lives.

If the Holy Spirit, then, facilitates or underpins all our growth by providing a direct line between ourselves and God, what exactly does this growth entail for each of us? I will now explore two answers to this question, using stories from my own life, concerning God's utilisation of personal gifts and our painful experiences.

****

The biblical premise is that we all have a unique set of gifts which are peculiar to each of us, even if the source of these gifts, as just explored, is the same. As Paul states in 1 Corinthians 12:4:

> There are different kinds of gifts, but the same Spirit.
> There are different kinds of service, but the same Lord.
> There are different kinds of working, but the same God works all of them in all...

NINE STEPS TO WELL-BEING

Following this declaration, what God wants for us regarding our personal growth, and as also illustrated by Jesus Christ in the parable of the talents (Matthew 25:14-30), is that we should not hide these personal gifts or ignore them. The further assumption is that, as God utilises our gifts or talents, it will also give us joy, satisfaction, and well-being. As we engage in activities reflecting who we are, so we will receive love and blessings in giving to others when we exercise these gifts. However, if this is what God wants for us in his love – and is why, indeed, he has created us in particular ways – then it is important for us to identify who we are and what motivates us, and not pretend we are something we are not. But here is the problem – truthful and authentic self-identification is often much more difficult to practice than to preach, which means we can easily become distracted from using our God-given talents, whatever they are.

Since learning to read, I have always been bookish and I have always enjoyed writing. Later in my life I discovered that I also enjoy communicating – with those who are interested at least – what I have found out about the world and the many different understandings of it. In addition, I have been motivated, in my adult life especially, by my awareness of injustice. I am deeply concerned that some people have a lot, while others, many others, seem to miss out. Putting these things together, by my late twenties and early thirties I ended up working for an organisation campaigning for disabled people's rights. As a researcher and political lobbyist in London, I highlighted the concerns of disabled people; much of my job involved communicating with journalists and politicians about these concerns, aiming to change policies and practices. So far so good, you might say – I was able to identify who I am and God, in his love for me, was helping

GROWTH

me to exercise and develop my motivations and the talents he had given me accordingly.

However, I also remember reading a letter during this time which started me pondering. A missionary friend of mine was sending me regular correspondence. He was employed by a church in Thailand doing all sorts of, what would be for me, impossibly difficult missionary-type things – preaching on public transport, setting-up soup kitchens for the homeless, visiting schools and 'spreading the good news' about Jesus Christ. The thought of doing any of these type of activities, for all sorts of reasons (some good and bad), filled me with dread, and still would – but this also made me feel guilty, as I asked myself certain, what we might call, 'beat-myself-up' questions.

Why couldn't I do these things? Isn't the life he leads much more of a sacrifice than my kind of life? Shouldn't I commit to a life of the kind he is leading and ignore what I seem to be motivated to do? Isn't running with what you are motivated to do the easy option, and even self-indulgent? Then, as I was thinking about these questions, God hit me with a response of the kind that is direct and sure; and as I also illustrated in Chapter Two, he answered in the first person (I) to me in the second person (you). His response was brief, to the point, and felt like a loving chastisement: 'I am not interested in what you can't do I am only interested in what you *can* do.'

I was taken aback by this response, but could see very clearly that I needed to not only accept my limitations, as I saw them, but positively embrace them, anticipating that God in his power would develop and nurture those talents, skills, and motivations I do have, and leave what I don't have for other people, like my friend in Thailand. In other words, it is no good pretending I am something I am not – this way leads to unnecessary guilt, a waste of energy and lack of focus. What I should focus on, though, is those things I can do, and trust in a loving all-powerful God to develop these capabilities and lead me to places which might seem difficult now, but will feel exciting and empowering for me in the future – but only because this future is consistent with what I am motivated to do, and what I will be able to do well.

This basic insight was, and remains, a very liberating thought, and has informed – thankfully – my personal development, choices, and growth, ever since. It has stopped me being filled with angst that I cannot do what others might do, and instead focus on the talents and skills which have been given to me. Reflecting again on Paul's observation in 1 Corinthians 12:14: '... the body is not made up of one part but of many', my job has been to find my part and play it, without looking over my shoulder at what others are doing, playing their different roles. It is only from this position – our own authentically gifted position – that God can utilise our particular and unique talents for personal growth, and so lead us to places we didn't even think capable of being in. What, though, about utilising my painful experiences for the same purposes?

Here, I want to explore what, for me, has been so far the most painful experience of my life. It is what I referred to in passing in Chapter Four, namely the break-up with my first wife. Cutting a very long story short, after over twenty years of marriage and two children (then eleven and eight years old), she told me that she had slept with a woman about three months previously. I knew this woman, as she lived in the same town and had visited our house often. I was also aware that she and my wife were developing a close friendship, but

GROWTH

obviously, up until this point, I assumed that this was all there was to it. Initially, I was assured by both of them that the affair was a once-off, that both of them felt dreadful about it and that it wouldn't happen again. However, it soon became clear that their relationship was deepening. It wasn't just a regrettable one-off lapse, but had led to a much more permanent shift in their relationship, and, of course, in my relationship with my wife too.

This is not to say that my relationship with my first wife was perfect by any means – after twenty years of marriage, what relationship is? It is also certainly not to say I was entirely blameless – for sure there was, and is, no excuse for the affair, and in *that* sense I was not at fault, but I know, for all sorts of reasons, I often wasn't the easiest person to live with, or the best husband I could or should have been. Nevertheless, whatever way you look at it, and however blame is apportioned, their relationship caused a massive rupture in our marriage. After initially being told it wouldn't happen again, my wife was involved in about a year-long on-and-off affair. This was followed by another eighteen months or so during which my wife chose to sleep in a separate room to me, but was not sleeping with her lover either. Her motive was that in not sleeping with either of us she could 'clear her head' and make a final decision about what and who she wanted. During this period, my wife and I went to marriage counselling with a Christian counsellor and we also had many long conversations about where our marriage was heading and what should happen.

However, despite these attempts to assess the situation, the last eighteen months were dreadful for all of us as my wife, never good at making big decisions, remained paralysed about what to do. I, in the meantime, after dealing with the

113

initial trauma, found myself becoming increasingly stronger emotionally. As a result, when we had not been sleeping together for about a year, I started to realise that if she slept again with her lover, I would be justified in leaving my wife, and that I could, even *should*, leave her. Once I realised this, I also made this clear to her. Predictably perhaps, roughly six months after I had said this, I was told by my wife that her physical relationship with her lover had recently resumed. In response, I very calmly packed a bag, took off my wedding ring, placed it on the dining room table, and left to start a new life.

However, over seven years later, and as I am writing this book, this new life meant me meeting and marrying a wonderful woman, Lyn, who has enriched my life hugely. The first big lesson here, then, is do not assume that when things go wrong, and even go very badly wrong, that God hasn't anticipated this fact. But, because he loves us, he has an even richer blessing in store for us, if we continue trusting in him and we are prepared to share our love with others. As is illustrated so well in the story of Job (and throughout the bible), God is with us in the midst of trouble and hurt, and, even though it sometimes might not feel this way, he will never leave us.

Throughout the ordeal leading up to the eventual break-up with my first wife, I can honestly say that I did not doubt that God's love was with me and holding me. I doubted the eventual outcome, for sure, but, as explored in Chapter Two, this is different to believing in a God who is for us and not against us, regardless of the outcome or the circumstances we find ourselves in. As the psalmist in Psalm 23:4 states:

GROWTH

Even though I walk through the valley of the shadow of death, I will fear no evil, for you are with me; your rod and your staff, they comfort me.

The point is that what this passage from scripture, and others beside, does not guarantee, is that God will make this valley of death disappear, as if by magic or trickery. Nevertheless, by walking through this valley with God, we learn to trust in his love, in *any* circumstances.

In addition, though, we are also promised that the journey through the valley of the shadow of death will end, and so is not a permanent state of affairs. Consequently, immediately after the earlier passage, and in light of my relationship with Lyn, I am able to wholeheartedly say to God, with the psalmist in verse 5 that: "You prepare a table before me ... You anoint my head with oil; my cup overflows."

Moreover, I can cap it all, and declare with the psalmist in verse 6:

Surely goodness and love will follow me all the days of my life, and I will dwell in the house of the Lord for ever!

In short, then, through emotional pain and trauma my personal growth and well-being is facilitated by knowing and experiencing the reality of God's love more, and that his support is wonderful and profound in whatever circumstances, as are his rich blessings.

The second big lesson has been rediscovering and deepening my relationship with my children as they have grown up, and are growing up. When painful situations emerge in our lives, what also often happens – as is frequently reported – is that our priorities are put into proper focus. We see more clearly what is important and so we learn to value and not take for granted the relationships that count in our lives. This lesson should include our relationship with God as he walks with us in life's troubles, as just described, but it also includes our relationships with significant others. For sure, the break-up of my first marriage has made me reflect on how I could take marriage for granted (which is a lesson I can hopefully take to my marriage with Lyn), but also I have seen the importance of maintaining and nurturing a loving relationship with my children, and not taking them for granted either. When they both lived with their mother after our break-up (and one still does), I undertook to see them at least twice a week, and so ensured – with Lyn's steadfast support – that they have remained a priority in my life.

Moreover, my first wife and I have also made it clear to the children that our separation does not have any bearing on the fact that we are their parents. I know our initial separation was a terrible shock to both our children, but the obligation on both of us has been to ensure that our divorce does not, as far as possible, have a detrimental effect on their development, and our relationships with them. With God's grace, I think we have achieved this. Also, as I have repeated on many occasions, including to my children, I am deeply indebted to my first wife for the way she has parented them and for the many lessons I have learnt from her about good parenting over the years. Consequently, and despite the odds perhaps, both our children seem very well adjusted and happy and are learning well the lessons of having good quality, loving relationships with those around them, and nurturing the talents and gifts God has given them.

The more general lesson is that God, in his love for us,

will continue to bless us and our relationships, despite bad circumstances and even the bad choices we might make. According to the psalmist, in Psalm 37:24: 'Though he stumbles, he will not fall, for the Lord upholds him with his hand.' Therefore, if we are open to God's love and forgiveness being manifested in various ways throughout our lives, we can rest assured that he can find a way through for each of us, even though mistakes are made and wrongs are committed, with him supporting all those affected, in their pain and hurt.

Following this theme, the third big lesson for me has been learning the importance of forgiveness and of 'moving on'. I discussed the meaning and importance of forgiveness in Chapter Five, and so I won't repeat the arguments here. Suffice it to say, consistent with one of the central themes explored, my decision to work through the long process of forgiving both women was not a noble or heroic choice – that is, a choice born from some kind of selfless duty toward them. Rather, it was a choice I needed to make, in the first instance at least, *for me*. Their needs for forgiveness, which I am sure, were real enough, felt secondary to this main motivation.

I quickly realised, especially after I finally left my first wife, that if I didn't choose this path of forgiveness I could easily become angry and bitter and that this would be bad for me, my children and for any of my future relationships. As Paul instructed the Hebrews in 12:15:

> See to it that no-one misses the grace of God and that no bitter root grows up to cause trouble and defile many.

I am extremely grateful, again depending on God's help that I took this path of forgiveness sooner rather than later, otherwise I am really not sure where I might have ended-up. I certainly would have been in no fit state to receive from and nurture a relationship of the kind I now have with Lyn and it is likely that any anger or bitterness harboured would have spilled over into my relationships with my children, to their – and my – lasting detriment.

Finally, the fourth big lesson I learnt from this experience was how to handle and be connected with my emotional dispositions a lot more. This has led to a better relationship with God and others around me. In the extreme circumstances I was experiencing, my emotions became raw and heightened; it was difficult to ignore the importance of emotion in my life. But, having gone through these circumstances, I now listen much more attentively to my emotional condition and have been able to handle and control myself more effectively than I did in the past. I can tell much better, for example, when I am becoming irritated or annoyed because I am anxious deep down. Recognising this allows me to identify what is really troubling me and so I can address it directly – in prayer and/or in my relationships.

I have also been able to acknowledge the importance of recognising when I am feeling sad and alone and not being ashamed of these emotions. Simple lessons, you might say, in developing 'emotional intelligence', as it is sometimes referred to in counselling circles, but ones I have found extremely difficult to learn in my life. I have the tendency, as men often do, to concentrate on what I think and how I understand things, rather than on what I feel. In short, getting in touch with my emotions and reading them more accurately, has enabled me to connect with people better emotionally,

GROWTH

including myself, and with God. What I have also learnt in the process, is that God's love is, in the middle of all these feelings, communicating with me, supporting me, healing me, and taking me to new places of rich blessing and well-being as I grow further into his love. I have, in other words, learnt, and I am still learning, the lesson in Proverbs 3:5-6, to:

> Trust in the Lord with all your heart and lean not on your understanding; in all your ways acknowledge him, and he will make your paths straight.

Chapter Nine
Victory

The intention, in this final chapter, is to summarise the main themes explored in the preceding chapters, and show how these lead to a life of well-being and victory. I refer here to a life where we are able to experience and acknowledge God's love and many blessings and overcome the difficult and sometimes painful circumstances we find ourselves living through on a daily basis, however big or small. The foundation of a victorious life, understood in Christian terms, is to submit to God's love and give over the whole of our lives to him, so depend on him. In the process, he will take our burdens and give us rest, peace, and joy (also see Matthew 11:28). But how does this happen exactly and why should it?

As I explored in Chapter One, we must first be open to conversion which offers a radical new way of perceiving and experiencing the world – one that is Christ-like (also see John 3:1-7). This openness to conversion requires, first of all, recognition and acknowledgement that our lives are not as they should be. When we submit this disconnection between what is and what should be to God, we start along the conversion road. Our attitudes and experiences of life are changed by the love of God and as we are 'born again'; by faith in his love and power we can start to trust that our lives will be transformed for the better (also see Romans 12:1-2).

However, we must also acknowledge that his love can be found in many places, and not just confined to Christian or religious circles – he is found in secular art, music, literature, films, media, philosophy, and culture, as well as in the rich and varied relationships we have with people who would not describe themselves as Christian, or as being religious at all. We must therefore be open to radical conversion, whatever its source. Our ears and eyes should be receptive to whatever God is teaching us and we should exercise our faith accordingly (also see Philippians 4:8). Moreover, we must apply this faith and these lessons about God and his character to whatever circumstances we find ourselves in.

As I explored in Chapter Two, faith is not, though, a belief that all the difficult circumstances we encounter will immediately be made right for us, nor is faith a belief that once-and-for-all answers will be provided for why we are experiencing these troubles (see, for example, the book of Job in the Old Testament). Rather, faith believes that God's love is with us, in these troubles – so supporting us through them, regardless of the outcome and our understanding of them. For sure, God's love often intervenes to change these circumstances in the here-and-now when we ask him, but this is not guaranteed by his love for us. What *is* guaranteed is that his love, if accepted and embraced, will sustain us through these times. He stands with us and so we are no longer alone and, in his good time, he will lead us out of these troubles to other new places of rich blessing (also see Psalm 23).

Standing with us, the Lord Jesus Christ also reveals his divinity, as I explored in Chapter Three – by means of his

God-like characteristics which are shocking and surprising, given the stupendous claims made about Jesus as Christ our saviour, in scripture. God, by becoming one of us in Jesus Christ (see John 1:14), has completely and utterly empathised and identified with what it is to be human. Therefore, God, the father, is no longer just 'on high' – as God the distant, mysterious, other-worldly, creator of all things. But, by being one of us – God the son, or the Son of Man even – he knows and experiences what it is to be 'lowly' and of this world, feeling often 'disconnected' from his life here. As the life of Jesus (of God made a person) is told through the gospels, we can see that God loves us, by knowing and experiencing what it is to be flesh and blood – to experience joy and pain, to laugh with others, to cry with others, to be wronged by others, to be lonely, to be friends with others, to be misunderstood, to be heard and not heard, to be exhausted and replenished; and, finally, to be rejected and abandoned, even if this involves dying by being nailed to a cross, and deserted by his closest friends.

However, as I also explored in Chapter Three, through the apparent defeat of a loving God who is nailed to a cross and left to die, he triumphs by using this death (*his* death) as a way of fully experiencing the burdens and sins of the world (1 John 2:2). His unjustifiable suffering is turned around as it becomes a once-and-for-all place where all wrongdoing, all brokenness, all pain, and all burdens, are let go of – and where God, in his love for us, assumes complete responsibility for everything which has gone sour and bad in the world. In other words, he demonstrates his love for us by becoming sin for our sakes (2 Corinthians 5:21) and so proclaims, contrary to any justifiable reason, that it is all his fault. By taking on the punishment of wrongdoing himself,

VICTORY

God made a human in the person of Jesus Christ, becomes completely divorced or disconnected from God the father. 'My God, my God, why have you forsaken me!' is the cry Jesus makes on the cross as he is torn apart, for our sakes and for our wrongdoing (and see John 1:29).

Our job then, as Christians, is to acknowledge the unjustifiable character of this event and recognise that it is we who need forgiveness. At the same time, we need to realise that this ultimate feat of a loving God, in taking the blame upon himself, makes us completely right with him (see 1 Peter 2:24). This outcome is not fair or just, for sure, but is the free gift bestowed upon us through the love of Christ (see Romans 6:23), and one, which if we are to accept, should prompt us to offer our lives back to him in order to be transformed (see Romans 6:15-23). We can accept this promise of transformation with the expectation that things will change for us, in ways that will bring us closer to the love and blessing of God. We can accept the fact of his resurrection, his power and love, transforming our lives today. His triumph, after becoming sin for our sakes and assuming responsibility for all that has gone wrong in the world, is to rise again after death – this being the hallmark of Jesus Christ's divine character, and the guarantee that his love in our lives is the supreme power exhibited in the universe, even over death (see all four gospels).

In Chapter Four, I explored how we might engage with this transformative power in our prayer. I identified that, in some ways, prayer is like conversing with other people, but in many ways, it is not. Unlike people, and unlike close friends even, God knows for sure what we are going to say, before we say it (Psalm 139:4); he knows our deepest yearnings and longings completely, and much better than anyone else, including ourselves (Psalm 38:9); he is not physically with us, but is always with us spiritually (1 Timothy 6:15-16); and he never gives us convenient answers to prayer simply because we want to experience the world our way, and given *his* ways are often mysterious and impenetrable (Romans 11:33).

Therefore, if we are to be transformed by God's loving power through prayer, we must first accept his authority and be still and silent in prayer before we engage in speaking to him and hearing his response (Psalm 46:10). Once we do start speaking, though, we must be as honest with him as we can, as there is no place to hide from God and there is no possibility of deceiving him (Jeremiah 23:24). We must, then, lay bare our frustrations, anger, ambitions, motivations, desires, hopes, fears, joys – all of what we are – to him, knowing that he has already seen and heard it all. During this process of engaging with him, we will then be able to ask him things without presuming that we will be given a solution according to our own wish-lists. Rather, we can presume that God, because he loves us, can take care of us and should be trusted with everything. Once this trust has developed, we can expect that our lives will change radically as a result (and see Mark 11:23).

In Chapter Five, I explored what is, for many of us, the biggest difficulty we must confront when we bare ourselves to God – the problem of forgiving others for hurts committed against us, or committed against others close to us (whether now or in the past), and receiving the blessing of forgiveness for those hurts we have committed in turn (also see Psalm 32). The main problem with forgiving others is that it entails acknowledging that the person who has committed the wrong – either to us or to others – is to blame, and so there are no excuses (also see Mark 11:25-26). Yet, in forgiving, we are expected to relinquish or give up our record of the wrongs committed, even though we are justified in keeping this score. Forgiving then is – on the face of it at least – not fair as we give up our right and, even more importantly perhaps, our need to punish the culpable wrongdoer.

Consequently, forgiving is often the most difficult thing we must do, as it involves a letting go of our rightful need to punish. This does not mean that the person who committed the wrong should not be punished for other reasons (for example, see Romans 13:2). However, if forgiving involves a loving act of the forgiver – by her relinquishing her own rightful need to punish – then it is important to highlight the benefits which ensue to the forgiver for forgiving. According to Chapter Five, these benefits are, broadly, two-fold.

First, by letting go of the justifiable anger we are liberated from the debilitating emotions which prevent our experiencing the healing process and peace of Christ. Anger, although needing to be honestly expressed, often finds a bitter root, however subtle or hidden (Hebrews 12:15). We, therefore, should go to God with the expectation of being healed from our hurts and being replenished and unburdened by the love of God. Again, his love will be expressed in many different forms, through our relationships (with family, friends, and even strangers); through art, music, books, and various cultural endeavours; and in the numerous other encounters we have with the stories and lives of people now and in the past. Opening ourselves up to receiving God's blessing from these very different places of love, allows our healing to take place, as we engage with the source of all love and joy – that is, God our creator.

Second, in forgiving others for wrongs, however small or big, it also opens us up to being forgiven ourselves – that is, for the inevitable wrongdoings committed by us to others (Matthew 6:14-15). These wrongdoings may or may not be on the same scale as the wrongs committed against us, but they are wrongs nevertheless and so also need to be confessed and thoroughly dealt with. We are all flawed and no-one is without blame, however small or big our wrongdoing (1 John 1:8). If we do not acknowledge this basic fact about ourselves, then this too will prevent us from receiving the full blessing of the love and forgiveness of Jesus Christ who died, once-and-for all, for all our transgressions (also see Isaiah 53:5).

In Chapter Six, I took a different tack and explored the importance of scripture in our lives – of meditating and digesting the various lessons learnt from the stories told of God's people struggling with God's love (see both the Old and New Testaments, and see Genesis 32:22-31), as well as in the stories of Christ's life and teaching (in all the gospels) and the experiences and teaching of the early church as it grappled with the realities of Christ's death and resurrection (the remainder of the New Testament). Chapter Six explored how the bible should not be understood as a 'car manual' for life, providing once-and-for-all neat solutions to life's troubles and questions. But rather, the bible points to a God who is often mysterious and unfathomable. Because God is beyond our understanding, he is beyond many of the so-called 'answers' we might provide in response to reading it (also see Job 11:7-12).

However, Chapter Six also explored how we encounter, via scripture, the uncompromising love of God which is profound and far-reaching. His love is expressed in bible texts as he demonstrates his steadfast commitment to blessing us – that is, if we are open to receiving his love and his power and

VICTORY

authority in our lives, despite life often feeling extremely difficult. So, meditating on and studying scripture, although not giving us all the answers as we *understand* them, does provide an arena in which we can directly encounter a loving God – so moulding and shaping who we are, as we are exposed to his word, dialogue and engagement with us (Psalm 1:2-3).

In Chapter Seven, I further developed this theme of engaging with God, through examining what is the meaning of church. Church is not a building, given we believe in a God who declares that he does not live in temples made of human hands (see Acts 7:48). However, we also cannot assume that the people we meet in church will satisfy our desire for genuine human connection with those who believe the same as we do. Certainly, we can engage in deep and connected relationships with fellow Christians – relationships which may be sustained over many years – but we must also acknowledge that frequently it doesn't quite work this way (also see 1 Corinthians 1:10-17).

The practice of going to church, when it is most superficial, is where we engage in polite niceties rather than being a place of honest unburdening. Consequently, members can become disconnected from each other, in all our diversities, strangeness, and flaws. Church history, too, demonstrates that while often the church has championed the cause of the oppressed and exploited, it has also, at various times, oppressed and exploited people. Therefore, we need to own-up to the sins of the church world-wide and repent and change our practices, as we also need to engage in contributing to the universal church (The Body of Christ), being open to the many varieties of groups and individuals who inhabit it. Acknowledging this variety encourages us to see the universal church as a place where we can celebrate diversity, and be of genuine belonging for all. We can also expect to find God in surprising places – both in Christian and non-Christian contexts – so we should be open to the many varied and unique gifts which all people possess and can use (and see Romans 12:4-8).

Finally, in Chapter Eight I examined the nature of personal growth – of journeying with God, and increasingly enjoying the blessings of his love and peace in our lives. The chapter explored, first, how this growth is facilitated via the 'third layer' of God's character (in addition to God as the Father, and God as the Son) – God as the Holy Spirit (see, for example, John 14:15-31). The main issue examined was how the Holy Spirit is often mistakenly relegated to an 'it' rather than being elevated as a 'he/person' – and that while the 'itness' of the Holy Spirit is easier to comprehend than 'his' personhood – the latter more accurately reflects the spiritual manifestation of Jesus Christ in our lives.

Jesus Christ has come back to us in this spiritual persona, partly because if he had remained in this world physically after his death and resurrection, this would have made redundant us choosing to have faith and to love him. We would have had no choice but to believe in his divinity, if all generations could feel and touch him as physically being alive, after his death, so effectively bullying us into submission. In addition, via the person of the Holy Spirit, Jesus can transcend the physicality of time and place and be with all of us always and everywhere (also see Acts 1:1-11). The power of the Holy Spirit, underpinning our growth, then, is the love of Jesus Christ himself, as we live out the power of his resurrection and freely accept him into our lives and grow to depend upon him. In the process, we can also enjoy and

VICTORY

participate in his loving power which triumphs over all those things that threaten our well-being, including even death itself (also see Romans 8:11-17).

In the second part of Chapter Eight I examined what we might specifically utilise to experience personal growth – most notably, our gifts and our experience of pain. Both these aspects of our lives are very personal and individual, but God can use them to our and his advantage as we engage with the power of the Holy Spirit. Regarding our gifts, God has given us unique talents and attributes which, in his love, he wants to use for our and others' benefit (Luke 19:12-27) – that is, assuming we open ourselves up to these being developed and nurtured by the Holy Spirit.

What God, though, is not interested in, is us pretending we are something we are not, thereby ignoring or downgrading the talents and attributes which he has given us. Nevertheless, this type of pretence is common as we often look over our shoulders at others who have those attributes we don't have. Our job, instead, is to focus on what we *do* have, and what we *can* do, so that our gifts are utilised to the full (also see 1 Corinthians 12:12-27). However, once we start using our gifts, we will be blessed in our lives with deep satisfaction, joy, and well-being. We will be doing things we are motivated to do and, subsequently, we will be taken to unexpected places which develop our talents still further and even in ways we would find now hard to imagine (Luke 19:12-27).

Regarding the pain we all experience in our lives at some time, Chapter Eight also explored how pain can be, in the long-term, a platform or springboard for receiving deeper blessings from God according to his loving character. It is when we are in pain that we often learn the most difficult lessons, but for precisely this reason, these lessons become the most important and most valuable in our lives. For example, the mistaken priorities which we often regularly order on a daily basis can be challenged to the core when we experience pain or loss (also see Hebrews 12:7-13). Our reordering of these priorities, prompted by our painful experiences, can even be a 'life-saver' as we engage more truly and authentically with what is, and what should be, of value.

Likewise, it is in our pain that we can better experience the closeness of God's love, as he walks with us through these painful circumstances (for example, see Psalm 23:4), and we can believe and expect an even more wonderful place of blessing when these trials are over, as they will be (Psalm 23:5-6). Moreover, in our pain, we often learn most acutely about ourselves – especially perhaps our emotional tapestry – and how we are often woven in complex and uneven patterns. Most notably, pain exposes our vulnerability and frailty, and therefore shows us who we really are deep down, without the usual props which often distract us from our fundamental weakness. Pain, therefore, becomes a platform for self-exposure, which if faced and addressed, can allow us to grow further into the love of an all-powerful God, as we in trust and faith, hand over our vulnerability and frailty for him to deal with (also see Proverbs 3:5-6, and 2 Corinthians 12:9-10).

****

Finally then, where does all this take us regarding a life of well-being and victory? In the process of making these various steps in our encounters with God, we open ourselves up to the divine power of love and transformation, and

VICTORY

abandon the pretence of trying to achieve so-called independence (whether from God or others), trusting in our own strength and understanding (also see Romans 12:1-6). We learn how to be still with God, to rest in him and accept his peace, knowing and experiencing both his authority and love for us in our lives. We relinquish any expectations that once-and-for-all neat and tidy answers will be worked-out by us, or that, with the wave of a magic wand, the difficult circumstances and troubles we experience will instantly disappear. Instead, and much more long-lasting (indeed *ever*lasting), we do expect to change in these circumstances through the power of God's love. We can go to an all-powerful and all-loving God with an open mind and heart, in faith that our responses and attitudes to our troubles will be transformed, whether slowly or suddenly, or both. For sure, in his love, he can and often does intervene in our circumstances to change them (Matthew 17:20), but, *whatever* happens, he provides us with a rock to stand on – faith in his love, forgiveness, and the power of his resurrection. Consequently, we can steady ourselves in life's storms and chart a course through them with his reassurance, peace and well-being living in us.

Therefore, we are never alone in our hurts, troubles and joys, as God is always with us, liberating us from the oppression of life's burdens, whether from now or in our pasts. He gives us the freedom to love and live life to the full and, with his Holy Spirit, be forever replenished and nourished – for our benefit, and for those around us. He provides us many places, often hidden places (truly heavenly places), where we can give and receive love, and where we can readily forgive and be forgiven. Moreover, in these places, we can learn and move on from our mistakes and the

NINE STEPS TO WELL-BEING

hurts done to us and we can rest and be satisfied with who we are, and what we have to offer. In short, claiming the gift of well-being and victory in Christ's love, by always asking him into our lives to change us and empower us, is claiming a life of joy and lightness of burden – and all thanks to God and Christ our saviour, Amen!

Acknowledgements

So many people have positively influenced my thinking and experiences as a Christian over the last thirty-odd years, informing what is written here, it would be impossible for me to list them all – although some I have mentioned by name in the proceeding chapters. However, regarding the production of the book particularly, it would be negligent of me not to also acknowledge specific contributors. These are, firstly, and in alphabetical order, Reverend Ruth Bierbaum, Reverend Canon Dr Ian Davies, and Reverend Ernesto Lozada-Uzuriaga Steele. They were all kind enough to read earlier drafts, and their theological insights, and attentions to the detail of my arguments, helped me immensely in improving and clarifying the content. I also would like to thank my copy-editor Clodagh Springer of *Ultimate Proof* who made extensive comments on the latest draft. Her ability to spot my mistakes and inelegancies concerning my written English, and her observations regarding my theology and interpretation of scripture were very gratefully received.

On a more personal note, I thank my wife Lyn so much for her support in this whole endeavour. She not only took the trouble of reading an earlier draft, and made many typically insightful and pertinent suggestions regarding the precise meaning of passages, but also has steadfastly encouraged me throughout the process of producing and publishing the book, and during its numerous iterations. As a mark of my gratitude, the book is dedicated to her, alongside my children, Georgia and Luke – for the love and inspiration they all have given me. It is also dedicated to the memory of my dear friend Monty, who died in the summer of 2013, after a very brief illness.

Finally, despite the many improvements made to the book because of these contributions, of course I take full responsibility for the words and arguments presented here. I am sure there remain many points of agreement and disagreement regarding what I have said and recommended, and I look forward, in hope, to engaging in many future discussions as a result. Anticipating this outcome, after all, is consistent with the central premise of the book; that we best see ourselves as questioning journeyers, rather than as possessors of once-and-for-all neat and tidy answers – and as we walk with Christ on all our paths to liberation, joy, peace, and well-being.

Steven R. Smith is Professor of Political Philosophy and Social Policy at The University of South Wales. As well as having an international academic reputation in the fields of social ethics and social justice, Professor Smith has been a Christian for over thirty years. Since being dramatically converted in his late-teens, he has worshipped, preached and been in leadership roles in various churches since. He is also a media commentator on contemporary issues and their bearing on Christianity and wider spiritual matters.

Life After Death:
Some of the Best Evidence

Jan W. Vandersande Ph.D.

Outskirts Press, Inc.
Denver, Colorado

The opinions expressed in this manuscript are solely the opinions of the author and do not represent the opinions or thoughts of the publisher. The author represents and warrants that s/he either owns or has the legal right to publish all material in this book.

Life After Death: Some of the Best Evidence
All Rights Reserved.
Copyright © 2008 Jan W. Vandersande Ph.D.
V3.0

Cover photo used with permission.

This book may not be reproduced, transmitted, or stored in whole or in part by any means, including graphic, electronic, or mechanical without the express written consent of the publisher except in the case of brief quotations embodied in critical articles and reviews.

Outskirts Press, Inc.
http://www.outskirtspress.com

ISBN: 978-1-4327-2549-5

Library of Congress Control Number: 2008927542

Outskirts Press and the "OP" logo are trademarks belonging to Outskirts Press, Inc.

PRINTED IN THE UNITED STATES OF AMERICA

Table of Contents

Introduction i
My Introduction to Psychic Phenomena 1
Mental and Trance Mediumship 13
    Mental Mediums 14
    Trance Mediums 23
Direct Voice 51
    Leslie Flint 51
    John Sloan 68
Materialization 81
    Johannesburg Materializations 89
    Alec Harris 99
    Tom Harrison's Circle 121
    Jack Webber 138
    Carmine Mirabelli 141
    Current Materialization Mediums 143
    Christmas Sittings with Mickey and Sara 149
My Meeting with a Magician and Victor Zammit's 153
    Challenges
Conclusion 157
Bibliography 161

Acknowledgements

This book would not have been possible had it not been for Mickey and Sara Wolf who in 1970 invited my wife Marlene and me to attend one of their séances. This lead to a friendship that lasted eight years and to us sitting with them in a large number of séances during those years. The psychic phenomena witnessed and the experiences gained during that time made it possible for me to be able to critically read the literature on psychic phenomena and as a result write this book describing some of the best evidence for survival after death. Mickey and Sara are now in the spirit world but I would still like to thank them.

I would also like to acknowledge Professor Jack Allen, who gave me four photographs of ectoplasm and materializations that he took at a sitting. He gave me the photographs and told me to do with them what I wanted to do. These photographs are in this book. Jack is now also in the spirit world but I would still like to thank him.

My thanks also go to my wife Marlene who helped remember many of the details of the numerous sittings we had with Mickey and Sara and to my daughter Colette and son Mathew who helped proof read the manuscript and provided useful comments.

Finally, I would like to thank Tom Harrison for allowing me to use some of the photographs of ectoplasm and materializations from his book.

Introduction

Nearly every person at some point in their lives has thought about death and the possibility of life after death. Most of those who are firm believers in a religion accept their religion's belief of a life after death. However, there are still many believers and those who do not practice a religion, who would like to know what happens after we die and not base it only on "faith". That is why in this book I would like to present the most compelling evidence I have collected for life after death. I have spent nearly a lifetime investigating and reading about psychic phenomena.

This book is not meant to be a discussion of as many types of evidence for survival after death as possible, but only those cases which I believe are the most evidential based on my own experiences. Many of these experiences will be discussed in great detail. I will thus not discuss evidence, no matter how good it might be, that I have no experience of. I will thus not discuss cases such as reincarnation, NDE (near-death experiences) and apparitions.

There exist a large number of cases that strongly support the survival after death case and many of those have been well researched and documented by very reputable and knowledgeable individuals. Still there are those who do not accept the evidence, no matter how convincing. They argue against it because they do not believe that personal survival after death is possible or they say they need to experience the evidence themselves. I myself was a doubter. That was until I witnessed the convincing evidence supporting the case for life after death. Some contemporary philosophers consider the idea of personal survival after death as theoretically impossible and unintelligible. These people will never be convinced with evidence no matter how persuasive the case. They have made up there mind and that is the end of the discussion. For those of you who have an open mind and are willing to examine the evidence presented in this book, it will hopefully make you think about the possibility that we do survive death.

By definition a scientist only believes what can be proven scientifically. Using the scientific method a researcher conducts an experiment, collects the data and gets a certain result. These results can then be duplicated (or not) by anyone, anywhere by performing the same experiment. I would agree with that since I am a scientist by training: I have a Ph.D. in physics obtained by conducting original research. However, when it comes to experimental evidence for psychic phenomena such as photographs, recordings and the presence of numerous credible witnesses, things all of a sudden change. When it comes to this kind of evidence most scientists won't accept or believe the results, no matter how convincing it is and how reliable, well-known or famous the researchers and witnesses are. Some very famous scientists, including Nobel Prize winners, have done psychic research and some have written books about that research (I will discuss some of that evidence in this book). Unfortunately, it is inherently difficult to duplicate psychic experiments because it is difficult to recreate the exact conditions under which the original experiments were conducted. Specifically, there have been only a small number of physical mediums (those who produced direct voice and materializations) in the world that were capable of reproducing their results and nowadays there are only a few. In this book I will present the evidence that some of these truly excellent mediums have provided and have reproduced, often under strict test conditions, numerous times.

Unfortunately, the upshot is that most scientists won't believe the experimental evidence for psychic phenomena since it would affect their view of reality. Also, they would face the ridicule of their colleagues if they expressed belief in psychic phenomena. I should know because it has happened to me. However, my experiences, as I will describe in detail, were so convincing that I did not care what others thought about me.

The explanation used by many skeptics to explain psychic phenomena is the "super-ESP" hypothesis (ESP- extrasensory perception) first mentioned by Professor H. Hart in 1959. This hypothesis basically states that all psychic phenomena, which suggest or indicate survival after death can be explained in terms of ESP by living persons (mediums, observers, etc.) by using a comprehensive form of telepathy, clairvoyance and precognition (these terms will be defined later). As I will show in the following chapters, this hypothesis is much more far-fetched and unlikely in most cases than the survival explanation.

There is also the standard fall-back option the critics, skeptics, and debunkers use to explain away psychic phenomena and that is fraud. According to them every psychic and medium who provides evidence for survival (whether it be messages, direct voice or materializations) are frauds. This position is ludicrous. There are a preponderance of very well-documented cases where the possibility of fraud has been completely ruled out. Anyone who is not willing to accept this is either not familiar with the history of psychic investigation or has already decided that survival is not possible no matter how convincing the evidence. It should, however, be stressed that there has been and still is a lot of fraud when it comes to psychic phenomena. Whenever money can be made by providing "survival evidence" for those who have lost a loved one, it is done fraudulently on many occasions. Over the past 150 years (the current age of modern psychic phenomena) many fraudulent mediums and psychics has been exposed. However, the exception does not prove the rule. Just because there have been many fraudulent psychics does not mean that they are all fraudulent. I will describe many cases where fraud has been totally ruled out.

Finally, there are those individuals who believe they are psychics (channelers or mediums) and believe that they provide evidence for survival. However, most of them are not very good and provide very little, if any, proof of survival. I have had sittings with many such "psychics" and most of the time the sitting was a waste of time and only occasionally were there a few "hits" (correct information unknown to the psychic). I do not believe these individuals are fraudulent, they just believe they have psychic abilities. I will describe several sittings with truly good mediums and thus show what a really good sitting is like.

The purpose of this book is not to try to convince the perpetual skeptic. It is meant for you who are genuinely skeptical, or agnostic, about the possibility of life after death. The evidence for life after death presented here is the best I have experienced myself or have found in the literature in the areas in which I have had my own experiences. Read the book with an open mind and just maybe the evidence presented here will make you consider the possibility that we do survive death.

My Introduction to Psychic Phenomena

My interest in religion and philosophy started my freshman year at Swarthmore College (in Swarthmore, PA.). Even though my majors were physics and mathematics, I took several philosophy and religion courses during my first two years there and really enjoyed them.

One night during my freshman year, I was watching a TV program about a prisoner trying to escape from prison. The plan was that he would hide in a coffin with a prisoner who had just died and the prison janitor would dig him out after the burial. He did as planned, was buried in the coffin with a recently deceased other prisoner and waited to be dug up. He waited and waited but nothing happened so he eventually lighted a match and looked at the dead body and saw it was the prison janitor! That was really the first time I truly realized I was going to die one day. From then onwards I started thinking more about death and the possibility of life after death. Taking the philosophy and religion courses increased my understanding about the different world religions and the various beliefs regarding life, death and life after death.

After graduating from Swarthmore I went to Cornell University where I got my M.Sc. in Physics in 1969. While there I bought some books on psychic phenomena (although at that time not much was available) and did some reading on the subject but otherwise did not give it much thought.

After receiving my masters degree at Cornell I went to South Africa to work on my Ph.D. in Physics studying the thermal properties of diamonds at the University of the Witwatersrand in Johannesburg. After about a year in South Africa, I met Marlene Mittens and we were married four months later. Marlene also had an interest in what happens after death and in psychic phenomena so we decided to look into it by going to Spiritualist church meetings. At these meetings they usually had a medium who would give messages from supposed "dead relatives". We received some messages but they were not very good and provided no evidence of life after death.

We did meet some people our age at these meetings and we decided to form our own development circle (a small group of people (typically from 3 to 10) that sit around in a circle to try to develop their psychic abilities and hope that one or more of them develop into a medium). One of the sitters, Basil, became a trance medium and he had several regular "spirit entities" speak through him. These entities were interesting to listen to but they never really provided any evidence. We suspected it was more likely the medium Basil talking rather than the "spirits".

It was not until we met Mickey and Sara Wolf that we really started to experience psychic phenomena. We met Mickey and Sara for the time when Marlene and I went shopping for some furniture for our new apartment. Mickey and Sara owned a furniture shop that sold mainly pine furniture. The shop was located right across from the University where I was working on my thesis. We were looking for a dining room table and chairs. I sat on one of the pine chairs and said how hard they were and then said they would be perfect for our circle because we would not be able to fall asleep. Sara then asked if we sat in a circle to which we replied that we did. They then asked us more about our circle and then started telling us about their circle. They mentioned that one of their sitters was Professor Jack Allen, a Professor of Anatomy at the University Medical School. They then invited Marlene and I to an upcoming sitting at their home. From that first meeting in 1970 until Mickey had his heart attack in 1978 we sat with them regularly. We became very close friends and met socially quite often for dinner or movies.

Our first sitting with Mickey and Sara was an experience we would never forget. Besides Marlene, myself, Mickey and Sara there were four other sitters, who occasionally sat with Mickey and Sara. We all went into the séance room at around eight o'clock. This room was set aside specifically for séances and spiritual healing. The room was quite small- about 15 feet by 15 feet. The one window was well covered and taped with a thick black curtain so no light could come in. The room was arranged in such a way that there was a curtain rod with a black curtain across one corner of the room. The curtain opened from the center by pulling each half to the side. Behind the curtain there was room for two or three chairs. About eight chairs formed a semi-circle in front of the curtain. Mickey and Sara sat on the two chairs behind the curtain. In front of the curtain stood a "trumpet", which is a cone-shaped "megaphone" made out of aluminum (or cardboard wrapped with aluminum foil) about one and a half feet in length. It had two luminous paint bands about an inch wide around the bottom and the top and some luminous spots in the middle. It could clearly be seen in the total darkness.

Mickey and Sara were both mediums and both went into trance (a sleep state). Sara was the main medium who went into deep trance quite quickly (within a minute or two) at the beginning of the sitting by just relaxing and closing her eyes. She said that she never had any recollection of what happened during the sitting. Mickey was usually in a light trance and most of the time did hear what took place during the sitting. He was told by the spirit guides that he provided "power" besides that taken from Sara so that the phenomena could take place.

Once Sara was in trance the sitting started with a spirit entity called Brian speaking through Sara. Brian was Sara's main control and always came through first and closed every sitting we had with Mickey and Sara. Brian had a very characteristic voice that we recognized immediately at each sitting and never changed all the years we sat with them. Brian stated that he was American and died when he was a teenager. He claims he was buried somewhere in upstate New York. He can best be described as the master of ceremonies; directing all the activities in the circle, introducing other spirit entities, speaking to the sitters, making jokes, etc.

Brian would either speak from behind the curtain through Sara, using her vocal cords, or his voice appeared to come from outside the curtain and at the height of a tall standing person. Sara was quite small, around five feet and two inches and remained seated throughout the whole séance. Brian was thus in that latter case not speaking through Sara but through an ectoplasmic "voice box" and his voice was magnified by the trumpet which sat there in mid air right in front of the voice box.

The terms ectoplasm and voice box will be used very often in this book so it is best to describe them briefly here. I will discuss them in more detail when discussing specific mediums and evidence.

Ectoplasm is a whitish substance which comes from the medium's body through one or more orifices such as the nose, the ears, the mouth and the solar plexus. Typically when ectoplasm initially comes out of the medium it looks quite transparent, like fine silk. This silk-looking ectoplasm would then solidify into partial or full materializations of spirit entities or into a rod-like shape to move the trumpet. The ectoplasm always returned to the medium's body when the materializations were finished. I know this all sounds hard to believe but Marlene and I have seen ectoplasm. Some materialization mediums as well as pictures of ectoplasm and materializations are discussed in detail and shown in the chapter on materialization.

Ectoplasm was given its name by Professor Charles Richet in 1905, when he was president of the Society for Psychical Research. He derived the name from the Greek meaning "exteriorized substance". The German authority Baron von Schenk-Notzing, who called it "teleplasma" produced a chemical analysis (around 1913) as follows: "colorless, slightly cloudy fluid with slightly alkaline reaction, traces of sputum, mucous membrane granules, potash, cell detritus, skin discs and minute particles of flesh", much the same as discovered by Dr.Dombrowski of the Polish Society for Psychical Research in 1916. (This was done in 1913-1916 so they could not get the kind of chemical analysis as you would get nowadays). The above analyses support the fact that ectoplasm actually does come out of the body of the medium.

There have been a few reported cases of serious injury to the medium when some someone grabbed or shone light on the ectoplasm. This typically happened when skeptics at those sittings tried to unsuccessfully expose the medium for being fraudulent. Great care thus has to be taken to ensure that the proper sitters, who would not do something foolish, are invited to a sitting. Mickey and Sara were always worried about this happening so they were very careful in who they invited to their sitting, especially since both of them sat in the cabinet (in their case behind the curtain). Most materialization mediums sat behind a curtain but a few sat in a cabinet made out of wood.

An ectoplasmic "voice-box" is produced by the spirit entities using ectoplasm drawn from the medium. This ectoplasm is fashioned into a replica of the physical vocal organs. The communicating spirit then concentrates his or her thoughts into this voice-box, creating a frequency of sound vibrations that the sitters in the room can hear. The voice-box is independent of the medium and is often located outside of the cabinet, usually in front of the curtain at head level (of an average height individual standing) or even higher. Occasionally it is at ground level when there is a "lack of power". As an aside: the materialization medium, who is in trance, usually does not feel the ectoplasm leaving his or her body and feels no pain.

Arthur Findlay in his book "On the Edge of the Etheric", evidence from which will be discussed in the next two chapters, describes a spirit communication in which they discuss a voice-box, called a "mask" by them. They state that the mask is made of ectoplasm drawn mainly from the medium as well as from the sitters and made in such a way to vibrate our atmosphere and hence produce sound. The spirit wishing to speak enters the mask with his or her spirit face. Sufficient cohesion is established between the spirits organs and the mask so that when the spirit entity speaks the ectoplasm of the mask is moved and sound is produced. This description of the voice-box is slightly different from that given above but both have the same basic principle: the voice-box or mask is made from ectoplasm drawn from the medium and the spirit entity speaks through it. The voice-box is separate from the medium so that the medium's vocal cords are not used, as is

Life After Death

the case in trance mediumship.

After this brief diversion to discuss ectoplasm and the voice-box, I will now get back to our first sitting with Mickey and Sara. Hearing Brian speak through a voice-box was exciting enough for Marlene and me since we had only heard trance mediumship up until then, but what we were to experience next was truly amazing. The trumpet, standing on the floor in front of the curtains, started lifting up from the floor and started flying around the room. Even though it was totally dark we could clearly see the trumpet because of the luminous bands and spots painted on it. The trumpet flew around like a bee would around the room; quite fast up to the ceiling, then from one side of the room to the other side. The trumpet would occasionally gently touch Marlene or me on the knee or on the top of the head. The trumpet never collided with the walls or the ceiling of the room or with anything else or anyone in the room. There is absolutely no way anyone in the room, whether Mickey or Sara or one of the other sitters, could move the trumpet like we witnessed in the pitch dark that evening. Try taking a stick about a foot long and try to gently tap several people sitting on chairs in a semi-circle on the head in the pitch dark, without bumping into anything. Even if you know where they were sitting, it is still impossible.

The movement of the trumpet could only have been performed by spirit entities using ectoplasm shaped in the form of a rod (in the chapter on materialization two photographs of an ectoplasmic rod attached to a trumpet are shown). The spirit entities can obviously see in the dark and have the necessary intelligence to shape the ectoplasm in the form of a rod and then move the trumpet as I have described. In all the years that we have had sittings with Mickey and Sara, the trumpet has always moved and has never bumped into walls, the ceiling or any of the sitters by accident.

Could there be any other explanation for the movement of the trumpet, other than by ectoplasm being directed by spirit entities? Night vision googles did exist in those days (the 1970's) but were very expensive and not all that good. It would have been almost impossible for any individual in South Africa to have purchased one. Also, trumpet movements like I have just described have also been observed in the 1920's (see the chapter on direct voice and Arthur Findlay's sittings). Night vision googles did not exist then, so can be ruled out as an explanation.

Skeptics like to use "super-ESP" (super-extrasensory perception) to explain anything they have no rational explanation for. Could the subconscious mind of the medium have moved and directed the trumpet to do what it did? There is evidence that some mediums can move very small objects (like toothpicks) short distances. There is no evidence that large and heavier objects can be moved the distance that our trumpet moved. Also, how can the subconscious mind of the medium "see" in the dark so that, even if it could move the trumpet, it would only touch the sitters and did not collide with anything else? This "super-ESP" explanation is a lot more far-fetched than the ectoplasm-spirit entity explanation for which there is photographic evidence.

This trumpet moving phenomena, while not proving survival after death, does demonstrate a non-physical (spirit) intelligence that can move and direct objects in our physical world. So in some way it does imply a spirit realm. In the chapter on materialization I will present evidence that spirits of the dead can materialize using ectoplasm.

Most of the time Brian spoke through Sara, while she was in trance, using her vocal cords, rather than speaking through direct voice. Some have called this type of communication possession of the medium by the spirit entity.

The spirit entity impresses his or her mind on the medium's vocal cords with the resultant speaking of the spirit through the medium. Some spirit entities have stated that that while in trance the medium's spirit body temporarily leaves the physical body to "make room" for the spirit entity.

There has been a great debate between believers in spirit communication and skeptics about the extent the medium's mind or subconscious influences what the spirit entity communicates. I will discuss this in a lot more detail in the chapter on mediumship but will briefly describe our experiences with Brian and Sara here.

We have had sittings in which we were sure that when Brian spoke it was really Brian speaking and not Sara because he said things that Sara did not know or could have known (I'll give a good example in the chapter on mediumship). We have also had sittings in which we suspected that it was Sara's mind influencing what Brian was saying. In the latter case, it occasionally happened that Brian would talk about things that Sara had just read, strongly believed in or used expressions she would typically use. We have noticed that this "influencing" what the spirit guide (mainly Brian) said happened most often when Sara was tired, not feeling well, or had her mind on other things. When she was like this she usually only went into a light rather than a deep trance.

Mediums do have off days. Communicating with the spirit world is not like a water tap that you open and close at will. You must have the right conditions and the medium must be in the right frame of mind. Even the best mediums have had off days when nothing happened or when mostly meaningless messages came through.

Skeptics have suggested that the medium's spirit control is actually a secondary personality of the medium, or a fictitious entity made up by the medium's subconscious mind. These claims will be discussed in detail in the chapter on mental and trance mediumship.

If Brian was indeed a secondary personality of Sara or a fictitious entity made up by Sara's subconscious, then you would not expect him to present evidential information that Sara did not know. But he did just that on many occasions during the eight years we sat with them. So as far as Marlene and I are concerned, Brian was a real spirit entity communicating through Sara by trance or direct voice. However, we do believe that at times Sara's mind or subconscious definitely influenced what Brian communicated and we might have been talking to Sara rather than Brian in those cases.

Now I will come back to our first circle with Mickey and Sara. After Brian had welcomed all the sitters and had spoken to each one individually, he introduced the next spirit entity to come and speak to us. The next spirit entity to speak was Madie, who spoke through the voice box and the trumpet was used to amplify her voice. She spoke with a German accent and spoke very slowly. She was a regular to speak at Mickey's and Sara's circles. She mainly spoke on philosophical topics, such as the purpose of life, love, death, the afterlife and other teachings that would be helpful to the sitters. Brian and Madie were the two regular guides that came through in every sitting we had with Mickey and Sara. Other spirit entities came through as well to give specific messages to some of the sitters but few came back at other sittings.

As I mentioned before Marlene and I had an experience we would never forget at this first sitting with Mickey and Sara. We became good friends with them and sat with them for the next eight years. During the first few years we sat quite regularly and then less frequently as Mickey and Sara got older. We also continued to sit in several different de-

Life After Death

velopment circles over the next ten years, up until we left South Africa in 1981. The mediums in those circles developed slowly and we never got the kind of results we got at the sittings with Mickey and Sara. During those initial years, after our first sitting, I read just about every book written on psychic phenomena. Also, when we traveled to England, which was just about every year, we had sittings at the Spiritualist Union in London.

In the next chapters I will present the best evidence for survival after death that I experienced myself as well as what I came across in the literature.

Mental and Trance Mediumship

Just about everyone is familiar with mental mediumship these days due to various T.V. shows such as "Medium" and "Ghost Whisperer" in which the star is a mental medium. Also, various mental psychics such as John Edward and James van Praag have their own T.V. shows and have been interviewed and have done demonstrations on shows such as Larry King Live and Oprah.

Mental mediumship is when the medium (or psychic) conveys messages from a spirit entity to the person for whom the message is meant (usually called the sitter). The medium either hears the message (called clairaudience), sees the spirit entity and/or symbols, images, signs, etc. (called clairvoyance), or just gets "an impression" that is communicated to him by the spirit entity (telepathic communication). The medium is fully conscious while this happens. This type of mediumship is also called channeling (i.e. messages are channeled from spirit through the medium to the sitter). Telepathy, clairvoyance and clairaudience are all forms of ESP.

Trance mediumship is when the medium is in a trance state (like being a sleep) in which a spirit entity possesses or controls the medium and then speaks through the medium using the medium's vocal cords, to the sitter or an audience. Some mediums claim to have no recollection of what happened while in trance while others claim to have some recollection of what happened. Sara Wolf most of the times recalled which of her spirit guides spoke through her but she never recalled what they said.

Mental Mediums

Mental mediums or channelers are the most common psychics and vary from total frauds to a few excellent mediums who provide evidence of life after death. There are many individuals who either want to know if there is life after we die or those who want to try to communicate with relatives who have died (passed over). They go to a spiritualist church (these still exist in England, South Africa, and some other countries), visit psychic fairs, or see a psychic who advertised in the paper, or was recommended by a friend. Over the past 30 years I have had sittings with many psychics. Many of the sittings were free but for some I had to pay a fee (anywhere from to $10 to $200). I will discuss some of these sittings in detail.

The key to sitting with a mental psychic is to say just about nothing except "yes" or "no" and to show no emotion (if possible) to statements that the medium makes. Do not give your correct name (especially when booking in advance), never volunteer information and even remove rings (especially a wedding ring). In this way the psychic, if not genuine, cannot "cold" read you (i.e. make some general statements and draw information out of you that the medium then uses to make it appear he (or she) has given you correct information about you). Skeptics say that all the mental mediums either get information about you in advance or "cold" read you. They say that there are even books or courses that teach you how to do that. In many

Life After Death

cases the skeptics are probably right but a genuine psychic, who is good, will give you fact after fact and information that is mostly (if not all) correct. I would have to say that of all my sittings probably a large majority (say about 75%) were a waste of time. Very little, if any, correct information was given in those cases and what was correct was very general, like "you are married". Those "psychics" were either not very good, had an "off-day" or were total frauds just out there for the money. I am sure that there are many well meaning psychics who just aren't very good. They very likely get some facts right from time to time and consciously or subconsciously do some "cold reading" as well.

I would first like to describe in a bit of detail some of my better sittings. One of the most impressive was in Ithaca, N.Y. in May 1983. We (Marlene, I and our two children) had just arrived back from Chicago where we had bought a house. There was a psychic fair at the hotel next to the Ithaca airport and we decided to stop by and see what was going on. At the fair I asked the organizer who the best psychic was. His response was that they were all good, to which I replied that there were good ones and bad ones and again asked who was the best psychic. He pointed to a middle aged lady. We waited until she was available and paid her $10 fee for the approximately 15 minute reading. We said nothing except "yes" or "no", but she hardly asked anything. She just talked. The first thing she said was that we moving to the Midwest but that we wouldn't be there long. She said we would then be moving to the South-West and that as far as she could see we would be there quite a while. She then said that we should not take our second car to the Midwest. The rest of the reading that I can recall was about the kids and how well they would do (a very general statement). I don't remember her saying anything that was wrong or turned out to be wrong. Actually, she turned out to be exactly right. We moved to Chicago two months later and one year later I took a job at the Jet Propulsion Laboratory in Pasadena, CA. (the South-West). Marlene and the kids joined me a year later when our house in Chicago was finally sold.

In Ithaca we had an old Dodge Dart that I wanted to take to Chicago, but Marlene said we shouldn't. After the reading we decided not to take the car and we sold it a week before we left. The day before we left I got a call from the buyer of the car saying that the thermostat had failed and the car overheated about 20 miles outside of Ithaca. That would have happened to us had we taken the car. It would have caused delays and problems. We still live in the Los Angeles area 24 years later and our children have done very well both academically and financially.

Here is a psychic who made predictions about the future that all came true. They were not generic, general predictions but very specific ones involving places and times. She did not say "I see you moving". Most people move several times in their lifetime, so that would have been a general prediction that would very likely come true. Also, to make a lucky guess this accurate (Midwest, South-West and car problems) would be extremely unlikely. Skeptics would say that she picked up the information about the move to Chicago and the car dispute telepathically from Marlene and myself and just added the rest (a lucky guess). I will discuss this in considerable detail later in this chapter. Suffice to say at the moment that many scientists don't believe in telepathy (the paranormal acquisition of information concerning the thoughts, feelings or activity of another person) and the telepathy that has been demonstrated under laboratory conditions by parapsychologists is no where as impressive as demonstrated here by this psychic. To be exact, the telepathy experiments in the laboratory are very simple (Zener cards, outputs of binary number generators, etc.) and the "hit" rates are not that far above chance. So the psychic conceivably could have picked up something telepathically from us about a move and a car, but it is much more likely that the exact message she gave was a communication she received from a spirit entity, who could "see" the future.

Predicting the future accurately does not necessarily prove survival after death but it does seem to indicate that our lives are predestined to some degree. But then, if our lives are predestined (partly or wholly), what would the purpose of a predestined life be if there was no survival after death? So I would have to believe that if the future can be accurately predicted, then life has a purpose and in that case we survive bodily death. Also, the medium must receive the information she gives out from some source, which to me the most logical explanation can only be a communication from a spirit entity. This entity would have to be able to "see" into the future to provide this information. This capability seems more likely to exist in the spirit world then anywhere else.

I had another very accurate prediction about the future when we lived in Chicago. I worked there as a stock market analyst at the brokerage firm Rodman & Renshaw. An analyst friend told me about the psychic Joseph DeLouise who helped him with stock market predictions. I set up a meeting with Joe using a false name. Joe had no idea who I was so he knew nothing about me. At the sitting Joe said that we would move to California where I would work on the Space Program. He also got many other facts right but the main thing I remember was his California prediction. Several months later I got a job offer from the Jet Propulsion Laboratory (NASA) in Pasadena, California. I accepted the job offer and moved to California in September of 1984.

Marlene and the kids joined me in May 1985, after our house in Chicago was sold. Here was another prediction that was spot on and much too specific to be a lucky guess or a cold reading. Marlene had a sitting with Joe but she was not impressed. So Joe was not always smack on.

Coming back to mental mediumship/channelers in general, there are lots of examples of evidential messages that prove survival after death. Many of the mental psychics have been tested extensively and some have been shown to be genuine and very accurate. Examples are George Anderson, John Edwards and others. One of the best examples of testing mental mediums was done by Dr. Gary Schwartz and reported in his book "The Afterlife Experiments". I will discuss some of his experiments and results here.

Dr. Schwartz carried out several experiments in Tucson, AZ in 1999 with up to five mediums: Suzanne Northrop, John Edwards, George Anderson, Anne Gehman, and Laurie Campbell. The experiments were progressively better designed to totally rule out any fraud and/or cold reading. For cold reading to be successful the "psychic" needs to be able to obtain information about the sitter beforehand and/or be able to hold a dialogue with the sitter to lure them into revealing more information than they realize. Even if the sitter only says "yes" or "no", the medium can gain information by carefully watching reactions to his or her comments, facial expressions, voice inclinations, etc. Initial experiments were conducted so that the medium did see the sitters, who would answer only "yes" or "no". The accuracy of the facts given by the mediums averaged 80% for the experiments conducted in this fashion. This is a very high and impressive accuracy rate and is difficult to duplicate by just cold reading a sitter.

However, it was suggested that the mediums were obtaining information by observing the sitters, so to rule out

Life After Death

any possibility of cold reading, the experiment was arranged in such a way that the medium did not see the sitter, who now sat behind a curtain. For the first ten minutes the sitter did not even respond to what the medium said. Even during the "yes" and "no" part of the sitting, the sitter would nod "yes" or "no" with his or her head and the experimenter (who could see both the sitter and the medium) would say "yes" or "no". In this way the medium had no idea who the sitter was, nor could they get any clues from the sitter's tone of voice or facial expressions. Fraud could definitely be ruled out since the medium had no idea who the sitter was so he or she could never get information about the sitter before hand.

One of the sittings using these very strict test conditions was with John Edwards, who according to the sitter (who had written down a list of relatives, facts, etc. beforehand) was 90 percent overall accurate (silent period and afterwards). He gave very specific details about her grandmother, her dogs, her mother's wedding, etc. This was the best result obtained under these strict conditions.

There were three mediums (John Edwards, Suzanne Northrop, and Laurie Campbell) who each sat with the same five sitters, all in the same day, under these very strict test conditions. The number of perfect correct facts for the silent periods (first 10 minutes), when there was no feedback, averaged 40 percent of the facts given. This number is far above anything that could be explained by guessing or chance. The silent period results were significantly worse (40% compared to about 80%) than those for the earlier experiments which had no silent periods and were solely "yes"/"no" questions with the medium seeing and observing the sitter. Why should the results be worse during the silent periods if the mediums are doing what they say they are doing: passing facts and messages from spirit entities to the sitter? Two possible explanations come to mind: firstly, it is possible that the medium needs to see the sitter to make better contact between the sitter and the associated spirit entities and secondly, during Schwartz's silent period experiment there were three mediums giving sittings at the same time in close proximity. Some kind of interference between the communications from the various spirit entities and the mediums might have occurred, e.g., the spirit grandmother of one of the sitters would not leave when a new sitter came and Dr. Schwartz's mother came through to speak to him during one of the sittings, while he was the experimenter (passing on yes/no answers) at a sitting. So the mediums might not have always picked up (whether by clairvoyance, clairaudience or telepathy) the correct message for his or her sitter.

It must not be forgotten that these results were extremely successful. The 80 percent average for the earlier experiments is just fantastic and the 40 percent is very good. No one can obtain or can even come close to these kind of results by guessing, by cold reading or by chance. The most likely explanation for these results is that there are mental mediums, who can provide evidence of life after death. The only other explanation could be that the mediums provided the correct information via telepathy (having ruled out fraud and cold reading). This is the standard reply from those not willing to accept spirit communication, not withstanding that this kind of impressive "telepathy" has never been demonstrated in the laboratory under test conditions. Also, very often the medium provides information that the sitter did not know and has to confirm after the sitting. That type of information is definitely not the standard telepathy, whereby the medium picks up the information from the sitter. There is the possibility that the medium picked up the information using what is now called "super-

Life After Death

ESP". I will discuss this later in this chapter.

Certain skeptics, if you can even call them that, will conclude that any psychic event is due to fraud, or lying, or deception, no matter how impressive the data is. For those "skeptics" nothing will ever convince them that psychic phenomena are real. It is a waste of time trying to convince them. They have already made up their mind. They just ignore results such as those obtained by Dr. Schwartz.

Unfortunately there are a lot of "psychics" who take advantage of the bereaved who want to speak to a dead relative, the gullible, and those who want to have their future told. When money is involved so are charlatans, frauds, and those who think they have a psychic gift. One must therefore be very careful when sitting with a psychic.

I could present many examples from some of the top mental mediums but will only give one here. This is from George Anderson's book "We Don't Die".

Joel Martin, who hosted George's radio shows, invited George to a lunch with Joan, an old friend of his, who George did not know. At her hotel, while they were waiting for Joan, George picked up that there had been a death in Joan's family. When Joan arrived they went to the restaurant for lunch and the following took place (paraphrasing from George's book):

As soon as George took his first bite he began moving his head from side to side, while holding his throat with one hand and said he had a choking sensation. He said to Joan that he saw tragedy around her. George then made some statements and asked Joan several questions (based on what a voice, only he could hear, said and what he was shown clairvoyantly). She answered only "yes" or "no" to the questions asked her. In this way it was determined that Joan's mother had died tragically by committing suicide and somehow choked. George picked up that she hanged herself by jumping off a chair. He told Joan that she was telling him that she did it because she and her husband (Joan's father) had been fighting for years and she was depressed and had just had it. He had threatened that he would kill himself one day and she had decided to turn the tables on him and kill herself before he did. She apologized to Joan for what she had done and said that suicide was not the answer. George picked up that there was a dog on the other side to greet her when she passed over. Joan confirmed that her mother's dog had recently died. George ended by saying that he hoped he had not upset Joan, to which Joan replied that it was just the opposite. George had provided answers to several questions she had been wondering about.

This reading is typical of how the best mental psychics work. Here is a good example of a medium seeing (clairvoyance) and hearing (clairaudience) the spirit entity that is communicating with him. They make factual statements and ask some questions to which the sitter answers "yes" or "no". Notice that he is not trying to get information from Joan but most of what he says are statements to which she answers "yes" or "no". I find this a very evidential unexpected sitting that confirms the survival after death of Joan's mother. George did not know Joan, knew nothing about her and did not know they were going to meet her, so fraud can be totally ruled out. The only explanation besides survival could be telepathy, by which he picked up Joan's thoughts about her mother. There were really no major facts that Joan did not know or had to check, but there were answers to questions Joan had about her mother. So the telepathy explanation is a possibility albeit a remote one. All the facts that George was able to produce point more to survival being the only explanation. Interestingly, George was once tested for high levels of telepathy or precognitive ability but was found to be no better than average. This re-

Life After Death

sult would make the telepathy explanation even less likely.

Over a period of seven years starting in 1980 Joel Martin arranged for George to appear live on radio and television programs doing thousands of readings for complete strangers who called in by phone and who gave no identification. Speaking to these complete strangers he was time and again able to give names, details of how a loved one died, personal nicknames, allusions to shared experiences, accurate predictions for the future, details of health problems, etc., etc. Joel had researchers follow up many of the readings and they found that George had an accuracy rate of between 86 to 95 percent.

Numerous skeptics and debunkers appeared on Joel's shows and all of those admitted George was very accurate and not a fraud. Some of the more well-known debunkers were invited on the show but never came. These "professional" skeptics and debunkers ignore George Anderson because they would be made fools of. Joel specifically invited a well-known magician, but he never came!!

Trance Mediums

Trance mediumship occurs when the psychic, more accurately the medium, goes into a trance-state which is similar to, but not the same as sleeping. A spirit entity then uses the vocal cords and mouth of the medium to speak. Most mediums do not remember what was said through them while some have some vague recollection of which entities (usually their regular guides) came through but rarely remember what was said.

Sarah Wolf would "dose-off" quite quickly (within a minute or two) and almost always her regular control would come through first. All her regular controls (guides) had very distinct voices so you would recognize them immediately. Marlene and I often sat with Mickey and Sarah and we regularly spoke to at least three different spirit guides.

One sitting with Sarah I remember well because of an interesting prediction and that was made by Brian. It was the 1972 Christmas sitting and Brian spoke to each sitter in turn and told them something interesting or made a prediction. He got to Marlene and myself and thanked us for the gift we had brought (everyone brought a wrapped present which was given to charity). We had brought a black baby doll. Brian commented that we would have a baby next year, like the baby doll, but that it would not be black! The presents had not been opened yet, so Sara did not know it was a black doll but Brian knew. We had our daughter Colette the following November.

Here is a case of a spirit guide speaking through a medium in trance and making a correct prediction about the future. It could have been a lucky or educated guess about us having a child but the comment about it not being black like the doll we brought is very difficult to guess. Brian obviously knew what we had brought.

There have been many trance mediums who have been extensively tested and investigated and found to be genuine. The best known and most extensively tested was Mrs. Leonora Piper (1857-1950), who lived in Boston. She was investigated by such famous men as Professor William James (1842-1910), the Harvard psychologist and philosopher, Sir Oliver Lodge (1851-1940), Nobel prize winning British physicist, Frederic W.H. Myers (1843-1901) and Richard Hodgson (1855-1905), who was the secretary of the American Society of Psychical Research (ASPR). Hodgson had exposed many well know "psychics" and showed them to be frauds. He expected to do the same

Life After Death

with Mrs. Piper. He spent 18 years investigating her (from 1887-1905) and had hundreds of sittings. During the first few years he disbelieved in her psychic power. He believed that her spirit control, a Dr. Phinuit, was a secondary personality of Piper buried away in her subconscious. Somehow this secondary personality was able to read minds and to communicate information that came from dead people (i.e. discarnate spirits) and /or somehow tap into a cosmic reservoir of information using what is now called "super-ESP" (a comprehensive form of telepathy, clairvoyance and precognition). Dr. Hornell Hart coined the term "super-ESP" in 1959 but early researchers where already hinting at such a hypothesis to explain observed phenomena.

Then in 1892, a friend of his, George Pellew (G.P.), who had passed over earlier that year, started communicating through Piper. This communication by his friend was characterized by too much personality and too much purpose and persistence to attribute it to telepathy (tapping into another mind or cosmic reservoir) according to Hodgson. He reasoned that the medium might get fragmentary bits of information through telepathy, but not the fullness of a personality that spoke through Piper. So after 12 years of investigating Mrs. Piper, Hodgson changed his mind and stated that he believed in the possibility of receiving messages from the spirit world.

One of the things Hodgson did to test the entity that claimed to be G.P. was to invite family members and old friends of G.P. to sit with Piper. He wanted them to check their knowledge against that of the spirit entity claiming to be G.P. Hodgson actually brought in 130 people, some friends and relatives of G.P. and some absolute strangers to sit with Piper. No participants were allowed to give their names or give any details, if any, relating to G.P. Only 20 or so were friends of G.P. and all were greeted by their name when they sat with Piper. G.P. recognized pictures, books, remembered past experiences, etc. Not once in the years between 1892 and 1897 did G.P. ever confuse a stranger with a friend, or vice versa. Hodgson found telepathy an inadequate explanation. Sometimes G.P. talked accurately about friends not in attendance (some living miles away) making thought transference even more unlikely.

Another extremely impressive communication through Piper helped convince Hodgson about the genuineness of spirit communication. In that particular sitting the parents of a little girl, Katherine (nicknamed Kakie), who had died a few weeks earlier at age five, came to sit with Piper. They did not identify themselves but brought with them a silver medal and string of buttons that the child once played with. A transcription of the sitting reads as follows:

> "Where is Papa? Want Papa. (The father takes from the table a silver medal and hands it to Mrs. Piper, who is in trance) I want this-want to bite it. (She used to do this)...I want you to call Dodo (her name for her brother George). Tell Dodo I am happy. (Puts hands to throat) No sore throat anymore. (She had pain and distress of the throat and tongue)... Papa, want to go wide (ride) horsey (She pleaded this throughout her illness). Every day I go see horsey. I like that horsey...Eleanor. I want Eleanor. (Her little sister. She called her much during her illness). I want my buttons. Where is Dinah? I want Dinah. (Dinah was an old rag doll, not with us). I want Bagie (her name for her sister Margaret). I want to go to Bagie. I want Bagie."

Here is a case where the five year old child speaks

Life After Death

through Piper and gives incredibly convincing evidence for survival after death. There is no way Piper or a secondary personality could have given this communication because of the very characteristic language and names used by the child and because of the evidence provided.

In his second report on Leonora Piper, published in December 1897, Hodgson states: "at the present time I cannot profess to have any doubt but that the chief "communicators" to which I have referred in the foregoing pages are veritably the personages they claim to be, that they have survived the change we call death, and that they have directly communicated with us, whom we call living, through Mrs. Piper's organism."

An interesting aside is that Piper reported seeing the communicating spirits exiting her body as she (i.e. her spirit body) reentered it following the trance state. When shown 32 photographs, she reportedly correctly identified G.P. as having communicated through her body. Piper is one of the few trance mediums who reported seeing the communicating spirits. Sara Wolf told us that she could "sense" who was communicating through her but she did not see them.

It should be pointed out that Piper also had bad days when nothing happened. On those days her control Phinuit had nothing to say. He would fish for answers, ask questions of the sitters and repeat what they told him as if it were an incredible discovery. Anyone who sat with Piper on one of her bad days was likely to leave very disappointed or disenchanted. This goes to confirm that even the best mediums have bad days, which could be due to a number of factors: the "conditions" aren't right (whatever these conditions are, whether on this side or the spirit side), the physical or mental condition of the medium is not conducive to spirit communication, the sitters have brought the "wrong vibes" for spirit communication, etc. Marlene and I have had sittings with Mickey and Sara where nothing happened and what was said was meaningless. It happens from time to time, even with the best mediums. That does not mean that they are frauds, it just goes to show how difficult spirit communication really is. Unfortunately, some good mediums lose their gift with age and then resort to fraud, which then puts a cloud over (or discredits) their whole life's mediumship.

Richard Hodgson passed over in 1905 and within weeks he was communicating through Mrs. Piper to his friends. He gave them evidential information to convince them that it was indeed Hodgson. He specifically tried to give information that was of such a nature that telepathy could be ruled out.

Professor James sat with Piper quite often and sent relatives and friends to sit with her. He also stayed in regular contact with Hodgson and other psychical researchers in England. He firmly believed Mrs. Piper was a genuine medium, who communicated evidential messages to the sitters. He just did not know how to explain these evidential messages. From what I have read about him, it appears he did not go as far as saying her evidence was proof of survival after death. He was ridiculed and criticized by his colleagues for his interest in psychic research. Things haven't changed much in 100 years. That is still the case today.

Professor James believed that fraud among professional mediums did not undo the possibility of real supernatural phenomena. Actually, fraud might serve to corroborate truth. James stated:

> "If we look at human imposture as a historic phenomenon, we find it imitative; tricksters were only able to garner attention because they faked

something that did exist, fraudulent mediums are only persuasive by taking advantage of the reputation earned by the few legitimate psychics".

The most impressive evidence for survival provided by trance mediums is given by Arthur Findlay in his book "On the Edge of the Etheric". His mother died on February 3, 1936 and she communicated through two different mediums on February 9 and February 12, giving survival evidence. Findlay states that not one mistake was made by the mediums, everything was correct and some statements were unknown to him and found later to be correct. Neither medium knew his mother had died. Taking the sittings with the two mediums together, 188 facts were given to him, which were correct. No mistakes were made and there was no guessing. I will here give the details of the sitting on February 9 in Glasgow. Arthur was with his brother John. The medium was Mrs. Bertha Harris, who went into trance and her spirit control spoke as follows: (the number in brackets is the number of correct facts in the sentence or paragraph and are from Findlay's notes);

"You seem to bring an atmosphere of sorrow with you today. Someone has passed on within the past week. A lady, small, stooping, old. I should say about eighty years of age. Very closely connected with you. Nellie brings her with her. (10) The lady had no feeling of surprise when she passed over, only a feeling of great joy to touch dear Robert's hand." (1)

Mrs. Harris's control then referred to Robert (my father) meeting her when she passed over and also "an old gentleman who had passed on recently". "This old gentleman welcomed her, but was now looking after someone else" (Annie, his sister, just died). "The lady gives her name as Margaret, and Nellie" (my brother's deceased wife) "says": "Just as I came and brought the old gentleman in Glasgow and then in London, so shall I bring your Mother to you in London as I have brought her this morning". (6) (This reference is to Nellie bringing my uncle to Glasgow the day before his funeral to speak to John and then, on a later occasion, to speak to John in London).

"The lady mentions Mary and Elizabeth. She sends them both her love and gratitude. She has mentioned them in her Will, giving them recognition. It is a money recognition." "I always like to pay my debts," she says. "I have tried to repay them for all their kindness to me." Her last conscious remembrance on earth was Mary and Elizabeth standing beside her. "Elizabeth stroked my hand and face with her hand. She was alone with me at the time." (9)

I then asked: "Have you seen your old school friend?" and the reply was: "Yes, Annie, big woman. She would nearly fill the doorway." (2)

"Your mother speaks of a red rose which was placed on her robe in her coffin on her breast." She says: "Red is my favorite color, but why did you not put the rose in my hand?" (5)

"Your Mother had very small hands and feet; she was proud of her small feet, she took size two in shoes." (4)

The medium went on: "Arthur's daughter, your Mother tells me, is young and tall, but was not present at your Mother's passing, as she was away from home at the time." (5)

"Your Mother mentions John's boys, one of

Life After Death

them, who is seventeen, is tall, the other, Arthur-not this Arthur (pointing at me)- I am more concerned about. Carry out what she advises and push him forward." (5)

"Your mother mentions various small gifts she has left for people with cards attached bearing messages and names. Arthur's daughter's gift is a necklace." (4)

"Your Mother asks me to tell you she tried to retain consciousness till you, Arthur, and Gertrude arrived. You rushed up from a long distance. She did not succeed in remaining conscious, but so long as she was conscious she kept thinking of them coming." (4)

The medium's control then spoke to John, saying that he had recently had his birthday, but that he had not yet bought his Mother's present. He had first told her he would not buy a book, and then had changed his mind and decided to buy one. (4)

"She tells me", the control went on," that John's books are becoming numerous and that his library is becoming like Nellie's handkerchiefs. Then she goes on to say that John put a piece of paper in his waistcoat pocket and that had reference to his book." (5) (The reference to Nellie's handkerchiefs was good, because Nellie, when she was ill, bought so many handkerchiefs at one time that there was a joke about it. As to John putting a piece of paper in his waistcoat pocket, he had done so that morning to remind him to order the book at the Church Bookstall.)

"Your Mother mentions something in her bedroom with a small single drawer in it containing papers which will interest you both." When we said we did not know of such a thing, she mentioned a bunch of keys and we said we did not know anything about this bunch of keys. (5) (When we returned home we looked around her room and saw her dressing-case, which was a mahogany box about 18 inches by 18 inches. We could not open it as it was locked, and we asked for the key. This was on a bunch of keys. The dressing-case was opened, and after examining the inside we found a spring which released a single drawer in which we found quite a number of papers of interest. If we had not been told about this drawer it is unlikely we would ever have found these papers.)

The medium then referred to my Mother having pain in her stomach and weakness of her heart, also to sickness. She referred also to her having weak knees. She then referred to one eye being troublesome: "Not blind, you know, but sore and uncomfortable. She goes like this" (The medium's hand went up to her eye, as my Mother was continually doing when her eye was troublesome, her right finger going round her eye.) (8)

"Your Mother died of something wrong here." (The medium put her hand to her stomach.) "Your Father died of something here" (She put her hand on her appendix.) "Your Mother has left three grown-up people and three children." (Myself, my brother, my wife, my daughter and John's two sons.) (4)

"Your mother was very fond of her Bible, and a little old village church with a bell in a small pointed steeple. She could hear the bell ringing from her home." (5)

"Your Mother loved the hills but she now sees hills like those she could see from her home." (2)

"Your Mother has met Dr. Lamond; she hardly recognized him as he is looking so much younger than when she saw him last." (2)
"Your Mother refers to a picture of Nellie on the piano in a room with a high ceiling with a pattern round it. It is a colored picture." (5)
"Your Mother said that during the recent church service Arthur moved up to the end of the pew, and she came and sat beside him." (1) (This is correct about me moving up to the end of the pew, but, when I did so, the medium was in trance on the platform and could not have seen me. In any case, I was sitting far back in the church.)

Findlay concluded by stating:

"All that was said in the sitting we had occurred with the medium in trance. Mrs. Harris, just before we left her, when saying good-bye, mentioned that before we arrived she had received a message which she had not understood. When she was dressing that morning, Nellie had appeared to her and said that Arthur and John were coming to see her that morning. She did not know who Arthur and John were, but she mentioned this message to us as a matter of interest.
Everything reported above is quite applicable to my Mother and the other people mentioned. Ninety-six facts were given which the medium could not have known. Not one single statement was incorrect or even doubtful."

On February 12, 1936 Findlay had a sitting with Mrs. Abbot in a private room at The London Spiritualist Alliance. Mrs. Abbot went into trance quickly and her control stated the following (I will just give the highlights of this sitting):

"An elderly lady was present, from seventy-five to eighty years, belonging to me. She had recently passed over. (3) Among those who were waiting for her was a clergyman uncle, who, when on earth, thought Spiritualism was the work of the devil. He was an ardent minister, and used to wear a red hood, but he has now given up the foolish ideas which he preached." (4)

"Your Father and Mother are both in the spirit world, and they send you their love. All is well with your Mother. This is not the first time she has come back to you, as she came back on two occasions before, but the first time she could not get through well; the second time, she got through what she wanted quite well." (4)

"Your Mother learned a lot about the after life from you (Arthur) before dying. She feels much younger now. Your Father is very happy having her with him. Your father can never thank you enough for all you did for your Mother. He approves of your books." (3)

"For some weeks before she died your Mother's mind was very forgetful. She was losing a grip on earth life. She just slept away quite peacefully. When she arrived here she was not so surprised as many other people are, because of what you had told her. For some years before passing her legs were bad, but now she feels quite young again, and her great freedom of movement is one of the things that impresses her most in her new life."

Then reference was made to the two boys.

Life After Death

"They are Ian's sons." (Ian is Gaelic for John, and is his home name.) "One was named Arthur, but his name had been changed, owing to the confusion with you, to a name connected with the family. Your mother objected to the change at first, but now thinks it was a good idea to change the name." (6)

Then reference was made to her furniture, and "she had hoped that the big furniture would not be sold." (1) (This was her wish on earth.)

Reference was next made to old family papers and to old family photographs. "They are not old rubbish and, though you are not interested in them, you should keep them." (3) (Correct. She knew I was not especially interested in these, and she made this remark, in these words, when on earth, to me.)

I then asked my Mother what G.W.G. stood for. The control stated that she was laughing, and that, though she could not explain what the initials stood for, yet she was not that now. She was having to lie low and not say too much, as she felt somewhat subdued after all the opinions she had given on earth. She said she was not a G.W.G. any longer. (5) (Correct. G.W.G. stood for "Great Wee Girl" which we called her when she became opiniona-tive.)

"Your Mother was very autocratic, yet homely. She did not like to be pushed on one side, but liked to feel she was someone in the home. Her legs were rather bad towards the end, but now she can walk and feels bright and fresh. She so loved her country place and her garden, but now she is in a place where there is no fog and dullness. Three months before her passing her sight became bad, but she can now see clearly and further than before." (6)

Findlay then concluded by stating:

"The sitting lasted for an hour and a half. When Mrs. Abbot came out of trance I asked her if she knew my brother, and she said "No". She recognized me because she had seen me going about the London Spiritualist Alliance building, but that she never, to her knowledge, had met my brother, which confirms what my brother had told me that Mrs. Abbot did not know him.

Mrs. Abbot said, after coming out of trance that she was quite unaware that my Mother had recently passed on, and I do not see how see could have heard of it, or known about it, as, after the sitting I mentioned it to one or two others in the London Spiritualist Alliance, who had not heard of it. It was mentioned in The Times, but even if Mrs. Abbot had seen it, I do not know how she could have connected her name with me, in fact I am quite certain that she never knew my Mother had died.

The sitting was arranged by the secretary of the International Institute for Psychical Research, but no name was given. That being so, Mrs. Abbot had no opportunity to make enquiries, and, when I arrived for the séance, I walked up to her room and found her waiting. She said she had an appointment with someone at two o'clock, but she did not know who it was, and I told her I was the person for whom the appointment was made.

Everything stated is correct and applicable to my mother and the others mentioned. Ninety-two facts were given at this séance, none of which the medium could have known. At the two sittings 188 facts were given in all. Not one of the statements made was incorrect or even doubtful."

I have here given this lengthy quote from Arthur Findlay's book because these two cases are excellent examples of trance mediumship. Assuming that Findlay has accurately reported the sittings and the facts given (and I see no reason why he shouldn't have) then these two trance mediums (Mrs. Harris and Mrs. Abbot) are as good a trance medium as you can get. Through their spirit controls they provide accurate facts, information, details, and even facts that the sitters did not know and had to verify. The spirit controls did not ask questions of the sitters to try to draw out information, but just provided or transmitted information. I have sat with numerous trance mediums but have never sat with anyone as impressive as these two mediums.

I have never in the literature of psychic phenomena come across anyone accusing Findlay of not accurately reporting his sittings. I thus have to assume that the above quotes are correct and did occur.

I want to give one more well-documented and extremely evidential example of communication through a trance medium, proving life after death. The medium was Eileen Garrett (1893-1970), who herself insisted that investigations of survival evidence must be conducted under the most rigorous scientific conditions possible. She was extensively investigated and never proven to be fraudulent. She never asked for money for her sittings.

At a sitting in 1930 in London, the purpose of which was to try to get the deceased Sir Arthur Conan Doyle to come through and communicate with them. The sitting started as usual with her principal spirit control coming through first. Then another voice broke in, it was not Conan Doyle, but a man speaking in great distress. He gave his name as Flight Lieutenant H. Carmichael Irwin and he said the following:

"I must do something about it....The whole bulk of the dirigible was entirely and absolutely too much for the engine's capacity. Engines too heavy. Engines too heavy. It was this that made me on five occasions have to scuttle to safety. Useful lift too small. Useful lift too small...Gross lift computed badly- inform control panel. And this idea of new elevators totally mad. Oil pipe plugged...Flying too low altitude and never could rise. Disposable lift could not be utilized. Load too great for long flight...Load too great for long flight. Cruising speed bad and ship badly swinging. Severe tension on the fabric which is chafing... Engines wrong- too heavy- cannot rise. Never reached cruising altitude. Same in trials. Too short trials. No one knew the ship properly. Weather bad for long flight. Fabric all water-logged and ship's nose is down. Impossible to rise. Cannot trim. Almost scraped the roofs of Archy. Kept to railway. At

Enquiry to be held layer it will be found that the superstructure of the envelope held no resilience and had far too much weight in envelope. The added middle section was entirely wrong...too heavy, too much overweighted for the capacity of the engines."

Lieutenant Irwin was talking about a lighter-than-air craft called a dirigible, which was used in the early days of commercial air travel. They did not last for long because of their poor safety record. The R101 of the British fleet crashed into a hillside near the city of Archy in France two days before the sitting. Most of the passengers (48 out of

Life After Death

54) died in that crash. The information provided by Irwin, the commanding officer of the dirigible, through Garrett was not known to anybody at the time of the sitting. Irwin's observations were confirmed by a team of experts after a six month investigation. Garrett was actually asked by the British Ministry of Civil Aviation to attempt further communications with those aboard the doomed airship. She agreed and several other deceased people who had been aboard R101 communicated through her. One of the crew members gave very detailed technical details about what had gone wrong. Those statements were also confirmed by the official investigation by the team of experts.

Here we have a case of communication by spirit entities that were unknown to the medium and the sitters, giving initially spontaneous information and later upon request, and giving highly detailed information and observations that were later confirmed by experts. Also, no one knew about the accident at the time of the first sitting. This is one of the best and most evidential cases of spirit communication clearly confirming life after death.

The skeptics cannot say that this is a case of fraud or cold reading. The only possible explanation they could give is that Garrett obtained the information through some sort of "super-ESP" rather than spirit communication. I just cannot buy that argument. Think about it: there is Garrett at her sitting and her mind just happens to pick up this bit of information about the crash out of the trillions and trillions of thoughts, events, information, etc, floating around our whole planet. How does her mind know which bit of information to pick up? Her subconscious would have to have selective action, i.e. would know exactly where to go to get the information, which seems very unlikely if not impossible. Secondly, many skeptics don't even acknowledge telepathy exists, and thirdly, as I have already mentioned, ESP (telepathy) experiments conducted under laboratory test conditions have never ever been even close to being as impressive as the information obtained from the best mediums. So, how can you then claim that ESP, specifically telepathy, can do the job which the super-ESP hypothesis requires of it. The best and most plausible explanation is that the spirit of the deceased lieutenant was directed by spirit guides to the Garrett sitting so he could speak through her. This communication proves survival after death, something the skeptics could never accept so they will think up any alternative explanation, no matter how far-fetched or implausible it might be.

We now come to one of the major criticisms that the skeptics have against trance mediums: that their spirit controls are nothing more than secondary personalities of the medium. Most trance mediums tend to have one or a few regular spirit controls that "take over" the medium's body for part of the sitting and communicate through it. These controls act as "masters of ceremony" and often pass on messages from other spirit entities (as in some of the cases described above). They look after the interests of the entranced medium. Brian was Sara's regular and main spirit control.

The skeptics usually cite two very well-known trance mediums: Mrs. Leonora Piper (discussed above in detail) and Mrs. Gladys Leonard (1882-1968), who have both been extensively investigated over many years and found to be genuine. Actually they were never found to be fraudulent.

The evidence received through Mrs. Piper was so outstanding and impressive (as discussed above), that Mrs. Eleanor Sidgwick (1845-1936) (who was a leading psychical researcher of her time) published a lengthy article on her in the Proceedings of the Society of Psychical Research. Some of the communications that came through Mrs. Piper

Life After Death

have been discussed above. Mrs. Sidgwick came to the following conclusion in her article: the "spirit" personalities who professed to communicate through Mrs. Piper were actually dramatizations produced by the medium's unconscious mind, in a state of self-hypnosis. She did, however, believe that some of the viridial communications that came through Mrs. Piper came from the dead and therefore imply genuine communications with spirits. What Mrs. Sidgwick called "dramatizations" others would call secondary personalities or aspects of the medium's personality.

Hodgson in his first report on Mrs. Piper stated that her trance was genuine. He performed just about every test he could think of such as; poke her, pinch her and put detergent etc. in her mouth while in trance, but none of these affected her trance. However, her trance personality, Dr. Phinuit, who was her main control from 1884-1897, was not what he claimed he was. Hodgson never found evidence that the French doctor existed in reality. Also, "Dr." Phinuit could barely speak French, if at all, and knew nothing about medicine. Hence, Hodgson, Professor William James and Professor Charles Richet (French Nobel Prize winner) all three believed that Phinuit was a secondary personality of Mrs. Piper. They believed that Phinuit was a coping device, a subconscious way for the medium to protect herself against whatever mental battering took place in the trance state. Some of her other controls that followed Phinuit were certainly fictitious and were also considered to be aspects of Mrs. Piper's own personality.

Similarly, Mrs. Leonard's control Feda and Mrs. Garrett's control Uvani were considered by some to be aspects of their personalities. The skeptics thus state that we would have to abandon the idea that the controls of trance mediums are spirits of deceased people temporarily controlling the medium's body. There is no doubt, based on the detailed evidence, that some controls of many mediums are fictitious and aspects of the medium's own personality. To generalize to all controls and all trance mediums is clearly not possible. Not enough information, details and research is available to determine this. Sometimes controls speak as if they could directly see the séance room and what happens in it while the medium is in trance. Often, they speak as if they could both see and hear a spirit (of a deceased person) who wants to communicate, and then pass the message on to the sitters, while very often describing the spirit entity in detail. In these cases it has to be a spirit, who has taken over the medium's body. A secondary personality could not see what is going on in the séance room, nor could it see spirit entities who want to communicate on that side and describe them.

Often the spirit entity, rather than the control, would speak through the entranced medium. In that case the spirit gives the messages, information, proof, etc. directly, rather than having to go through the medium's control. The key to being convinced that the spirit entity is who he or she claims to be, are the personal characteristics such as voice, characteristic phrases, gestures and mannerisms, which relatives or friends should recognize. A good example of this is given above in the case of Hodgson recognizing his friend George Pellew speaking through the entranced Piper. Hodgson claims that telepathy could not account for the fullness of the personality of Pellew, which he recognized. Super-ESP, if it can do what its proponents claim, might be able to get the correct facts about a certain deceased person, but it is very hard to believe it could get all the personal characteristics so that the medium's secondary personality could give a realistic impersonation of the spirit entity it is claiming to be. Personal characteristics and mannerisms, which are recognized by sitters, are the strongest evidence

Life After Death

for spirit communication by a deceased person. Skeptics argue that super-ESP can acquire the information and personality patterns required for the production of both the fictitious communicators (secondary personalities of the medium) and also of the spirit personality supposedly communicating. I have difficulty seeing how super-ESP can do all of this especially considering it is a hypothesis with very little evidence to back it up. Remember, telepathy has been shown to exist under laboratory conditions, but certainly no where as impressive as the psychic abilities of the mediums described above.

I would now like to give a case where a sitter received both incorrect information from the medium's fictitious control and also correct information from the spirit friend communicating directly through the medium. Dr. van Eeden, psychical researcher, had numerous sittings with the medium Mrs. Thompson in Paris between 1899 and 1901. Van Eeeden brought from Holland to the sittings a necktie which had been worn by a friend of his who had committed suicide some 15 years earlier. During the initial sittings he was given information by the medium's control that contained both correct information but also inexplicable faults and mistakes. Up to the sitting on June 7, 1901 all the information had come through Nellie, Mrs. Thompson's so-called spirit control. But on that date the deceased friend tried, as he had promised in earlier sittings, to take control himself and speak through the entranced medium. Here quoting van Eeden:

> "The evidence became very striking. During a few minutes, though only a few minutes, I felt absolutely as if I were speaking to my friend myself. I spoke Dutch and got immediate and correct answers. The expression of satisfaction and gratifica-

tion in face and gestures when we seemed to understand each other was too true and vivid to be acted. Quite unexpected Dutch words were pronounced. Details were given which were far from my mind, some of which, as that about my friend's uncle in a former sitting, I had never known, and found to be true only on inquiry afterwards."

"But being now well on my guard, I could, exactly at this most interesting few minutes, detect as it were, where the failures crept in. I could follow the process and perceive where the genuine phenomena stopped and the unconscious play-acting began."

"When I read the notes from of the sitting again it is impossible for me to abstain from the conviction that I really have been a witness, were it only for a few minutes, of the voluntary manifestation of a deceased person".

Here we have a sitting where the sitter, a psychical researcher, recognized the personal characteristics and gestures of the spirit entity, a friend of his, communicating through the entranced medium. He did, however, comment that what he believed was a genuine communication did not last very long and that the medium's subconscious then started taking over the communication. He believed that her spirit control was an artificial creation of her mind (later called a secondary personality of the medium).

This case shows that genuine trance mediumship exists, but that both good and wrong information can be given during a sitting. As I have mentioned before, having a sitting with a really good trance medium is rare. The best trance mediums have good and bad sittings and are not always correct. I believe that it just shows how difficult the com-

Life After Death

munication with a spirit entity is, when trance mediumship is involved. We have to deal with the subconscious of the entranced medium and with the spirit entity either telepathically (?) communicating with the medium's control or trying to take over the medium's body and use her vocal cords to speak. None of that is easy. Direct voice, which is discussed in the next chapter, is less common than trance mediumship but when it happens it is usually easier to determine if it is genuine.

The question now arises: how did Mrs. Piper (and similarly Mrs. Leonard and Mrs. Garrett and any other mediums with fictitious controls) communicate such excellent evidence through a control or guide that supposedly was fictitious and nothing more than an aspect of her personality? In the case of a real control (the spirit of a deceased person) it is this control that takes over the medium's body and then passes the messages from communicating spirits to the sitters. This was supposedly not happening when the fictitious control was talking. Mrs. Sedgwick believed that the evidential material Mrs. Piper produced while in trance was derived telepathically either from the dead or the living and injected into the "presentation" her control (her secondary personality) was giving. So probably in most cases, the medium somehow receives the correct evidential information from the spirit of the deceased and then gives it out through either a genuine control or a fictitious "control" to the sitter. It is not important how the information is transmitted from the spirit entity to the medium as long as the information is evidential and there is no fraud involved. It is interesting to note that Mrs. Sedgwick did believe in real survival evidence.

Skeptics, of course, say that all information is obtained telepathically by the entranced medium from living people, in cases where all fraud can be ruled out. I have already addressed this point earlier several times and find this a very unlikely scenario. Especially considering additional experiments carried out by Hodgson and James on Mrs. Piper and by Sir Oliver Lodge on Mrs. Leonard. They used "proxy" sitters in their experiments. A sitter would go for a sitting with Mrs. Piper or Mrs. Leonard and ask about a certain person (they were told to ask about) that they themselves would know nothing about. The entranced medium could thus not telepathically get the information from the proxy sitter since that sitter knew nothing about that person. In most of these proxy sitting cases both mediums provided excellent evidence for survival (written down by the sitter and confirmed afterwards).

So where did Mrs. Piper and Mrs. Leonard get this information? Telepathically (or some kind of communication) from the spirit of a deceased person is far more likely than the medium happening to pick up the right information from the subconscious mind of a certain living person who happens to know the right information or pick up the right information from existing records/information (the trillions and trillions of bits of information floating around our planet).

Carl Jung, the well-known psychiatrist, proposed the idea of a "universal subconscious" and others talk about the Akashic records (a universal (cosmic) reservoir of mind that contains a complete archive of human experience). There is no evidence that either exists. The medium could "just" tap into this "universal subconscious" or into the Akashic records and get the information she needs (easier than "googling" it on your computer!!). As discussed earlier this is referred to as "super-ESP" whereby mediums obtain all their information by telepathically tapping the memory stores of living persons or tapping into the "universal subconscious" or cosmic reservoir and clairvoyantly

Life After Death

scanning the archives, records, etc. How would her mind (subconscious) know where to get the right information pertaining to the sitter or the person who the questions were being asked about? It seems a lot more plausible that a spirit entity gave the medium the information by means of whatever process impressing it on her mind.

It should again be pointed out that the best trance mediums could not perform perfectly every time and occasionally nothing at all happened at a sitting. Even Mrs. Piper, Mrs. Garrett and Mrs. Leonard had sittings where either nothing happened (no communication) or there was some spirit communication that was vague, trivial, or useless. The explanation usually is that the conditions weren't "right". This sounds like a feeble excuse but when you think about what the medium is trying to do it makes sense. The medium, who has a gift, is trying to receive a message from a spirit of a deceased person. This type of communication is not like turning on a light switch. We are not even sure how exactly this communication between the mind (subconscious?) of the medium and a spirit works. We assume it is some type of telepathic communication. The physical, mental and emotional condition of the medium is very likely extremely important. A medium who, for example, is in a bad mood or who has had a fight might not be in the right kind of receptive condition to receive the spirit message. That could easily explain no messages, or garbled messages, or nonsense messages, etc. No one can be in a perfect mental state at all times. That is why trance mediumship can never be 100 percent proved under laboratory test conditions. This does not mean that trance mediumship does not exist or is fraudulent or nonsense, it just means that it can be excellent at times or poor at times. That is exactly what happened with the best mediums. Also, does it matter if it is a spirit entity that communicates the evidence through the entranced medium (by taking over the medium's body) or if it is a secondary personality of the medium? I am sure that in some cases it is the former and in other cases the latter. In the case of channelers it is the medium that receives the evidence from spirits of the deceased (hears, sees, telepathically, etc.) and gives it to the sitter.

I have had sittings with mediums (channelers, not trance mediums) in London at the Spiritualist Union quite a few times (about 6-8 times) and in two of those sittings the medium picked up absolutely nothing. In two other sittings just about no evidential information was provided and in the remaining sittings some correct names and some evidence was provided. Only one of the mediums gave more correct than incorrect information. I am sure the mediums could not cold read me and most of the correct information was more than just generalities (i.e. you are married). It thus appears that these mediums picked-up some of the spirit entities tried to communicate. This goes to show that to get a really good reading is truly rare.

Sittings here in the U.S. have not been much better except for the sittings in Ithaca and Chicago, which I have described earlier. Similar to London, most of the sittings here resulted in very little or no evidence. To have both a good receiver (i.e. a good medium) and the "right" conditions, whatever they exactly might be, does not happen too often. To say that the medium is a fraud or no good is not always justified if the conditions aren't right. However, do remember that a lot of fraudulent and not very good mediums exist, who make a good living off of it.

In this chapter I have given some evidence given by both mental mediums (channelers) and trance mediums that I believe shows that there is life after death. I have also in some detail discussed the arguments and hypotheses the

Life After Death

skeptics and critics use to try to debunk this evidence. Their main argument using the all encompassing "super-ESP" is as far as I am concerned a lot more far fetched than communication with spirits of the deceased.

Direct Voice

Direct voice, as described earlier, is the communication by spirit entities through an ectoplasmic voice box rather than using the vocal cords of the medium. The ectoplasm is drawn from the medium and made into a replica of the physical vocal organs. The spirit entity then through the voice box creates sound vibrations that we can hear. The voice box is independent of the medium. I have described, in an earlier chapter, how in the first sitting Marlene and I had with Mickey and Sara we heard Sara's guide Brian speak both through her, while in trance, and also through the voice box. The voice box appeared to be located outside the curtains of the cabinet, since that is where the voice appeared to come from. The two different ways Brian communicated could clearly be distinguished.

I would now like to present in detail the evidence provided by two of the best known direct voice mediums. The first one is Leslie Flint and the second John Sloan. I believe both these mediums to have been totally genuine and honest and their evidence extremely impressive, as I hope I can show here.

Leslie Flint

Leslie Flint was born in England in 1911. He grew up in poverty and had no formal education. His first job was at the cemetery. While he was a teenager he went to a Spiritualist church where the medium told him what he had done that morning at the cemetery. She also told him about one of his guides, who wanted him to develop as a medium. Lastly, she told him that he would become very famous. Some time later another medium told him the same thing.

He was invited by someone at the Spiritualist church, who had heard the messages given to him, to join their home circle so that he could develop his mediumship, if he indeed had that gift. At that time he got a letter from a woman in Munich, Germany. She was given a message for him in her home circle that he must develop his mediumship. She was given his address and sent him a letter with that message. At the home circle he got the same message as in the letter.

Flint then decided not to return to the circle in spite of the messages he got. However, he received another letter from Germany stating that he must develop his mediumship. So he decided to return to the circle. At the very next sitting he "fell" asleep. When he awoke he wanted to apologize for sleeping but was told he had been in trance. He was told that his guide spoke through him and told them that he, Flint, must continue his development. That circle developed internal friction and he left.

Several years later when he was 22 he was asked to join another circle, that of Mrs. Edith Mundin. He sat in that circle for several months with nothing happening. Then he started going into trance again and he also became clairvoyant (saw spirit entities).

His development as a medium now entered its last and most important phase. It started at the movies! While there he started hearing strange whisperings around him and people sitting around him started complaining and telling him to shut up. It happened several times so he stopped go-

Life After Death

ing to the movies. These whisperings around him were the earliest manifestations of the voice phenomena. He also started getting these independent voices in the circle he sat in. These voices were located in space a little above his head or slightly to one side of his head. These voices of dead people (now spirit entities) spoke directly to friends and relatives and their voices were recognized as being their own when on earth. Sometimes the voices were only a whisper, hoarse and stained and at other times they were clear and fluent and easily recognizable. Flint was wide awake when the voices were talking so he heard everything. A direct voice medium is usually in trance, but Flint wasn't.

At that time the spirit entities told him to give up everything so he could serve through his mediumship. He now started charging for his sittings so he could support himself. They would have open circles, after their home circles, and he charged at those open sittings.

At one of those open circles a Mr. Noah Zerdin was given some very evidential information by his first wife who was in spirit. Afterwards Noah warned Flint that he was risking his life every time he held an open circle for direct voice. He was told that it was dangerous to let any Tom, Dick or Harry attend. The reason Noah gave was that ectoplasm, taken from his body to form the voice box, was involved when the spirits spoke through this voice box. If any of the sitters either through malice or curiosity would shine a bright light on him, this ectoplasm would then rush back into his body with such violence that it would at best result in a violent shock or at worst cause internal hemorrhage and possibly death. This might sound far-fetched but it has happened to several well-known mediums. I will discuss one case in the chapter on materialization. Noah told Flint that there would always be those who doubted the genuineness of the direct voice and try to expose the medium involved. Flint was baffled and surprised that his genuineness should be doubted since there is no way he could speak in hundreds of different voices and accents, both male and female, which were heard at his many different séances. Noah suggested that Flint join his home circle, which had experienced sitters, and stop with his open sittings. Flint did as Noah suggested and joined his home circle.

After months of sitting in the Zerdin circle a big London meeting was organized at which Flint would demonstrate his direct voice to hundreds. It was a success and at regular intervals he gave public demonstrations in some of the biggest halls in London in front of audiences of up to two thousand people. He sat in a cabinet which was sealed to keep the light out since darkness was needed to produce the voice phenomena. The demonstrations were highly successful and much evidence of survival was provided by the many different spirit voices that came through.

Flint was tested over and over again to prove that the voice phenomena were genuine. One typical example was where he was securely roped to his chair and just before the light was turned off a measured amount of colored water was poured into his mouth and he held it there for the duration of the séance. Once the light was turned off and after the usual short wait, his regular control, a cockney boy called Mickey, spoke in his usual clear and distinctive voice. Various voices spoke after Mickey until the séance ended and the lights were turned on again. Flint then returned his mouthful of colored water into the glass and everyone saw that the amount was only fractionally less than the original amount. It is impossible to speak with a mouthful of water, try it!

Flint admitted that he also had sittings that were failures. Sometimes he and his sitters would wait in the dark room for an hour and nothing at all would happen. It just shows and confirms that psychic phenomena cannot be produced at will no matter how good the medium. Marlene and I have had similar sittings were nothing happened with Mickey and Sara and with other mediums. There is no doubt about it that even genuine mediums can have off days when nothing or hardly anything happens at a sitting. As mentioned before there could be several reasons for this, with the main one being that the medium is not well either emotionally or physically so that he or she does not have enough "psychic power" to produce the phenomena or to receive communications from the spirit entities. Also, "conditions for communication" (what ever they might be) might not be right so that spirit entities just cannot come through the medium or telepathically communicate with the medium.

Now to some of the evidence that Flint has provided in his many sittings. Typically, at a private sitting, which is how Flint earned a simple living, the sitter or sitters would make a booking usually under a false name or only a first name. They would sit down with Flint in a dark room and after a couple of minutes Mickey, Flint's regular control, would talk to the sitters briefly and then introduce a relative or friend of the sitter or sitters. These entities would give their name and start talking to the sitter giving personal details proving that he or she is who they claim to be. They would typically tell the sitter that he or she is not dead but alive in the spirit world. The private sitting would typically last from half an hour to an hour.

I will now give some specific detailed communications given by the independent direct voices that provide excellent evidence for survival after death. The details and any quotes have been taken from Flint's book "Voices in the

Dark" (MacMillan London, 1971).

The first case is a group séance where Air Chief Marshal Lord Dowding, a convinced Spiritualist, was an honored guest. Flint's guide Mickey introduced a young airman in these words: "There is a chap here from the Air Force who wants to get in touch with his parents. He is so excited I don't know if he will manage to speak but I'll try to help him." Shortly they heard the voice of the airman asking them to contact his father and mother. He had been to see them often, he said, but they could not see him. He told them he was killed when his plane crashed over Norway when he was twenty years old and he was his parent's only son. Please tell mother I'm alright now, he urged, she is so unhappy it is making her ill.

No one in the group could identify this communicator so a sitter Mr. Walter West asked for the boy's full name and address and promised to get in touch with the parents if it were possible to do so. "Thank you very much", replied the dead boy, "I had three Christian names, Peter William Handford and my surname was Kite." He then gave an address in Grange Park, north of London, where his parents were still living. But that was not all, Peter Kite next spoke to a man in the group saying, "I know you, you are Mr. Turner, you took out my tooth." None of the other sitters knew Mr. Turner was a dentist nor did they know his name. Mr. Turner said he remembered Peter Kite coming to him for treatment some years before but he did not know he had been killed nor even that he had joined the R.A.F.

After the séance Mr. West went to Grange Park and found the house where Peter Kite had said his parents lived. The dead boy's mother, Mrs. May Kite, answered the door to Mr. West's ring and when she heard what he had to tell her she readily accepted an invitation to attend a special group séance with Peter's father. Lord Dowding was also

Life After Death

invited because they felt that his presence at the first séance had helped Peter Kite to manifest.

Almost as soon as the light was turned off Mickey came to tell them that Conan Doyle wanted to say a few words to Mr. and Mrs. Kite before their son came to speak to them. Doyle, who in his lifetime finally became convinced of Spiritualism after years of sitting with mediums, then spoke very sympathetically to the parents who had no knowledge of psychic matters. He explained to them how after Peter's plane crashed he had found himself alive in a new more subtle body which resembled in every respect his physical body which he could see lying motionless in the wreckage of his aircraft. At first, Doyle told the couple, their son had been bewildered because although he could see the body which he recognized as himself he felt so gloriously alive and well he simply did not realize he was dead. When two peasants came to investigate the wrecked plane Peter was puzzled when they seemed neither to see nor hear him, but soon some friends of his whom he knew to be dead came to explain his new condition of life to him and to take him to his new plane of being.

As soon as Conan Doyle had finished speaking Peter Kite excitedly greeted his father and mother. "I've got the dog, Mother", he said laughingly, "it's an Alsatian." This was a reference to a joke he had played on his mother only a few days before his death. Peter had been fond of dogs and he had telephoned his mother to say he was sending home an Alsatian he had acquired. Mrs. Kite was not a dog lover and the thought of a huge Alsatian tearing round her house had appalled her. After teasing her for awhile Peter had relented and reminded her it was April 1.

"I saw you putting my photograph in your bag with the ones from Norway before you left home", went on the spirit voice. Mrs. Kite told the sitters she had changed her handbag before leaving for the séance and had transferred its contents including her son's photograph and some which had recently been sent to her of his grave in Norway.

"You are keeping the garden in good trim", said Peter. "I like the part you have made into a garden of memories. Do you know the birds nesting in the cherry tree can see me even if you cannot?" The parents told the sitters that six years before when Peter was killed they had apportioned a patch of garden as a memorial to him and in it they had planted a cherry tree in which birds were building nests at that time. "I often go to my room and you haven't changed a thing in it." Peter continued. "My model plane is still there and all my books and the wallpaper I didn't like!" It was true that the parents had kept their son's room exactly as it had been on the day he was killed and he had never cared for the wallpaper in it. "I'm glad my car is still going but it's a bit small for you, Dad, isn't it?" Mr. Kite agreed Peter's sport car fitted him a bit too snugly; he was a large somewhat overweight man. "I'm saying all these silly little things so you will know it's really me speaking and that I do come to see you, above all I want you and mother to know I am more alive now than I ever was."

For close on forty minutes the voice of Peter Kite went on piling evidential detail on detail, details trivial in themselves but in the aggregate giving his parents incontrovertible proof of his identity and his continued existence.

This is a very impressive and evidential communication. No one knew the communicator. He gave his name, the address where his parents lived and then a large amount of evidential information to his parents. Assuming that this was a true account of the two sittings, and I have no reason to believe they weren't (no one has ever proven Flint to fraudulent or a liar), then there is absolutely no way Flint could have researched and acquired all this information.

Life After Death

The only explanation the skeptics can use to "explain" the exceptional results is their old standby of "super-ESP"; the medium must have telepathically acquired the information from his parents and/or from the nebulous universal subconscious/Akashic records and then communicated this information through a secondary personality. As discussed before I find that explanation far-fetched and unlikely to be correct. The explanation that appears much more likely and believable is that the spirit of the dead Peter Kite communicated through the voice box and not a secondary personality of Flint. I can believe that it is possible that a secondary personality can speak through a medium in trance (as was discussed in the chapter on trance mediumship) but to have a secondary personality speaking via independent direct voice using an ectoplasmic voice box is a lot harder to believe. Actually I just don't see how that is possible, especially in the case of Flint, who was not in trance during the séance. I know of no one who, with his or her mouth taped (or not taped) can produce a clear voice speaking at a short distance from his or her body without using his or her vocal cords. A ventriloquist needs his or her vocal cords and could never produce a voice if his or her mouth was taped. To have had Flint's subconscious mind produce the voices seems even more far-fetched. There is no evidence at all for that being possible. Thus in the case of Flint the only possible explanation is that spirit entities spoke through the voice box and provided evidence for survival after death.

I will give a few more cases that provide excellent evidence for survival after death.

A certain Mrs. Grover booked a sitting with Flint when she lived in London with the hope that she might bring comfort to her younger daughter by making contact with the girl's husband who had recently died. At the sitting Bill, Mrs. Grover's son-in-law, spoke to her calling her "Gerry" as he did in his lifetime and asking about her health. Then in a voice fraught with strain said: "Mummy Bear, Daddy Bear and Brumas." He repeated this pointless phrase many times then said in a puzzled way: "I don't know why I am saying this except to prove identity." Mrs. Grover was not only disappointed with her sitting. She was mystified since the phrase which had been repeated with such urgency meant nothing to her whatsoever. When she returned home and told her daughter about the nonsensical message she had been given at her sitting. Bill's widow was radiantly happy. The silly phrase which Bill had uttered so often and with so great an effort was the code message the girl and her husband had agreed to try to communicate to the other should one of them die first.

Some years later Mrs. Grover had another sitting with Flint at which Bill manifested. Here follows Mrs. Grover's own account of this sitting which she sent Flint:

> "We sat for several minutes and I was beginning to fear dear Mickey would not come through, but he did and, after his usual chat, he said: "Bill is here, Aunty Gerry." To my astonishment my son-in-law's first words were, "Gerry, you are very worried about your health?" I must explain that Mr. Flint had no idea I had been ill for a year before I left London with an internal complaint which was still troubling me. While I was in London on this visit I had taken the opportunity to see a surgeon and I had spent a whole day having X-rays and various tests at the London Clinic a few days prior to my sitting. The London surgeon had been called to Scotland to perform an emergency operation and for this reason his secretary had told me it would be some time before he could read my X-rays. Therefore I answered

Life After Death

Bill that I was rather worried about myself. Bill replied: "There's no need for you to worry at all. I have seen your X-rays and there is no malignancy. You will not need an operation, surgery cannot cure a bug! But in the future you must be careful about your diet and avoid roughage." My son-in-law was a doctor and a specialist in radiology during his life on earth. It remains to add that on the day following this sitting the surgeon's secretary telephoned me to say that the surgeon had just seen the X-rays and she repeated almost exactly the reassuring words Bill had said to me in Mr. Flint's séance room".

The following case was taken from a letter Mr. Robert Bolton, then living in New York, wrote to Psychic News, a British weekly psychic news paper, in which he describes what happened at a group sitting for 75 people at the W. T. Stead Centre in New York City (taken from Flint's book):

"After various spirits had spoken to their friends, Mickey announced the presence of one who was known on earth as Carl Schneider. No one in the room responded, no one apparently knew him. Mickey persisted, declaring someone in the room knew him and that person must speak up to help him communicate. "I know a man of that name", said Mr. Boltan, at last, "but to the best of my knowledge he is alive and well." Nothing daunted, Mickey asserted Carl Schneider was on the other side and he was about to speak. Carl's voice was then heard and he and Mr. Boltan conversed. "When did you pass away?" inquired Mr. Boltan. "About twelve months ago, maybe a little over a year, the spirit replied." It was Carl's voice! I recognized its unmistakable husky quality, declared Mr. Boltan after the séance. Mr. Boltan found the return of his friend Carl Schneider so totally unexpected he was in a state of agitation until he could confirm whether his friend was alive or dead. On the morning after the séance the first thing he did was to call a telephone number Carl had once given him. When the phone was answered he asked to speak to Carl Schneider and the answer came: "I am sorry, but Carl passed away." Because he could still not believe it, Mr. Boltan then asked; "Are you sure?" The voice at the end of the other end of the line replied: "I ought to be. I am the one who found him. He committed suicide about a year ago".

This is another impressive spirit communication. Information is given by a spirit entity, which is not only unknown to everyone present but is even rejected as untrue, yet which is subsequently proven to be correct. Again, telepathy can be ruled out since no one present knew the information about the spirit entity Carl and the survival hypothesis seems a lot more acceptable than some "super-ESP" hypothesis, which is used by skeptics to explain anything they cannot explain.

The next case is an example of a large demonstration in Kingsway Hall in London. Flint sat in a stuffy cabinet, about seven feet high and four feet square, covered with tarpaulin so no light could come in, while the hall was fully lighted. The cabinet sat in the middle of the stage so everyone could see it. A microphone stood about 20 inches in front of the cabinet.

As usual Mickey spoke first, but this time, unusually, he told the large audience that Mickey was only the name

Life After Death

by which he was known in the world of spirit and to his medium. He said that in his life on earth he was called John Whitehead and he sold papers outside Camden Town underground station until he was run over and killed by a lorry when he was ten years old. I'm a lot happier over here than I ever was on your side, he assured the crowded hall, "you could say kicking the bucket was the best thing I ever did." This caused a general laugh and tension throughout the hall relaxed noticeably.

The next spirit voice claimed to be Jack Hickinbottom, who used to live at 76 Albert Street, Tipton, Staffordshire. From the gallery a woman's voice answered, "Yes, son, I am here". Mother and son then talked together over the illusory gulf of death about such trivialities as the color of a mackintosh, the name of the neighbor's dog and the nature of the son's last illness, all of which in themselves of no importance whatsoever, but to the mother who had traveled from her home in the Midlands only that morning and knew no one in London they provided convincing evidence that it was actually her son, dead for eight years, she was speaking to.

The next communicator from the other side gave his name as Roy Marchant and was acknowledged by his parents in the audience. "Hello, Mother! Hello, Dad!" said Roy excitedly. "I want you to know I am not dead, I'm marvelously alive and I send all my love to you and to baby". His parents replied affectionately. Then Roy thanked his mother for a children's party she had given for his child. "Don't think of me as being a long way off, he went on. I'm not. I am often with you, I was with you in Switzerland! There isn't any real separation".

One of the most touching contacts of the evening began very quietly with Mickey saying: I want to speak to the lady all in grey at the back because her boy's here. He was in the Navy. His name is Jim. A woman at the very back of the gallery called: "Is it for me?" The moment her voice was heard, suddenly and loudly came the pathetic cry: "Mum! Mum! I'm so glad you've come!" "darling, darling!" Was all the mother could reply. "I'm not dead you know", Jim assured her anxiously, "I'm alright!" In trying to bring conviction Jim's anxiety increased. "I wasn't drowned. I'm ALIVE!" The shouted word rang through the hall, fraught with the pain of not knowing whether the comfort he sought to bring would be fully understood. Mickey intervened at this point to provide the anticlimax which restored a smile to every face. Jim's a darned more alive than you are lady, I'll tell you!

Finally, here is one of Flint's more unusual sittings:

The sitter gave her name as Mrs. Bowering and she appeared to be somewhere in her late sixties. They went into the séance room and sat down without any preliminary chit-chat and Flint turned out the light. Mickey spoke to the lady almost at once. "There's a man here who says his name is Fred and that you are his wife, Alice." "Yes", said Mrs. Bowering, "Fred is my husband. Can I talk to him, please?" Shortly, a man's voice spoke and he and Mrs. Bowering had an intimate and personal conversation about their past together until suddenly he said laughingly: "fancy you taking the trouble to have my body taken out of it's grave after all these years and having it cremated! I see you are wearing the ring you buried with me on your finger at this moment! I've met Bowering over here, you know, and we like each other very much. As a matter of fact it amuses both of us that you should have my ashes in one urn on the mantelpiece and his ashes in another." Mrs. Bowering then inquired if Mr. Bowering could speak to her and soon the voice of another man greeted her. "You know, Alice, he said, even though you've put Fred's urn and mine on the

Life After Death

mantelpiece we are not really there. We are here and we come often together to try to help you as well as we may but these ashes really have nothing to do with us anymore." To Flint's astonishment Mrs. Bowering then told both her late husbands she had met a man called Wilson and she was seriously considering marriage with him. She wanted to know if either of them would object to this. Both Fred and Mr. Bowering said they had no objection at all and the only thing they wanted was the happiness of Alice. Flint found this story of the ashes of the two husbands in urns on the same mantelpiece so hard to swallow that when the light was turned on he asked the lady if it was true. She said it most certainly was.

I have already mentioned that Flint was extensively tested and gave an example with the colored water in his mouth. Flint feels that he has been one of the most tested mediums. Here follow a few more "tests" of his mediumship:

Rev. Charles Drayton Thomas was a member of Flint's home circle and also a member of the council of the Society for Psychical Research. This Society was founded in 1882 in London by a group of scholars and scientists whose avowed purpose was to make a systematic investigation of certain phenomena which appear inexplicable on any generally recognized hypothesis.

Rev. Thomas devised a test to prove that the voices were not produced by Flint's lips. He reported the results of the test under his by-line in the Psychic News of February 14, 1948 (taken from Flint's book):

> "On February 5, I placed over his tightly closed lips a strip of elastoplast (band-aid). It was 5 ½ inches long and 2 ½ inches wide and very strongly adhesive. This I pressed firmly over and into the

crevices of the closed lips. A scarf was then tied tightly over this and the medium's hands tied firmly to the arms of his chair; another cord was so tied that he would be unable to bend down his head. Thus, supposing he endeavored during trance to loosen the bandage, it would be quite impossible for him to reach it. Anyone can discover by tightly closing the lips and trying to speak how muffled and unintelligible are the sounds then produced. My experiment was designed to show that under the above conditions clearly enunciated speech and plenty of it could be produced by the direct voice. The experiment was entirely successful. Voices were soon speaking with their usual clarity and Mickey emphasized his ability several times by shouting loudly. Some twelve persons were present and we all heard more than enough to convince the most obdurate skeptic that the sealing of Mr. Flint's mouth in no way prevented unseen speakers from saying anything they wished. At the close of the sitting I examined the cords and the plaster, finding all intact and undisturbed. The plaster was so strongly adhering I had considerable difficulty in removing it without causing pain."

On another occasion the conditions under which Flint was tested were:

His lips were sealed with plaster, a throat microphone was attached to his throat and wired to amplifiers so that the slightest sound made through his own larynx would be amplified enormously, the researchers were able to watch his every movement in the dark by means of an infra-red telescope and finally, his hands were held by a sitter on either side of him.

Brigadier Firebrace, also a member of the SPR, was present at one of the tests and wrote a letter to Flint stating:

"I well remember the test sittings I had with you and Drayton Thomas. At these sittings, during the séance we had an infra-red telescope focused on you and you had a throat microphone round your throat. There was an electronic expert present who watched the instruments which were attached to the throat microphone. I can well remember that under these conditions we got direct voice without any indication on the instruments that it was registered by the throat microphone. But the voices were fainter than on previous sittings I had had with you. An interesting point was on the final occasion when with a voice speaking faintly the infra-red telescope suddenly fused; the voice immediately doubled in volume. This indicated to me that infra-red rays weaken mediumship in some way. I must add you could not possibly have known that the infra-red telescope was out of action. Altogether an impressive exhibition of mediumistic power."

The tests performed on Flint rule out, beyond any doubt, that his lips/mouth produced the voices. As far as I am concerned there is thus no doubt that the voices are produced independent of the medium and represent the voices of spirit entities. Any skeptic or critic who is not willing to accept the results of the tests and all the independent reports by sitters, who sat with Flint, is not willing to face reality. I just cannot see how the "super-ESP" hypothesis can explain the voices. The hypothesis that the medium's subconscious or his secondary personality in some way produces the voices is extremely unlikely to give it any credence.

To summarize this section on Leslie Flint, all I can say is that Flint was one of the truly great mediums who provided outstanding evidence for life after death. He was tested numerous times and was never found to be fraudulent.

John Sloan

Arthur Findlay in his book "On the Edge of the Etheric" describes his sittings with the medium, John C. Sloan, who lived from 1869 to 1951. At the time of Findlay's first sitting with Sloan in 1918, Sloan had already been sitting for around 30 years. His mediumship included trance, direct voice, materializations, clairvoyance and apports. When Findlay sat with him, Sloan's mediumship was mainly direct voice and trance.

Findlay's first sitting in Sloan's circle was on September 20, 1918. Findlay had been invited to the sitting a few days earlier by someone who he had met at the local Spiritualist church. There were 12 people at the sitting and he was not introduced to anyone. So no one knew who he was. Even the person who invited him did not know his name. The sitting was in a small room in complete darkness. Sloan sat on a small stool. Two trumpets (also called megaphones), rubbed with phosphorus so they could be seen in the dark, were placed in the center of the circle. These two trumpets started moving around the room once the medium was in trance. These trumpets floated around the room, as high as the ceiling, and gently touched the sitters on any part of their body, on request, without mistake. For example, someone would be lightly touched on the point of the nose, another on the top of the head, another's

Life After Death

hand would be touched and so on, but never a hard knock, always gently. At times the trumpets moved around very fast but never flew into anything. The reason I described the trumpet phenomena that Findlay experienced with Sloan is because we experienced exactly the same phenomena with Mickey and Sara (described in detail earlier). Many other circles (some described in other sections) have also observed this trumpet phenomena just as described by Findlay. As I have discussed earlier, it is impossible for any human being to move the trumpet as described above, in the total dark. It is not humanly possible. The only conclusion there can be is that spirit entities/intelligences moved the trumpets and that they can "see" in the dark. It is hard to imagine that the medium's subconscious can move the trumpets, as observed, so I have to rule it out as an explanation.

Coming back to Findlay's first sitting, for about three hours dozens of voices, men's, women's and children's voices, spoke to the different sitters. He was told all the voices were those of "dead" people. Every voice was different and the mannerisms were different, in fact each voice had a different personality. Everything the voices said was claimed to be correct by the sitter who was addressed.

Eventually, the trumpet stopped in front of Findlay and his father, Robert Downie Findlay, started speaking to him. He spoke to Findlay about a private matter that only he and his father and a dead friend of his father knew about. The dead friend also spoke to Findlay about details of the private matter. That was Findlay's introduction to a séance with direct voice. No spy system, fraud or impersonation could explain what had taken place, since no one knew who he was.

During the next five years Findlay attended 39 seances with Sloan, sometimes at his house and at times in places of

Findlay's choosing. Eighty three different voices spoke to him or his friends, who he took with him to some of the séances. At times he sat alone with Sloan and the voices spoke even when his ear was within an inch of Sloan's mouth, which was silent. Two and/or three voices sometimes spoke at the same time.

Of the eighty three different voices that spoke to him and his friends, two hundred eighty two separate communications were given. He considered one hundred eighty of those to be what he called "A1" messages in which it was impossible for the medium or any other person present to have known the facts given. One hundred he considered as "A2" messages in which by means of newspaper or reference books the medium could have found out about the facts.

I will now give Findlay's summaries of two "A1" cases and one "A2" case:

Case 1 of the "A1" Group:

> "I (Findlay) took my brother with me to a séance shortly after he was demobilized from the Army in 1919. He knew no one present and was not introduced. No one except myself knew that he had been in the Army. No one present knew where he had been during his time in the Army. His health had not permitted him to go abroad, and he was stationed part of the time near Lowestoft at a small village called Kessingland, and part of the time at Lowestoft, training gunners. With this preliminary explanation I shall now give you the following summary of my notes on this case:
>
> During the course of the sitting the trumpet was distinctly heard moving about the room, and various voices spoke through it. Suddenly it tapped my

Life After Death

brother on the on the right knee, and a voice directly in front of him said, "Eric Saunders". My brother asked if the voice was addressing him, and it replied "Yes", whereupon he said that there must be some mistake, as he had never known anyone of that name. The voice was not very strong, so some person suggested that the company should continue singing, and, while this was going on, the trumpet kept tapping my brother on his knee, arm and shoulder. It was so insistent that he said: I think we had better stop singing, as some person evidently is most anxious to speak to me. Again, he asked who it was, and the voice, much stronger this time, repeated, "Eric Saunders". Again my brother said he had never known any person of that name, and asked where he had met him. The reply was: "in the Army". My brother mentioned a number of places, such as Aldershot, Bisley, France, Palestine, etc., but carefully omitted Lowestoft, where he had been stationed for the greater part of his Army life. The voice replied "No, none of those places. I knew you when you were near Lowestoft". My brother asked why he said near Lowestoft, and he replied: "You were not in Lowestoft then, but at Kessingland". This is a small fishing hamlet about five miles south of Lowestoft, where my brother spent part of 1917. My brother then asked what company he had been attached to, and, as he could not make out whether he said "B" or "C", my brother asked if he could remember the name of the Company Commander. The reply was "Macnamara". This was the name of the officer commanding "B" Company at that time. By the way of a test, my brother pretended that he remembered the man, and said: "Oh yes, you were one of my Lewis gunners, were you not?" The reply was: "No, you had not the Lewis guns then, it was the Hotchkiss". This was quite correct, as the Lewis guns were taken from them in April 1917, and were replaced by Hotchkiss. My brother asked him two or three leading questions, such as the name of his (my brother's) billet, which he answered correctly, and then Saunders said: "We had great times there, sir; do you remember the General's inspection?" My brother laughed, and said that they were continually being inspected by generals, to which one did he refer and he replied: "The day the General made us all race about with the guns". This was an incident my brother remembered perfectly well and one which caused a good deal of amusement to the men at the time. He told my brother he had been killed in France, and my brother asked him when he had gone out. He replied that he had gone with the "Big Draft" in August 1917. My brother asked him why he called it the Big Draft, and he said: "Don't you remember the Big Draft, when the Colonel came on the parade ground and made a speech?" This reference was to a particularly draft sent out to France that month, and was the only occasion on which my brother remembered the Colonel ever personally saying good-bye to the men. He then thanked my brother for the gunnery training he had given him, and said it had been most useful to him in France. My brother asked him why he had come through to speak to him, and he said: "Because I have never forgotten that you once did me a good turn". My brother has a hazy recollection of obtaining leave for one of the gunners, owing to some special circumstances, but whether or not his name

Life After Death

was "Saunders" he could not remember.

About six months after the above incident my brother was in London, and met, by appointment, the Corporal who had been his assistant with the light guns in his battalion at the time. My brother told him the above story, and asked if he remembered any man named "Eric Saunders". My brother had been training gunners for nearly two years at the rate of about a dozen a fortnight, and beyond putting them through their examinations, and taking a general oversight of them, he never came into sufficiently close personal contact with them to get to know many of their names. The Corporal, however, whom my brother met, was more with the gunners, but did not remember any person by that name. Fortunately, however, the Corporal had brought with him an old pocket diary, in which he had the habit of keeping a full list of men under training, and other information. He pulled it out of his pocket, and together they looked back until they came to the records of "B" Company during 1917. Sure enough the name appeared there, "Eric Saunders", f.q., August "17", with a red-ink line drawn through it; f.q. stood for fully qualified, and, though my brother knew the meaning of the red-ink line, he asked the Corporal what it meant. "Don't you remember, Mr. Findlay, I always drew a line through the men's names when they went away. This shows that Saunders went out in 1917."

Unfortunately my brother did not ask Saunders the name of his regiment, and consequently I could not trace his death, the War Office, without this information, being unable to supply me with any details beyond the fact that over 4000 men of the name Saunders fell in the war. Men came to Lowestoft from all over the country for training, so my brother had no record of Saunder's regiment.

Even allowing for this it is a remarkable case, as it is fraud and telepathy proof. Not only did no one present know my brother, but my brother did not know the speaker, and cannot even today recollect him, as he was passing hundreds of men through their training, all of whom would know him, but he never had an opportunity to know him individually. This case contains 14 separate facts; each one was correct, and each one comes up on my "A1" standard."

I agree with Findlay's summary of this case. Fraud and telepathy can be totally ruled out (there is no evidence what so ever that Findlay in any way fabricated what happened at these sittings- he has never ever been shown to be fraudulent). "Super-ESP" whereby the medium's subconscious taps into some "super database" or "universal subconscious" or 'cosmic reservoir", retrieves the needed information and then has his secondary personality, pretending to be the spirit entity, give out this information, seems a lot more far-fetched of an explanation than a genuine message from an entity in the spirit world. Also, as I mentioned before, how does "super-ESP" explain the direct voice, where the spirit entity speaks through the trumpet using the ectoplasmic voice box, as observed in Findlay's (and Flint's) circle? I can accept that in the case of trance mediumship the medium's secondary personality can at times speak through the medium (discussed in the previous chapter), but I cannot see how a secondary personality can speak independent of the medium as in direct voice. And if it could, how could it speak with a characteristic voice that is recognized by the sitter? No, "super-ESP" does not provide the explanation for the observed phenomena. Spirit communication does.

The second "A1" case is the following one:

"Sloan's séance was scheduled to begin at 7:15 PM, and on my way to it I called on a lady friend (Mrs. Wood Sims) and asked if she would care to come with me to a séance. As it was then past seven she hurriedly got ready and came with me. She mentioned casually to me that she had just returned from a visit to friends in England, and I heard her make the same remark to someone else just before the séance began, but no details were given-just the casual remark. During the séance a voice spoke to her, giving the name of her host's (where she stayed on her visit to England) deceased son, saying: "I saw you when you were staying with my father at Leeds". Several other voices spoke to her, giving their names, and sent messages to her host at Leeds. Two of these she did not know, but she said she would tell her host they had spoken, and pass on their messages.

Mrs. Wood Sims afterwards told me that her host had replied that he had known all these people on earth, and their messages were quite intelligible to him (at a later date I met this gentleman, and he confirmed what Mrs. Wood Sims told me). This Lady's brother, also at this sitting, spoke to her, calling her "Anna", a name only he used, as she is never called by that name. He said his name was "Will", but "Bill" to her, which was correct, and then correctly referred in detail to some advice he gave her before his death. "If you had only taken it, how different your life would have been", he said. "It is only too true", said my friend to me afterwards. Finally, his face materialized before her, and she assures me that it was his face in every detail."

The above two cases are only two of many that Findlay reported. In total he had on record 180 facts he called "A1" and he claims all were as good as presented in the above two cases.

I will now give what Findlay called an "A2" case:

"A lady, a friend of mine, died. She belonged to a well-known family. Consequently an obituary notice of about a quarter of a column appeared in the Glasgow Herald, giving particulars of her family and immediate ancestors. This, consequently, brings this case under the "A2" category, though I know of nothing to associate her with me or my family in the mind of the medium. Sloan, I am sure, was not aware that I knew her. I am sure Sloan had never heard her name and knew nothing about her or her family, but, as some critics make out that a case loses its evidential nature if the information given can be traced to print, I place this one accordingly in the "A2" category.

A week after the funeral, at a sitting I and a few personal friends had with Sloan in the séance room of our Society, her son, Cecil, who was killed in the war, spoke to my brother stating that he was so happy now, as he had his mother with him. I asked if she were present, and he replied she was, but not yet fully conscious that she had passed over. I asked if she could speak to me, which she did. Her conversation showed that she was not quite conscious of the change. She said she wanted her husband, naming him correctly, and wanted to know what had happened. I might add that the nature of her illness had not been published, and was only known to a few of her intimate friends. I explained to her the change that had taken place, that she was now an inhabitant of the etheric world, that she had left forever this world of physical matter, that she had gone through the change called death, and then I said: "Do you not recognize who is standing beside you?" referring to her son who had just spoken to me. "No", she said, "I can see no one". Here her son interposed with the remark; "Mother cannot you recognize me yet?" Her father then spoke to me, telling me things I afterwards found in reference books to be correct. Then her brother spoke, giving his correct name and where he lived on earth. Towards the end of the séance, after other voices had spoken, the lady returned and again spoke to me. "Have you not seen Cecil?" I said. "No; where is he?" she replied. Then her voice suddenly changed from one of sadness to joy, and we her exclaim, "Oh, Cecil, my darling my own darling boy." Then there was silence. In a few minutes another voice spoke: "He is taking her away with him; she will soon be alright."

I had been a participant in a great drama. I had been privileged to have had the unique experience of witnessing the return to consciousness of one the world called "dead", and her meeting with her son, who had given, so the world thought, his life for his country. I had witnessed, when she was with us on earth, her terrible grief when she had heard of his death, her wonderful courage, and I was present at the final act when see and her only son became reunified. How I should have liked to tell her sorrowing husband of my experience, but I knew how use less it was, so I refrained from doing so.

To describe, in a few words, what took nearly two hours to unfold, to make one conscious of the rare personal touches which accomplished it all, is, of course, impossible. The circle consisted entirely of my own personal friends, in the séance room of our own Society, and they were all deeply affected, especially my wife who knew the lady well. Had Sloan been a great actor, knowing intimately the personalities concerned, and their family history, he could not have carried through, with such success, the various impersonations, whereas he knew nothing about her family, or my friendship with her and her son."

Again an impressive case even though an important fact did appear in the newspaper. The chance of Sloan seeing the obituary and finding all the additional information is extremely unlikely if not impossible. Actually, as Findlay states in his book, Sloan was a very simple man who did not read, had no education and most important took no money for any of his sittings.

Fraudulent "mediums" charge for their "performances" since the whole purpose of being a "medium" for them is to make money. Many genuine and good mediums do not or have never charged for their sittings. They gave/give their sittings for the benefit of the sitters, many of whom have lost loved ones so need comforting. In many cases there was proof that their deceased loved ones are still alive. Sloan is a prime example of a medium who never charged, since he had a job, and provided impressive survival evidence. Mickey and Sara never charged for their sittings since they had a small retail business. Their sittings were always in the evening or on the weekends. Some of the best known genuine mediums do become professional mediums and charge/charged for their sittings. Leslie Flint was a professional medium but made a very meager living from it.

To conclude this chapter on Flint and Sloan, two of the most impressive direct voice mediums, I state without any doubt that they have provided excellent evidence for survival after death. As discussed above, fraud and telepathy can be ruled out and the "super-ESP" hypothesis is a lot more far-fetched than the survival hypothesis, especially in the case of direct voice. Direct voice does away with the argument that the medium's secondary personality is communicating.

Materialization

Materializations, especially full-body materializations, are the rarest and the strangest of all reported paranormal physical phenomena. Anyone who has witnessed genuine materializations has truly seen something unique. Portions of human bodies, such as hands, which move, grasp, carry things, etc., or entire bodies which speak, breath and walk like living beings materialize (i.e. form) from ectoplasm. This ectoplasm comes (pours) mainly from the medium's nose and mouth (sometimes from the solar plexus as well) and then when the seance is finished the ectoplasmic hands, bodies, etc. dematerialize as the ectoplasm returns to the medium. Materialization is so controversial with many proponents and critics that I will first describe historical cases of interest and the controversy they created, before describing in detail those cases and mediums that I believe offer evidence for survival.

At the end of the nineteenth century and beginning of the twentieth century there were numerous reports and photographs of materializations. Some very well known, well educated and highly respected investigators reported and published photographs of materializations taken under strict test conditions. Sir William Crookes, a physicist and chemist, in 1874 published his work "Researches into the Phenomena of Modern Spiritualism". He describes sittings with a medium called Florence Cook and the materialized entity called Katie King. He shows photographs of Cook in trance with the fully materialized Katie King next to her (these photographs can be seen on the International Survivalist Society website: www.survivalafterdeath.org). Critics have tried to explain away these materializations by claiming that the medium Florence Cook and the materialized entity Katie King are the same person, i.e. the medium was dressed up in a costume pretending to be the materialization. This criticism breaks down with the photograph showing Cook and King together demonstrating they were two separate entities. Crookes claims that his experiments were held under strict test conditions. He recorded physical differences in complexion, hair coloring, height, blisters, skin type, face and finger sizes plus manners and ways of expression between the materialized figure Katie King and the medium Florence Cook. All physical comparisons were apparently different, proving that they were two separate entities. Several of Crookes' friends (scientists, physicians, etc.) attended the séances and were convinced of the genuineness of the materializations. Dr J.M. Gully, a physician, wrote to Crookes in 1874 and stated;

> "To the special question which you put regarding my experiences of the materialization of the spirit-form, with Miss Cook's mediumship, I must reply that, after two years' examination of the fact and numerous séances, I have not the smallest doubt, and have the strongest conviction, that such materialization takes place, and that not the slightest attempt at trick or deception is fairly attributable to any one who assisted at Miss Cook's séances."

The psychical researcher A.N. Aksakoff (1832-1903) reported on a séance he attended on October 22, 1873 in

Life After Death

Cook's home. He stated that Florence was tied to the chair with tape and ropes inside the cabinet. Her hands were tied behind her back and the knots of the rope were sealed. Katie King appeared as usual during the sitting, dressed in white with hands and arms bare, and spoke to the various sitters. During the sitting, Aksakoff asked Katie if he could look into the cabinet and he was allowed to. He reported that he saw Florence in a deep trance, sitting on her chair, with both hands tied behind her back. So it can be concluded from this account, assuming it was reported correctly, that Florence did produce materializations, as long as she did not have an accomplice masquerading as Katie (and there is no evidence for this).

But then there are those who claim Florence Cook was a fraud. Mr. W. Volckman at a séance on December 9, 1873 believed Florence and Katie King were the same person since there was a resemblance according to him. To prove it he seized the entity Katie King, dressed completely in white (presumably ectoplasm), and ended up fighting with three sitters while the spirit entity escaped back into the cabinet. In the cabinet they found Florence in her black dress and bound to the chair with the same tape used to confine her at the beginning of the sitting. Volckman's evidence of "fraud" is thus very debatable and based only on his opinion, but Florence's reputation as a physical medium received a blow from which it never fully recovered. She was again supposedly exposed on January 9, 1890, by Sir George Sitwell who seized the spirit entity and found Florence masquerading in her underclothes. These two accounts differ markedly from the accounts of Crookes, his friends and his photographs. Who is right and could one of them be lying? It could be that no one lied. It is well known that physical mediums (those producing movements of objects without contact, direct voice, materializations, etc.) can have off days when nothing happens and often (but not always) start losing there powers when they get older. It is very possible that a medium becomes fraudulent when he or she cannot produce at a certain séance and does not want to disappoint the sitters. Unfortunately this is known to have happened with genuine mediums.

The questions remain: was Florence Cook a fraud, an occasional fraud or a genuine medium? Did those who exposed her lie about it? Were Crookes' photographs genuine? I don't know the anwers to these questions. However, there just appears to have been too much evidence witnessed by many credible sitters to suggest that at times Florence Cook did produce materializations. Let's examine some other controversial cases and then I will come to cases I believe are genuine and evidential.

Baron Dr. von Schrenck-Notzing, a Professor of considerable social standing and a well-known investigator of physical mediums, published his book "Phenomena of Physical Mediums" in 1920. There are some 225 photographs with mediums and ectoplasm, all taken under strict controlled test conditions. In all his experiments the female medium put on a costume, specifically made for her, in the presence of a female sitter and then was examined by the Professor. The costume was made out of fine transparent material to rule out the possibility of hidden pockets, veils and other material. Only the medium's naked body was under the costume. After each experiment an examination of the medium and the cabinet, in which she sat, was undertaken to further eliminate the possibility of fraud.

Photographs taken at an experiment with the medium " Eva C" (whose real name was Marthe Beraud) in March 1911 showed the medium's hands being held by Prof. Schrenck- Notzing and Professor Charles Richet, who had won the Nobel Price for Physiology and Medicine in 1913, while ectoplasm was coming up out of her costume at the throat area. Another photograph taken in 1913 with the female medium Stanislava shows ectoplasm coming from her mouth, under similar test conditions.

Critics have claimed that the medium "Eva C" was a fraud and they point to some of the photographs, which to me look suspicious as well. Professor Richet was claimed to be too believing as regards physical phenomena according to critics, especially when it came to "Eva C's" materializations. Prof. Richet in his book "Thirty Years of Psychical Research" published in 1923 states:

"...I saw a fully organized form rise from the floor. At first it was only a white, opaque spot like a handkerchief lying on the ground before the curtain, then this handkerchief quickly assumed the form of a human head level with the floor and a few moments later it rose up in a straight line and became a small man...who took two or three halting steps in front of the curtain and then sank to the floor and disappeared as if through a trap door, but there was no trap door."

Could Prof. Richet have been fooled and was it really "Eva C" dressed up to look like a materialization? "Eva C" is reported to have said that materializations started out as a joke, which was played with accomplishes and continued when Richet started attending her séances. In his book Richet takes cognizance of these allegations that he had been the victim of fraud, but maintains that trickery would not account for what he saw. He traces the allegations to the spite of a servant that had been fired for theft and exploitation of the lies by a sensation seeking newspaper.

Then there is the "medium" Eusapia Palladino (1854-

1918), who most investigators knew cheated when she could. It was suspected that she liked to see what she could get away with. She was investigated numerous times and there were some investigators who believed she was genuine (at least at times). Richet conducted several tests on Eusapia and the results were a frustrating mix of deliberate fraud and results he could not explain.

Richet brought in several witnesses, one of whom was the physicist Marie Curie, at a sitting with Eusapia in Paris. He and Curie sat on either side of the medium, each holding one of Eusapia's hands. Now quoting Richet: "We saw the curtain swell out as if pushed by some large object." He reached up and grabbed the bump behind the curtain. He felt a hand with sausage-like fingers, but there was nothing beyond the wrist. Eusapia had a small hand so the fingers could not be hers and Curie was still holding onto her other hand. Richet then tried another experiment. He placed smoked paper on a table some distance from the medium. Pale hands appeared and pressed against the paper. After wards Richet found that the dark film of the smoke had worn off in places, but Eusapia's hands remained clean, untouched by the smoky residue. It is at this time that Richet invented the word ectoplasm (exterior substance) to explain the observed phenomena. It thus appears that at times Eusapia did produce phenomena, but her deliberate fraud at times cast a cloud over her mediumship.

Many so-called mediums have been caught red-handed trying to fraudulently produce partial or full materializations. The sitter has to be knowledgeable about what to look for before, during and after the séance. The best proof is when both the medium (inside the cabinet) and the materialization (outside the cabinet) are visible at the same time in red light and accomplishes have been ruled out. It is not clear whether Richet saw the materializations under these conditions. It is thus possible that he may have been fooled in certain instances. The reason I have described the work of Crookes, Schrenck-Notzing and Richet is to show that well educated, skilled researchers, who published books with photographs of materializations, appear to have been or could have been fooled by fraudulent mediums in certain cases. We will never know the truth. These cases show how controversial and complex the whole concept of materialization is.

Magicians and illusionists (I will just use the word magician to describe both) have been and are the most vocal critics of psychic phenomena so I would like to present a controversial case with a magician on either side of the controversy. The case deals with Helen Duncan, the Scots materialization medium, who has been claimed to have been one of the best materialization mediums but by others claimed to have been a fraud.

In 1931, she gave five séances at the National Laboratory of Psychical research in London. According to Harry Price, a skilled magician, Helen secreted yards of cheesecloth with which she impersonated several "spirits". He took a large number of photographs of supposed cheesecloth phantoms which he claims all show warp and weft of the material, selvedge creases and even dirt marks. Even rubber gloves and safety pins were in the photographs. Helen had been thoroughly searched before the séance and enclosed in a one-piece garment designed by Price but she was still able to produce the "materializations". Price claimed that Duncan possessed a secondary stomach into which she swallowed the cheesecloth, etc, to be regurgitated at leisure during the séance. He published a report about Duncan claiming that Helen's former maid came to him and supported his theory concerning regurgitation.

This report by Price appears at first glance to be very

damaging for the mediumship of Helen Duncan. However, a report published in 1932 by Will Goldston, the eminent magician who founded the Magician's Circle, claims just the opposite. He sat with Helen in March 1932 at a home in North London. The medium's cabinet was a curtain drawn across a corner of the room. During an hour and a half eight different forms manifested. They were of all ages, both sexes, and each possessed an individual speaking voice. He carried on a conversation with a small female called Violet who told him she was eight years old and permitted him to feel her hand. He then concluded that, so far as he was aware- and he was a magician of lifelong experience- there was no system of trickery which could have achieved the astounding results which he witnessed that evening with Mrs. Duncan. Nor was he aware of any system of ventriloquism or voice control which could so perfectly simulate the voices of eight different people. After the sitting Mrs. Duncan drank two cups of coffee and ate two tea cakes. Naturally, the question is how is it possible to absorb all that food and drink into the stomach that is already packed with cheese cloth? He had no answer for that but did not think it was possible.

He then had a second séance with Helen which he considered to be a test séance. He had enlisted as co-examiners Henry Rigoletto, Dr, A.E. Neale, and Dr. O.H. Bowan. All three were magicians of the widest experience. Previous to the sitting Mrs. Duncan had been stripped, examined, and entirely reclothed by two ladies who were present with them the whole evening, and who were strangers to Helen. They examined the room but could find nothing in the room, or, more particularly, in the cabinet, which gave them any grounds for suspicion. He sat about two feet from the cabinet. A dim red lamp was used for illumination, sufficient for him to see the curtains clearly and the outline of the medium.

Life After Death

The spirit forms that manifested on this second occasion were, he thought, a little lacking in clearness and power. Nevertheless, they were essentially of the same type- that is, shining with a curious phosphorescent sheen in the ruby light and entirely self-luminous. He said that he was completely at a loss to explain their appearance and disappearance by any material means. There was no sign or sound which he could possibly construe into evidence of fraud.

Here we have two completely contradictory accounts of materialization sittings with Helen Duncan by two highly respected magicians. Which one is correct? I find the explanation of a second stomach and the swallowing and regurgitation of yards of cheesecloth extremely far fetched and extremely unlikely. Try swallowing yards of cheesecloth and then try to regurgitate it without making sounds that the sitters could hear!! The accounts by Goldston seem much more believable and are very likely the truth. That does not rule out that in certain cases Duncan might have resorted to fraud when her powers were not there at a particular sitting, although that is sheer speculation.

Skeptics will say that all materializations are fraud and point at the many mediums who have been caught cheating. There are however too many cases that appear genuine (conducted under strict test conditions by reliable researchers) that eliminate the notion that it is all fraud. I will now discuss some of the cases I believe are genuine and which provide evidence for survival.

Johannesburg Materializations

Some of the most impressive photographs of ectoplasm and full materializations were taken by a dear friend of ours, Professor Jack Allen, who was Professor of Anatomy at the University of the Witwatersrand in Johannesburg, South Africa. Mickey and Sara introduced us to Jack and his wife Lentchen at their home at a sitting. They had been sitting with Mickey and Sara for many years before we met them. We became good friends with Jack and Lentchen and we remained friends until we left South Africa. Jack had a keen interest in psychic phenomena and we spent a lot of time discussing what we experienced in our separate and group sittings.

Jack told me about his sittings with a medium whose name I was not given because he was a business executive high up in one of the top insurance companies in Johannesburg. The medium did not want it to get around that he was involved in Spiritualist activities. He was afraid it might affect his career. This medium, who I will call the Johannesburg medium, produced lots of ectoplasm and full materializations. Jack took several pictures using infrared film and red light.

The first photograph (picture 1) shows ectoplasm coming from the right nostril of the medium, who is in deep trance, and forming a ball-like shape on his right shoulder. There must be some "guiding intelligence" that directs the ectoplasm to move and form the shapes it does. The lump of ectoplasm on his shoulder could form a 'voice box" in the case of independent direct voice (as discussed in the previous chapters). As discussed in those chapters, the spirit entities would shape the ectoplasm into a "voice box" or "mask" and would then speak through it and not through the medium's mouth. That was how Flint, Sloan, Sara and others produced the independent direct voice.

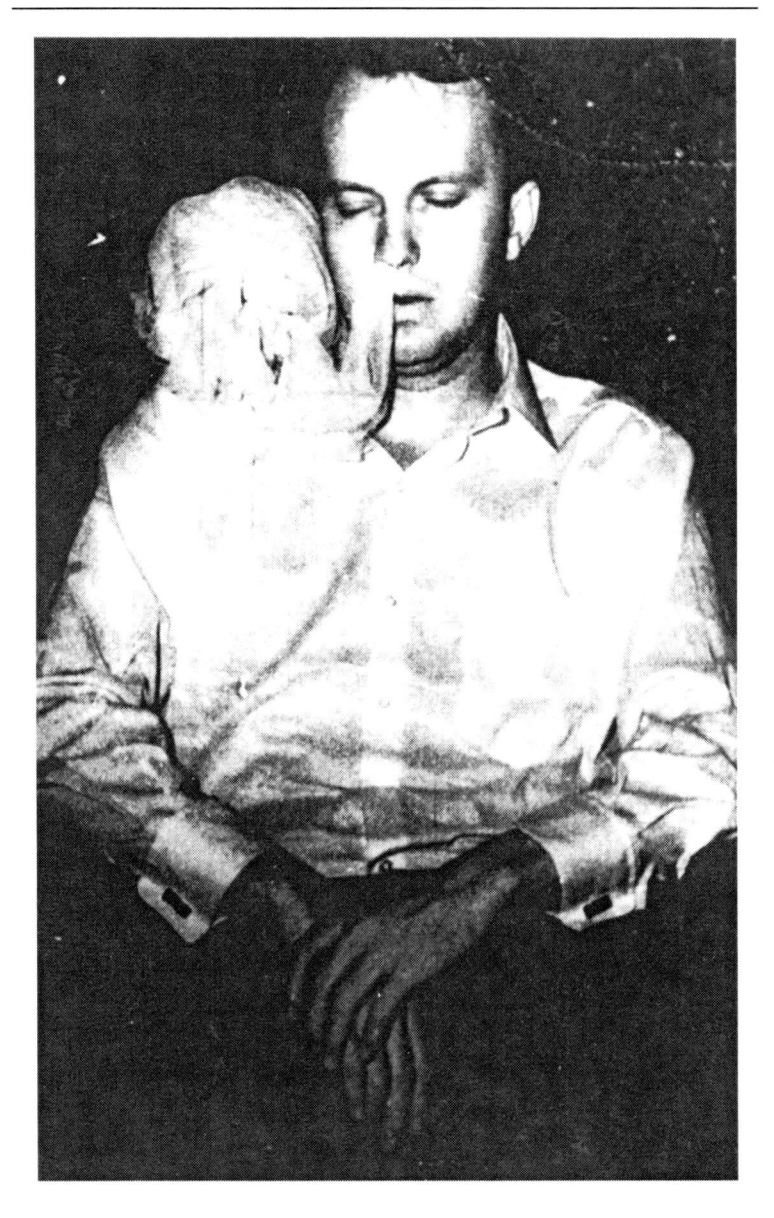

Photograph 1: Ectoplasm coming out of the right nostril of the Johannesburg medium.

The second photograph (picture 2) shows ectoplasm coming out of the left nostril of the medium. This time it drops over the medium like a sheet of very fine gauze. Marlene and I have seen ectoplasm in a transparent form like this at a sitting with Mickey and Sara and their medium friends Max and Kitty Gordon. Mickey and Sara and Max and Kitty were friends for decades and sat together for most of those years. Kitty was a very good physical medium often producing ectoplasm and materializations. On that particular evening Mickey, Sara and Kitty sat in the cabinet. With the red light on Brian, Sara's guide (the usual master of ceremonies), told us to open the curtains. We could all see the three mediums in trance sitting in the cabinet. Then ectoplasm started pouring out of Kitty's nose and started to form a gauze-like sheet similar to that in picture 2. One of the sitters was then told to pick up the end of the ectoplasm on the floor, hold it high (about 5-6 feet) and then pull it partly across the room (about 4-6 feet) while it was still attached to Kitty's nose. It was truly spectacular to see. The ectoplasm was slightly transparent. The person holding the ectoplasm was then told to drop the ectoplasm. It fell to the ground and disappeared (quite fast- within seconds) back into Kitty's nose. Besides the very clear sight of ectoplasm there was also a very noticeable smell; I would call it a smell very much like a perspiration smell.

Life After Death

Photograph 2: Ectoplasm coming out of the left nostril of the Johannesburg medium and forming a sheet that covers most of his body.

So, after this digression, coming back to picture 2, the ectoplasm looks exactly like we saw at a sitting with Mickey and Sara. For some to say that the ectoplasm as seen in pictures 1 & 2 is fraud is nonsense. Ectoplasm coming from the medium (nose, mouth, ears and/or the solar plexus), as rare as it is, has been seen by numerous lucky sitters, photographed many times and we have seen it ourselves. Obviously the ectoplasm was not a hallucination, as many skeptics would want you to believe, since it was photographed. No magician can produce ectoplasm in red light, in which everyone would be able to see it and him at the same time, and have it return to his body without using his hands or any other contraption. There are many photographs of "ectoplasm" that are clearly fraudulent and many that are very suspicious. The big difference between just about all of those photographs and the pictures shown here is that in those cases the medium was behind the curtain of the cabinet or in a closed cabinet so no one could see what the medium was doing. Also, in those cases very little happened in red light, most of it was in the dark to hide what the medium was doing (such as draping himself with cheesecloth or opening a trap door so accomplices draped in cheesecloth could come out and walk around the séance room). Fraudulent mediums and magicians need their hands to produce the "ectoplasmic" hands, heads and/or bodies to fool the sitters. The key is to see the medium and the ectoplasm and/or the full materializations at the same time in red light. Red light is used rather than white light since it has lower energy so will do no or less harm to the ectoplasm. Also, genuine materialization mediums would have no trouble with being tied very securely (such that not even a magician could get out) to their chair during the whole sitting. Many mediums have been securely tied up and still produced the same results. Besides the mediumship of the Johannesburg medium, I will describe a few other genuine materialization mediums later in this chapter.

The next photograph (picture 3) is of a full materialization, the rarest of all physical phenomena. The ectoplasm that came from the Johannesburg medium (as shown in pictures 1 & 2) built up and formed into a full human form that that walked and talked. At first glance it appears to be a person dressed up in a white sheet or sheets. It is clearly not the medium as can be seen by comparing the faces in the three pictures. In addition, the medium could be seen sitting in the cabinet by all the sitters when the curtain was drawn open. When one looks carefully at the materialization you can see that it is not just a sheet that was thrown around a person, but quite an elaborate outfit. This cannot be the medium or another sitter quickly putting on an outfit like this in the cabinet. Can it be someone who came in through a trap door or a door or a window? According to Professor Allen it was a room where he had sat several times and he and other sitters had checked that the door (only one) and window (only one) were always closed and locked. There were no trapdoors (just about all homes in Johannesburg have no basement) or secret doors (he had checked for that) for clothed persons to come in through. Also, with the red light on it was impossible for a person to sneak into the room through some secret entrance. Finally, it could also not be one of the sitters since others would have noticed in the red light that someone was missing. So the only conclusion can be that the "entity" is indeed a materialized spirit using ectoplasm from the medium. This materialization seen in picture 3 walked around the séance room and spoke to the sitters according to Professor Allen. Once the materialized spirit had finished speaking to a particular sitter or sitters, he would either walk back behind the curtain, where the medium sat, or would just slowly sink into the floor and disappear. In both cases the ectoplasm returned to the medium.

Photograph 3: A full materialization produced by the Johannesburg medium. Note all the folds and drapes of the "gown" covering the materialization.

The next photograph (picture 4) again is a full materialization, this time standing next to a sitter and holding her hand. I find this materialization impressive and very evidential. Firstly, this is not a man dressed up in a simple white sheet or robe. Note the details of the "gown" which shows many folds and layers. Secondly, note all the ectoplasm on the floor between his feet and between his feet and those of the lady sitter. If he was a man dressed up pretending to be a full materialization (as discussed earlier, there is no place he could have come from and he is not the medium) then it would certainly be very difficult to walk with all that "cloth" (or whatever it is) between his legs and being pulled behind him!! Thirdly, and this I find most interesting, note that the materializations beard in the picture is black. The first reaction might simply be that if the materialization is a fraud then the black beard is phony and has probably been glued on, giving a black image. I now want to show a photograph (picture 5) taken by Tom Harrison in the 1950's in England of a full materialization of his grandfather with a beard (a later section in this chapter discusses Tom's circle and all that took place in detail). Note that the beard of the materialization is also black. Tom had no explanation for why it was black, nor do I. But the fact that the two photographs of two full materializations taken continents and years apart, both show a black beard is strong confirmation that the pictures are genuine and not fraud. If the materializations were frauds and the beards thus false, then there would be no reason for them to be black. In the photographs the black color indicates that the light from the red lamps is totally absorbed and thus not reflected back (totally or partially) into the camera and onto the film. Any false beard, whatever it is made out of, would reflect some light and appear any color but black. The beards are unlikely to be ectoplasm, as the rest of the body is, since it is black and nothing else is. We just don't know the reason why both are black. It is indeed very interesting and very evidential since both photographs have it.

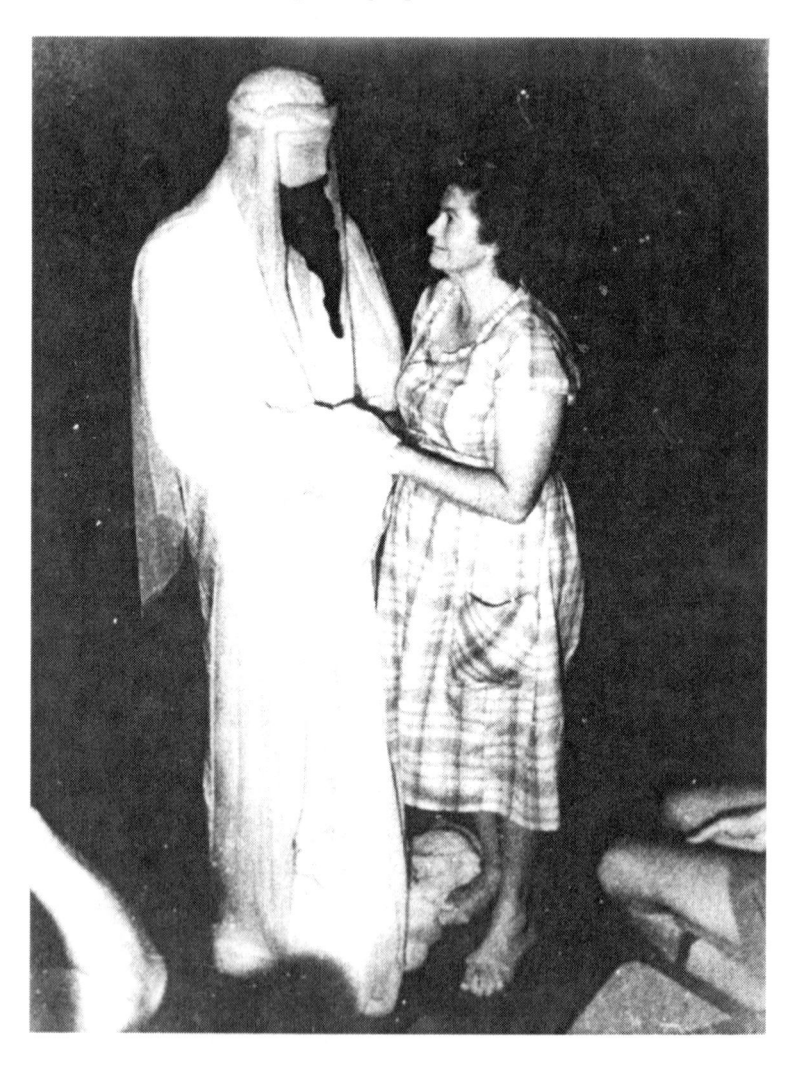

Photograph 4: A full materialization produced by the Johannesburg medium. Again note all the details (folds,

drapes, etc.) of the "gown" covering the materialization. Also note all the ectoplasm on the ground at the feet of the materialization and the sitter. Finally note the black beard.

This last photograph (picture 4) is one of the best full materialization photographs I have ever seen, but then of course there aren't many genuine full materialization photographs in the literature. The photographs shown in a later section of this chapter, taken by Tom Harrison, are very similar to pictures 1-4, as the picture of his grandfather with the black beard shows.

Photograph 5: An ectoplasmic materialization produced by Minnie Harrison of Tom Harrison's granddad. Note the black beard.

Alec Harris

During the more recent period (after 1940) there have been many circles where there have been materializations, but unfortunately very few or no photographs were taken. A good example of a materialization circle in which no photographs were taken were the sittings of Alec Harris, who was one of the most impressive materialization mediums ever. Alec's life and mediumship were recounted by his wife in her book "They Walked Among Us" (Psychic Press-1980).

Alec Harris was born in 1897 and married Louie in 1928. Initially Alec was not interested in psychic matters at all. Then in 1934 Louie's brother Ted became a spiritualist and worked as a medium giving demonstrations of clairvoyance. As a result Louie became interested and attended a spiritualist church meeting which impressed her. Alec wanted nothing to do with it. One day Alec visited a business associate and his wife. He was told by the wife, who was a spiritualist, that he (Alec) possessed mediumistic gifts. Alec did not believe it and still wanted nothing to do with it. He then only reluctantly did some table tipping (a way to communicate with spirit entities) with Louie and a message from his sister Connie, who had died in 1923, came through. Personal questions were correctly answered and the contact greatly moved Alec. He started using his mediumistic capabilities by first doing spiritual healing and then trance mediumship. A circle was formed and sittings were held regularly.

During that time the materialization medium Helen Duncan (discussed in some detail earlier in this chapter) came to demonstrate at their local spiritualist church. Alec's sister Connie materialized and communicated again thus confirming her survival of bodily death. Then on a further visit by Helen Duncan, Louie's father, Albert, materialized. To quote Louie from her book;

> "With that the curtains parted and my beloved father stepped from the cabinet. He came forward, his arms outstretched to my mother and a conversa-

tion between them ensued. The masking on part of the red lamp was removed and we looked closely at dad…every feature was clear."

Here is a report of a sitting with Helen Duncan in which materializations appeared that were recognized by the sitters and spoke to the sitters. Helen did not know Alec, Louie and their dead relatives so fraud was not possible. There is thus no doubt that at times Helen's materializations were genuine.

At about this time Alec and Louie began to experience physical phenomena in their own home. They originally used a red light when meditating but their spirit controls (guides) invariably extinguished them even to the point of destroying the light filament. Louie said of this "time and again this happened, I felt a growing annoyance as the pile of broken globes increased". It was clear that their spirit controls required darkness and Louie and Alec reluctantly complied. Initially no phenomena occurred but in time the trumpet moved. "It rose, and glided silently across the mantelpiece, coming to rest on the opposite side. The trumpet avoided two vases which stood in its pathway". To obtain the best results Alec was told by the guides that he had to be in a trance and use a "cabinet" (corner of room with a curtain across it). Alec did not like this because he wanted to see what was happening, not be in trance. However, he complied and did what they asked. The guides also suggested that he should be securely tied to the chair he sat on in the cabinet each sitting. A red light was allowed.

Initially, when sitting under these conditions, they experienced direct voice and partial materializations (hands and arms). A humorous and impressive séance took place on Christmas night 1939. After going into trance one of Alec's guides announced that an experiment was to be conducted. The sitters in the circle could hear different voices, including those of children, coming from the cabinet. This was followed by various items of Alec's clothing (such as his shoes, belt and sweater) being passed out of the cabinet by materialized hands. Suddenly Alec came out of the cabinet still in trance, but he was no longer wearing his pants. At that point Alec came out of his trance and noticed that he had no pants on. Louie went into the cabinet and saw the pants sitting in the chair just as if Alec's body was still inside them with the ropes still binding them. No one in the circle knew how it was done. The guides explained that they can materialize and dematerialize objects (usually called apports, but in this case Alex himself). Apports are items (usually normal everyday things) that are moved from one place to another without human contact through solid barriers such as doors and walls. The guides said that they dematerialized Alec in the cabinet and then rematerialized him outside the cabinet. This dematerialization/rematerialization happened several times to Alex later in his life at several different sittings. Mickey and Sara were at a sitting with Alec and experienced this and told us about it. Apports will be discussed in more detail later in this chapter. I realize that this dematerialization and then rematerialization is hard to believe, but I wanted to mention it because it has been well documented (such as here with Alec) in several cases that I believe to be real and genuine. Even I find it hard to believe, but I have seen ectoplasm disappear just like that so I have witnessed dematerialization.

In the 1940's the first full materializations started to appear in their circle. Initially, faces could be seen in balls of ectoplasm, then figures would start forming. As the weeks went by the figures grew stronger and stronger. Eventually, the coming of deceased spirits in ectoplasmic

Life After Death

bodies was a common feature at their circles. Louie noted in her book;

> "Now I began to understand about the great service it was said we had to perform. I envisaged the enormous possibilities this type of mediumship would provide for the bereaved".

Some of the most impressive evidential materializations will now be discussed.

The first case involves a woman Louie met at the local spiritualist church. A spirit was trying to communicate through the medium to give a message to that woman but was unsuccessful. Louie invited the distressed woman to their next circle. At the séance, once Alec was in trance, a full materialization stepped out of the cabinet. It was a young man who held out his arms to the woman and said "Mum, it's Derry". The woman gave an anguished cry, jumped from her seat and went to the young man. He put his arms around her. The mother broke down and wept in her "dead" son's arms. He gently comforted her and said: "I want you to be quite sure it is really me. Look, I've still got it". The solid materialization form took her hand and placed it on his chest. "Can you feel it, Mom?" he asked. Later they learned that the young man had had a deformed breast bone. To give his mother positive proof of his identity, he materialized his deformity to convince her, which he certainly did. Afterwards they were told that the young man had volunteered for service with the paratroops. His plane was shot down over Northern Africa.

This is a very impressive case of survival evidence. Louie and Alec did not know who the woman was and that her son had been killed during the war. Alec definitely did not know what he looked like and that he had a physical deformity. There are only two arguments that can be put up to try to refute this excellent evidence; firstly, that Alec produced the materialization using "super-ESP" powers and then produced the evidence using telepathy and/or these super-ESP abilities, and secondly, one can argue that Louie made up the story in her book. To me it seems the almost always used telepathy/super-ESP argument is more far fetched than the materialization evidence. How would Alec's subconscious have known where to get all the necessary information necessary to produce the perfect looking materialization that the sitter recognized and then give all the right facts while he is in trance?? No, it is too hard too believe that the subconscious mind can do all that. The well-witnessed and documented materialization makes a lot more sense. The best way to counter the argument that Louie made up all these sittings with materializations, is to quote accounts of sittings written by visitors to the circle, which were published in magazines and papers.

I will here quote verbatim a few of the most impressive accounts written by visitors to Alec Harris's materialization séances. The editor of the psychic magazine "Two Worlds" Ernest Thompson sat with the Alec Harris circle several times and wrote the following (taken from Louie's book):

> "At the first séance I had with Alec Harris 15 spirits materialized that evening. They were tall and short, fat and thin, male and female. Some were visitors from other lands, one being an American Red Indian who stood quite seven feet tall. As evidence of the genuineness of these manifestations Rohan, the spirit in charge of the proceedings, materialized and drawing the cabinet curtains to one side revealed the entranced medium sitting in his corner

Life After Death

upon a chair so that we could see them together. On two further occasions the materialized forms were visible simultaneously with that of the medium. As further evidence of the genuineness of these materialized forms Rohan permitted us to witness the entire process of materialization.

First of all, there appeared what seemed to be a white rod which trust itself along the floor from under the cabinet curtains. It moved as if it were alive and stopped about a yard in front of the curtains. The end began to enlarge into a ball until there was a mass of moving, pulsating ectoplasm about the size of a large stone. It became elongated vertically until it was the height of a human being. Gradually, as if it were being sculptured, there appeared a face and then a head. Soon the form was completely human, clothed in ectoplasmic draperies.

The materialized spirit began to walk about the room and was able to speak to us. As the power waned we saw the spirit dissolve and collapse into empty space. Then occurred the most wonderful and beautiful manifestation of the entire séance. A charming Spanish girl gracefully glided through the curtains and enthralled us with a dancing display. It was fascinating to watch her elegant movements. As she turned quickly on her toes, the hem of her billowing white dress flicked my cheek. It felt as soft and sensitive as gossamer.

Then she came to the main purpose of her visit, to prove human survival by demonstrating to us that she was indeed a female and not the medium (a male) masquerading in disguise. Slowly she parted her robes revealing, beyond all doubts, a nude female figure."

Jan W. Vandersande Ph.D.

This is a very impressive detailed description of what happens at a materialization sitting. Assuming that Thompson has given an accurate account of the sitting, and there is no reason to believe he has not, it clearly confirms that Alec does not dress up as materializations, but that they are genuine. The number of different materializations and the description of how they are formed rules out accomplishes who came in through trapdoors or secret doors. Can you imagine having 15 different accomplishes, especially considering that Alec did not charge for just about all of his sittings. I will now give another impressive account of a sitting with Alec.

In August 1946, Maurice Barbanell, the well-known editor of the weekly psychic newspaper "Psychic News", and the well-known medium Helen Hughes sat in a Alec Harris circle. Helen had apparently prophesied that very sitting in 1936. Maurice Barbanell wrote the following in "Psychic News" (taken from Louie's book):

> "There is in South Wales one of the most remarkable materialization mediums. At séances spirit forms not only show themselves in good red light, but hold sustained conversations- after having walked about ten feet from the cabinet.
>
> At a sitting which I attended I saw 30 forms materialize during two-and-a-half hours. Alec Harris does not use his gift professionally, deriving his income from his work for a government department. The sittings have to be held fairly late at night because his wife is engaged in an orchestra at a local theatre.
>
> It was not until almost 10.30 PM that 27 of us assembled in the séance room. As most of the sitters had come by coach from valleys about 25 miles

away, few got to bed before four AM.

The story behind the sitting is a fascinating one. About ten years ago, the medium's wife had a private sitting with Helen Hughes. She was then told that, if she and her husband sat in their home for development, they would one day obtain full-form materializations. Moreover, it was stated that Helen would witness the phenomena. She did at this séance I attended.

I was asked beforehand to make a thorough examination of the room, of the cabinet, and of the medium, who wore only a thin pair of trousers made of black material and a black vest. The black was deliberate, because the forms always appear clothed in dazzlingly white ectoplasm, which I noticed as usual did not reflect the red light (Author's note: it has to reflect light to be seen. He probably meant that the ectoplasm looks white rather than red). I was so close to the cabinet that several of the forms had to walk over my feet. On several occasions I handled the flowing ectoplasmic draperies, which were soft and silky to the touch. I shook hands with two forms. Their hands were firm and normal.

Helen Hughes received two outstanding proofs. One was the materialization of Douglas Hogg, a Battle of Britain pilot who has proved his survival to his parents through her mediumship. He showed his features distinctly and asked her to stand up so he could talk to her face to face. He gripped her by the hands, thanked her for all she had done, and kissed her, almost with reverence, on the forehead. She had no difficulty in identifying him: clairvoyantly she has seen him on many occasions.

Douglas Hogg also gave a greeting to Charles

Glover Botham, another medium through whom he has given evidence of his survival to his parents. The other spirit form to show himself to Helen was her Red Indian guide, a magnificent figure complete with headdress, who gave his name. The cast of his features was typical of his race. Another Red Indian guide, completely different in appearance, manifested and spoke to the medium's 13 year old son who had been brought up to regard spirit visitors as a normal part of life.

From the standpoint of evidence, the highlight of the sitting was the materialization of a man known to several people present and particularly to Tom and Mabel Hibbs, leading figures in the South Wales District Council of the Spiritualist' National Union. He came right out of the cabinet, walked about ten feet to the corner of the room and showed himself to Mrs. Hibbs. At first he did not give his name, though asked to do so, because he declared that he ought to be easily identified by his features and his voice. He was right! Mrs. Hibbs soon recognized this man, who had passed on recently, and who was one of the officials of the district council.

To appreciate the remarkable nature of the sitting, you must remember that it is very rare to get materializations venturing beyond the cabinet because there is an invisible lifeline connecting them with the medium. Yet the "dead" official, as well as several others, walked to the corner of the room, sat in a chair and carried on a long discussion. Some of the forms, after maintaining these conversations, were heard to say that they must go back to the cabinet for "more rations". They walked back and a few minutes later came out, moved across to the

Life After Death

corner of the room, sat down and continued where they left off. Several turned around and showed their backs, to prove they were solid figures. Once a form stooped to straighten a rug which had been moved by somebody else.

From the spectacular point of view, the most extraordinary incident was the materialization of a girl. She disposed of any suggestion that the results could be explained away by trickery by revealing part of her feminine form! Then one materialization parted the curtains so we could see the figure and the medium at the same time.

Frequently throughout the séance I heard some of the guides conversing with the medium in the cabinet. Apparently there are intervals when Alec is almost conscious.

It was an impressive demonstration of materialization at its best. The medium and his wife devote their spare time to Spiritualism and make a specialty of healing. Already they have several striking successes to their credit. But no skeptic could attend one of these materialization séances and still remain a skeptic".

This is another impressive description of one of Alec's sittings confirming the previous account by Thompson. I would just like to comment on one thing Barbanel said, that the materializations were connected by an invisible cord to the medium. I believe that the connection was not always invisible. Look at picture 4 and all the ectoplasm on the floor behind the materialization. It would not surprise me if that ectoplasm did not go back into the cabinet to the medium, connecting the two of them.

Magicians, in general, have been very critical of physical mediums, claiming that they are frauds and that the phenomena are produced by tricks, which they can detect and/or duplicate. To be fair magicians have exposed fraudulent mediums. So to have a magician attend one of Alec's séances and to confirm that the materializations are real would be a great coup. Mr. A.G. Fletcher-Desborough, a professional stage illusionist, attended a séance and wrote with conviction to the Liverpool Evening Express: (and I here quote from Louie's book):

> "I examined the cabinet which Alec Harris used. Having been on the stage as an illusionist and magician I knew exactly where to look for such things as panel and floor escapes, ceiling and wall slides. I was satisfied that nothing could make an exit or an entrance in any way. There was no chance for deception."

Now quoting Louie's account of what happened to the magician at the sitting:

"Of a short, stout man who materialized from the cabinet and went straight to him, giving the name "Bertie", he said: "It was my father. In a mumbling way of speaking, he gave a pet name used by my parents. No one but the family knew it."

Then a young man came who hobbled and walked with difficulty. He graped the sitter's hand and said: "Bertie! I am your brother, Walter." The form was recognized immediately by the conjurer. He explained that his brother had had a bad ankle shot away in the Boer War. "No one there knew I had a brother." He said. "So who learnt his name, and that he hobbled when walking in life? There certainly could have been no deception in this case."

Then from the cabinet walked a stiff, upright young fellow. Like the others the figure went towards the conjurer. Then he swerved and throwing out his arms "embraced my wife, saying in a very pathetic voice, "Mother, Mother, I'm your son Ronnie." This apparently was their third son, born under fire during the Sinn Fein rising in 1916. He was captured in Singapore Harbour by the Japanese and beheaded.

"He turned to me after embracing his mother," said the magician, "and put his head against mine. I recognized his voice."

Fletcher-Desborough concluded his article with the question: "Why all these manifestations on my behalf? Because I was an unbeliever."

This account is not just another impressive description of one of Alec's sitting, but an important account since it was written by a magician.

In 1957 their circle was visited by Professor T.J. Haarhof, Professor of Classics at the University of the Witwatersrand, Johannesburg, South Africa. He had remarkable evidence at that sitting. I quote from Louie's book:

"University men are usually very shy to acknowledge psychic phenomena because in most cases they cannot produce scientific proof. I was no exception until I was privileged to share a type of experience that enabled me reliably to correlate theory to fact.

Recently I had a new type of experience in which subjective factors were completely eliminated. It was at the house of Mr. and Mrs. Alec Harris. I want to say at once that no praise is too great for the motives, the integrity and self-sacrificing service of Mrs. Harris; and that the materializing powers of Mr. Harris are astounding, unique and entirely above suspicion.

I make these statements after many years of investigation and many disappointments and experience of fraudulent mediums.

Some ten years ago, in Johannesburg, I was brought into touch with a Greek philosopher, who gave me convincing proof of his identity and entrusted a certain very difficult task to me. He does not wish his name to be mentioned at this stage, but I was given descriptions of him.

The Harris circle knew nothing of all of this. But at the sitting a week ago, this philosopher materialized. He walked out and took me firmly by the hand. He brought his face close to mine. I saw that it corresponded to the descriptions I had been given. He held up his white robe for me to feel. The texture was that of linen but not so smooth. It had a fibrous yet silky quality.

He spoke to me in ancient Greek, which is certainly unknown to the medium. He said, "Auto Eleluthe" (I have come in person). He is one who very seldom "comes" and who had the reputation of being unsociable. But he came because, unknown to me, something happened of which I heard only the following day. Margaret Lloyd, through whom I had contact with him, had passed on in the Johannesburg Hospital. He wanted to encourage me to go on with the work and to say that help would be given in other ways. Otherwise I should have concluded that the work had come to an end."

Lastly, here is another case where the materializations speak in foreign languages unknown to Alec. (Again quoting Louie):

"At another sitting there was an eminent sitter, a medical man, Sir Alexander Cannon. The highlight at that sitting was the materialization of Mahatma Gandhi, who came especially for Sir Alexander. The materialization of the Indian holy man was exactly as he looked on earth. He was painfully thin, almost emancipated, as a result of many long fasts. Gandhi wore his customary loin cloth and the well remembered steel rimmed spectacles.

He conversed at length with Sir Alexander in Hindustani, a language familiar to the doctor, but certainly not to Alec. Our eminent sitter was "very impressed" with the materialization, particularly at the accuracy of the form's detail and the timbre of his voice. Sir Alexander knew the holy man well. Gandhi conversing in his vernacular tongue was even more convincing evidence as far as he was concerned.

But the doctor had further indisputable evidence. Two Tibetan monks materialized. They conversed with him in a little known tongue. Cannon mentioned he was one of the few people in the world who understood this ancient Tibetan language."

I always get nervous when famous "dead" people speak through a medium or materialize. In this case there was a good reason for Gandhi to materialize since he and Sir Alexander knew each other well. His materialization thus provided evidence for survival. It is not the case of a materialization claiming he or she was someone famous but then there is no one to confirm it. In the séances with Alec there is almost always a friend or relative present who recognizes the materialization.

Jan W. Vandersande Ph.D.

I now want to mention a few interesting observations that George Cranley gave in his account of a sitting he had with Alec Harris. George, who lived in Cape Town, South Africa, got an invitation to attend a sitting with Alec Harris in Johannesburg through a mutual friend. He flew up to Johannesburg to attend the sitting. I will now only mention the few interesting observations from George's account of that sitting.

The room was lit by a number of red bulbs. No dimmer switches were used, which made it very easy to distinguish everything very clearly. The séance lasted about three hours and about fourteen people materialized. One of the materializations was a Red Indian, his friend's guide, who went by the name of Black Feather. He was very tall, well over six feet. This materialization let George feel his chest and then let George hit him on the chest. George did so cautiously and then was told to hit him harder which he did. George hit him even harder but Black Feather never flinched. George's hand just bounced off him.

Anther materialization was a boy called Ginger who went around greeting all the sitters. George noticed that, as Ginger walked around, there was a trail of ectoplasm behind him that flowed under the curtains and back to the medium. I mention this observation because something similar can be seen in picture 4. In that picture there is a trail of ectoplasm on the floor attached to the materialization. We can not see where it goes to but it would not surprise me if it went back to the medium.

One of George's guides materialized and he spoke to him for about 10-15 minutes. Suddenly, the guide said he had to go. Here is George's description of what happened next:

> "I thanked him for coming, but still held onto his hand. Something made me look down at his feet.

As I did so I saw the bottom half of his body dissolving away, but his hands were still solid. Then his hands just melted away between my fingers yet my hands were still closed. The last thing I saw was his head slowly sinking to the floor saying, "I am going now", disappearing under the curtains like a streak of light".

This is a beautiful description of one way a full materialization dematerializes. Mickey, Sara and Professor Allen have all three described similar dematerializations to me. Similar reports can also be found in the literature. The ectoplasm sort of vaporizes (the best way to describe disappears or dissolving away) and rapidly goes back into the medium. It is amazing how the materialization can still speak even if only his head is the only part of his body still materialized.

The only argument that can be used to refute all this evidence is to say that Louie and the sitters all lied. That suggestion is just so far fetched since it would involve hundreds of sitters all lying. This is just not possible, especially considering the credentials of many of the sitters.

One of the main reasons I believe the evidence provided by the materializations in Alec's seances, is that Mickey and Sara sat with Alec several times and confirmed what happened in his sittings. Alec and Louie moved to South Africa in 1957 to be with their married son. Mickey and Sara sat with them in Johannesburg in the late 1950's. They told us about the numerous materializations they witnessed first hand. I clearly remember Mickey describing one of his guides, a Native American, who materialized at one of the sittings. Mickey was asked to come and stand right in front of the materialized guide, who was taller than he was. He was allowed to touch the guide while they were talking to each other. The guide told Mickey and Sara that they would be doing work similar to what Alec did and that they would be helping people. The guide proved to be right.

One of the stories Mickey and Sara told us was similar to one that appeared in Louie's book. It is a story that is hard to believe, but Mickey and Sara also witnessed it and I am willing to describe it here because I believe their account of it. It is the dematerialization and re-materialization of Alec to a place outside the séance room. I here quote Louie from her book:

> "We were giving a circle for the church. I always made a point of including among the sitters one of our regulars. Graham Watkins attended that night.
>
> Toi-Toi (one of their regular guides- a child) materialized. A man asked the spirit child, "Do you remember the night you took off Alec's trousers?"
>
> "Hush!" I chided, but before I could utter another word Alec's trousers came hurtling through the air. Amid the laughter, I found myself thinking, "Thank goodness the circle is nearly over." Then Christopher, a spirit friend, requested us all to leave the room very quietly.
>
> Knowing Alec did not like being left alone to come out of trance, Graham offered to stay behind with him. I said I would do likewise. But Christopher was emphatic. No, he insisted, we all had to go immediately. "Leave the medium's trousers by the cabinet," he added. As the sitters filed out, Graham saw my concern and whispered: " Don't worry. I will sit just outside the door. When I hear the slightest movement I'll slip in and see to Alec."
>
> Somewhat relieved, I went downstairs to make

the tea. The front door bell rang. I rushed to open the door. As I did so, I could not stifle a little scream as I saw my husband, now out of trance, standing there, a bewildered expression on his face and now wearing his trousers.

Graham, who had heard my scream, rushed downstairs to investigate. His face registered shock on seeing Alec in the doorway. Graham's expression of amazement was almost comical as he stammered, "But...but... he never.. I mean I never.. but how?"

He had not heard anything untoward from the séance room, and was mystified as to how Alec got out. Alec was not much help either. His only explanation was that he suddenly found himself in the front garden, with his trousers on. He had no recollection of getting there.

There was no normal way in which Alec could have left the room of his own accord. Graham guarded the door. The only window was permanently closed, fixed by a wooden frame, fitted for black-out purposes. In any case it had become warped by the sun and was immovable. On checking it was found to be jammed tight. There were no sign it had been tampered with."

This dematerialization of Alec in the séance room and rematerialization outside of the house just seems totally impossible to believe, but Mickey and Sara described and swore to a similar event at a séance they attended with Alec. I would be hard pressed to believe this except for the fact that apports (objects brought into the séance room from outside the room) have been well documented. In the next section I will mention the apports Tom Harrison regularly received in their circle. However, there is a big difference between dematerializing and then rematerializing a human being compared to an object. But I have no reason to doubt what Mickey and Sara told me. I guess that if the spirits can dematerialize any object and move it through a wall (or door) atom by atom or molecule by molecule, then they can do the same with a human being, no matter how impossible it sounds. Yes, it is hard to believe, but if a full materialization can take place, and I have absolutely no doubt it can (and hopefully the reader won't have any doubt either after reading all the evidence in this book), then the spirits can do almost anything under the right conditions.

Finally, I will describe how an attempted press "exposure" of Alec failed. It was in 1961 in Johannesburg and the Harris's had one more sitting planned before going on vacation. The sitters were all well known to a friend of Louie. At the last moment one of the sitters, who had booked two seats for the sitting, asked the friend if he could transfer the two seats to two acquaintances for whom he could vouch. Louie's friend agreed to the exchange, never expecting collusion. The two substitute sitters later turned out to be journalists. It was their intention to expose Alec, in what was believed to be a hoax to hoodwink gullible sitters. They requested to see the séance room by themselves and were allowed to.

When Louie placed the sitters immediately before the sitting began, she placed the two journalists in the second row on either side of her niece's husband. She felt they could do no harm there. However, there was an opening in the center of the front row for sitters in the second row so they could come to the cabinet should they be called by spirit friends.

The spirit friends took a long time to materialize and Louie felt that something was wrong. At last one of their

Life After Death

guides, Rohan, appeared, standing uncertainly in the aperture before the cabinet. Instead of coming out to greet the sitters he stood at the cabinet curtain opening and surveyed the two semi-circular rows of sitters. Louie now knew something was wrong. After a pause Rohan did come out and started welcoming the guests by taking the hands of each sitter in the front row. He was weary and not relaxed as he usually was. He went back to the curtain and pulled it open so that everyone could clearly see the entranced Alec and Rohan standing near him (all in red light). Rohan then came forward to take the hands of those seated in the back row. Now quoting directly from Louie's book:

> "Eventually, it was the turn of one of the substitute sitters to be greeted. As Rohan was about to take his hand in welcome, the man sprang forward and grabbed him! Throwing his arms around the spirit figure, he held on to him tightly shouting, "I've got you!" The sitter was obviously convinced he had captured the draped medium in the act of duplicity, masquerading as a spirit form.
>
> As Rohan's figure quickly dematerialized there was a loud groan from Alec in the cabinet. Then came a cry of pain as the ectoplasm swiftly returned to his body with the impact of a sledge-hammer.
>
> The treacherous sitter fell dazed to the floor as the "solid" body he had held so tightly minutes before disappeared. I threw myself on him, desperately flailing with my hands, sobbing: "Oh, don't! You'll kill my husband! You fool, you'll kill him!"
>
> The man looked up at me, his eyes wide, terrified. The realization dawned on him it had not been the medium he had grasped, but what it purported to be, a fully materialized spirit form. Meanwhile the

second imposter, taking advantage of the commotion that ensued, rushed to the window and pulled aside the closed curtains, having previously tampered with them during the "meditation" session earlier. This revealed his confederates outside the window. They had a battery of cameras focused on the séance room, on the cabinet in particular.

Lenses immediately clicked furiously as flash bulbs exploded. I glanced frantically in the cabinet's direction, and realized with profound relief that our guides were doing all in their power to protect their medium. They had swathed the curtains around Alec, completely enveloping him so that he was immune to the blinding flashes of light being so ruthlessly directed at him. I was utterly bewildered and sick with dread for Alec, knowing what he must have suffered by the sudden impact of the returning ectoplasm.

The two journalists made a dash for the door and escaped. They ran off into the night to join their confederates in a waiting car. The magazine, the imposters worked for, had promised readers in a previous issue it would give full photo coverage in the "exposure" of Alec's mediumship. No photographs were ever printed."

When Alec came out of trance he was patently very ill. He had a severe pain in his solar plexus that persisted for some weeks. A doctor was called. He treated Alec weekly for many months. Rohan, too, suffered adverse effects and needed, they were told by their spirit scientist, a period of recuperation.

The exposure attempt had definitely affected the health of Alec. He slowed down considerably and was a lot less energetic than before. It took a few years before he was anything like his old self again. He again started giving occasional circles but only for friends, not the public. But spirit friends had difficulty in materializing and sometimes only partially materialized. It was never again like the old days. Alec passed over to the Spirit World in 1975.

As I mentioned earlier, Mickey and Sara sat in Alec's circles many times. The stories they told us confirmed many of the facts described by Louie in her book. They described in detail many of the full materializations they witnessed.

I believe that Alec Harris was no doubt one of the most impressive (if not the most impressive) materialization medium who ever lived. He offered excellent and impressive evidence for survival. There is no doubt that he was genuine. No one could fraudulently produce as many materializations per sitting as Alec did and provide the evidence he did. Besides Mickey and Sara there were other very credible witnesses to his materializations, some of whom have been quoted above.

I will now describe the evidence provided by another very impressive materialization medium.

Tom Harrison's Circle

Another impressive materialization medium, besides Alec Harris, was Minnie Rose Harrison. In his book "Life After Death-Living Proof" (2004) her son Tom Harrison describes her mediumship, the many séances she gave and the evidence they received. He based his book on the detailed notes he kept of each sitting for the first two years. It is a book definitely worth reading and highly recommended. I will now briefly describe Minnie's mediumship and the evidence for survival that she provided.

Minnie Rose Harrison was born in 1895 and died in 1958. She was the youngest of 11 children. From her teenage years she had been clairvoyant and clairaudient and then developed into a deep-control trance medium. In 1946 a home circle was formed and called the "Saturday Night Club" by the sitters. The original purpose was to contact spirit friends through the trance mediumship of Minnie. The circle consisted of Minnie, her husband Thomas, her son Tom (the author of the book), his wife and some friends, at whose home the sittings were held just about every Saturday night. The sittings were held in the living room. The "cabinet" was a corner of the room with a chair and a curtain in front of it (just like Mickey and Sara and Alec Harris had).

They also had a trumpet that moved exactly the same way as in our circle with Mickey and Sara and as in Arthur Findlay's circle (both described earlier). To quote from Tom's book:

> "It was fascinating and exciting to watch the trumpet, which had three small spots of luminous paint on it, make rapid movements around the room, darting up to the ceiling, pirouetting around the room, gently touching some of the sitters on their knees- all in complete darkness, without knocking into the lampshades, or other pieces of furniture; quite remarkable".

From Tom's quote it can be seen that the behavior of the trumpet in their circle was very similar to what Marlene and I witnessed numerous times when sitting with Mickey and Sara and also very similar to the description by Arthur Findlay in his sittings with Sloan. This trumpet behavior shows a guiding intelligence by the spirit guides associated

Life After Death

with the circles. There is just no evidence the medium can move a trumpet by means of telekinesis or telepathy.

Initially the spirits spoke only through the trumpet in the "Saturday Night Club". Some of their regular visiting spirits were Sunrise, a Native American guide who was Minnie's main guide, Aunt Agg, one of Minnie's sisters (Aggnes Abbott) who died in 1942, Sam Hildred, the father of Gladys Shipman, in whose house the sittings were held, and Grammy Lumsden, Tom' s wife maternal grandmother.

One thing their circle experienced were apports. Very few circles have ever experienced apports. They seldom occur but in Tom's circle they were very common. Apports are every day items that are moved from outside the séance room to the inside of the room through the closed doors, windows, or walls. In just about every sitting they received fresh flowers as apports. According to their spirit guides the apport is first dematerialized, brought through the solid wall and then rematerialized inside the room.

The first reaction a reader probably has is that an apport is just not possible. How can a solid object be moved through a solid object? Initially, I was very skeptical myself, but there is enough solid, convincing evidence that apports occur. Tom Harrison mentions that they received apports just about every sitting and there is no reason to believe that he is lying. Also, Mickey and Sara told us that they got apports in Alec Harris's circles. A few other psychics have reportedly produced apports. We must keep in mind that if spirit entities can take ectoplasm from the medium and build it up into an ectoplasmic person that is often recognized by a relative or friend, speaks and walks around the room, then they can very likely dematerialize and then rematerialize solid objects. As a physicist I must stress that at the atomic level a solid object is like a piece of Swiss cheese (the one with lots of holes in it). So if they can break a solid object up into individual atoms then those atoms can easily be moved through a "solid" wall. The key is how to dematerialize and then rematerialize the object. Obviously, the spirit entities have a lot more scientific knowledge than we do since with our current scientific knowledge we would not know how to do that.

Getting back to Tom's circle, it was after eight months of sitting almost every Saturday night that they witnessed their first full materialization. Up until then they saw and felt ectoplasmic hands, but there was never enough ectoplasm for a full materialization. That particular evening they sat in red light and Minnie sat in the semi-circle of seven sitters (the "cabinet" with the curtain in the corner of the room had not yet been setup). Every one could thus very clearly see the ectoplasm come from Minnie's mouth (while she was in deep trance) and build up into a solid ectoplasmic person. That person took Tom's hand and gave him four carnations (apports). After that the ectoplasmic figure shrunk slowly towards the floor with the ectoplasm returning to the medium. Tom did not recognize the ectoplasmic figure but was told it was Aunt Agg.

During the next five sittings they had many spirits materialize. These spirit entities and the entranced medium could clearly be seen in the red light by all the sitters. It was thus definitely not the case of the medium getting dressed up in white robes or the case of some one coming in through a window or trap door. There is no reason at all to believe that Tom made up all that happened at their sittings so this is thus a case of genuine materializations.

Many of the spirits that materialized were relatives of the sitters such as Aunt Agg, Sam Hildred, Granny Lumsden and Ivy Hudson (the deceased sister of Tom's wife Doris). The sitters thus recognized these materialized spirits, all of whom came with personal greetings and messages.

Life After Death

At one of the sittings one of the regular sitters, Dr Jones, a surgeon, took the pulse of a materialized Aunt Agg. His comment was: "You'll live", at which Aunt Agg chuckled and replied "Thank you Mr. Jones, I am living and will continue to live". This showed that the materialized spirit was a solid ectoplasmic person with a pulse.

After numerous sittings the guides requested that a "cabinet" be used. In their case a corner of the room was portioned off with a black curtain (Mickey and Sara used the same setup), so that they could actually use a brighter red light. Minnie would now be behind the curtain so would not be affected by the brighter light. The spirit entities now materialized behind the curtain, in semi-darkness, which apparently took less power so as a result more entities were able to materialize at a particular sitting and stay longer in the brighter light. After several months the spirit entities walked out from behind the curtain and moved around the room. They were, however, always connected to Minnie by means of an ectoplasmic cord.

I would now like to describe a sitting of their circle in which extremely convincing evidence for survival was presented. This does not mean that the materializations of the relatives of the sitters are not evidential. It definitely is but some skeptic can always say that the sitters knew the relatives so "subconsciously" influenced the medium, or similar far-fetched attempted explanations. It is important to have a sitting with some one who was not known to the sitters or the medium.

This happened in October 1948. Roy Dixon Smith wrote a letter to "Psychic News", a weekly Spiritualist newspaper, in which he wrote that he was investigating Spiritualism and was particularly interested in "experiencing genuine materializations". One of the sitters of the Saturday Night Circle saw the letter and after discussion the circle decided to offer him the opportunity to sit with them. Roy was invited and sat with them on October 9, 1948.

Before giving his description of the sitting I will first give some biographical information about Roy. He served in the British Army in India where he met Betty in 1934. He married Betty in 1939 but their life together was very brief as Betty died of heart disease in 1944. That was when he began his determined quest for evidence of survival beyond death, through Spiritualism. He traveled far and wide in his search and sat with many well-known mediums and was given impressive evidence, but he never witnessed ectoplasmic materialization. He wrote a book in 1952 titled "New Light on Survival".

Roy was a complete stranger to all the sitters of the circle. I will now give a detailed account of Roy's sitting in their circle. The account is taken from Tom's book:

> "On the afternoon of October 9, 1948 I was met at the station by Mr. Shipman. He took me in his car to his home where I found that a bedroom had been placed at my disposal, and I was entertained freely and most hospitably for the weekend.
>
> They knew nothing whatever about me and had never heard of me (and vice-versa) until after my letter had appeared in the paper. The house was of the same general type as the one at Buckie (name of a town in Scotland where Roy previously had a sitting), my host and his friends likewise business and professional people of the same outlook and social background. The circle whom I met that evening consisted of Mr. and Mrs. Shipman, the parents of Mrs. Shipman*, Mrs. Harrison the medium, who is an intimate friend of the Shipmans' and a short and somewhat plump middle-aged lady bearing not the

least resemblance to Betty, her son and daughter–in-law, and a well-known local doctor. I mention all these details to show how utterly preposterous and ridiculous would be any suggestion of fraud, even had it been possible to produce thereby the results described.

My letter in the "Psychic News" said that I wanted these experiences to include in a book, and thus that anyone who might give them to me would, in a way, probably be rendering a public service; and that is why they answered my plea, but insisted, quite naturally, on my not disclosing their address to avoid being pestered by curiosity-mongers and others. For evidential reasons I revealed no details of my private life before the séance was over, and for the same reason they would have refused to have listened to them, since they were just as anxious as I was for genuine evidence.

The room in which the séance was held is much the same as the one at Buckie except that there is only one door, that being in the same relative position to the cabinet and the sitters as the window is in the Buckie house, while the mantelpiece is alongside and on the right of the corner that contained the cabinet. The cabinet in this case consisted of a single black curtain, which I helped to hang up myself across the corner of the room; it enclosed a space barely big enough to hold the medium on her chair.

The light during the séance was a bright red electric light bulb in a bowl suspended from the center of the ceiling. The room throughout the materializations was thus brightly illuminated and the forms and their faces clearly seen. The circle of chairs was arranged close up to and blocking the door, and thus a little farther from the cabinet than at Buckie. The door was locked and the séance commenced.

The first phase was direct voice in the dark through a luminous-banded trumpet (better called a megaphone) which darted about the room, sometimes high in the air, and often accompanying the singing like a conductor's baton. The trumpet hovered in front of the sitter to be addressed, and the voices came through, all being quite loud but some difficult to understand while others are perfectly clear. The circle guide, speaking through the trumpet, then gave an excellent description of Betty, remarking on her height, slimness, and beauty; all being facts unknown to anyone present except myself. Betty then attempted to speak to me; after prolonged and seemingly painful effort and a few exclamations to the effect that she couldn't do it, she managed to say, "I am your Betty".

During this phase, large pink carnations were apported into the room, one being dropped on each sitter's lap including mine. They were quite fresh and moist as if with dew. There were no flowers of this type previously in the room or, so my host told me, anywhere else in the house. The medium all the while had been sitting with the rest of us in the circle and was not in trance.

At the close of this phase, which seemed to me to last about a quarter of an hour, the red light was switched on. The medium took her seat behind the curtain and the materializations commenced. There were about a half dozen in all.

I was introduced to each one of them in turn; all being deceased friends and close relatives of the sitters and thus thoroughly well known to them. I rose from my chair, walked up to them and shook them by the hand, and we made conventional remarks to each other just exactly as everyone does when first meeting a stranger. They were swathed in white muslin-like draperies and cowls that were exact replicas of those worn by the forms in the Buckie séance.

They were solid, natural and, except for their apparel, exactly like ordinary people. In fact, had everyone been dressed similarly, it would have been quite impossible to distinguish these materialized forms from the rest of the company. Their hands felt perfectly natural and life-like in every respect and their hand grips were very firm. They smiled, laughed, and chatted to me and the others; all their features, complexions, and expressions being perfectly clear in the ample light.

I repeat (and surely I cannot be more explicit) they were exactly like you or me in muslin draperies, and they behaved as we would behave if we dropped in amongst a circle of friends and relations plus one stranger for a few minutes' visit, and they were welcomed accordingly and just as naturally and unemotionally as we would be. There were mutual cheery goodbyes as they departed, sinking apparently through the floor in precisely the same manner as the forms at Buckie.

My introduction to the first of them was "Come and meet Aunt Gladys" (he should have written Aunt Agg-he got the names wrong), the sister of the medium, and she was most charming and vivacious as she offered her hand and smiled and chatted to me. Then came "Grannie", and as I was presented to her the doctor said to me "Feel her pulse". The old lady chuckled, extended her arm, made some humorous remark about "mucking her about" or something to that effect, and I pressed my fingers into her wrist. All the sinews were there and the wrist felt and looked absolutely natural; the beat of the pulse was strong and regular.

"Now feel her feet", said the doctor, and I bent down and felt the foot that laughing old lady extended from her long draperies. It felt rather spongy or woolly and was apparently about to dissolve, for just after that the old lady bade us farewell and vanished. Then came a man with a twisted face drawn down rather grotesquely on the right side, as a consequence of which he could only mumble incoherently. I was introduced to him by name, and as I shook his hand my host explained, "He always comes like this. He died of a stroke".

I cannot remember the next two or three visitors very clearly, but what I said of the others applies equally to them; and by then the slight feeling of oddity at this amazing experience had left me, for it was all so absolutely natural. They all differed drastically in face figure, voice, and mannerism, and in every case their eyes were open; while, of course, the movements of their features as they laughed and talked by itself disposes of the suggestion of a set of masks, should the most unreasonable of skeptics have such an idea in mind, and should he also have such a strange opinion of human nature as to imagine that anyone would lavish free hospitality on a stranger for the sole satisfaction of tricking him.

The guide then announced the coming of Betty and asked us to sing one of her favorite songs. We sang "I'll walk beside you", in the middle of which a tall slim figure emerged from the curtain and stood silently in view.

I rose from my chair and walked up to the figure, taking the extended hand in mine. I examined the hand and it was just like Betty's and quite unlike the medium's. I stared into the face, and recognized my wife. We spoke to each other, though what we said I cannot remember, for I was deeply stirred and so was she and her voice was incoherent with emotion.

"Can he kiss you" someone asked, and Betty murmured, "Yes". I then kissed her on the lips, which were warm, soft, and natural. Thereupon she bent her head and commenced to weep, and in a moment or two she sank. I watched her form right down to the level the floor at my feet where it dissolved, the last wisp of it being drawn within the cabinet.

After I had resumed my seat, there was a pause, perhaps to allow me to recover some of my lost composure; and then the circle guide announced another visitor for me, giving the name John Fletcher, and saying that he was a clergyman who had been helping to inspire my book. Perhaps the clergyman guide referred to by the male medium in chapter 3, but of whose authenticity I was distinctly dubious.

A tall black-bearded figure then appeared, and when I reached him he gave my hand a very powerful hearty grip, expressed his delight at this meeting between us and my realization, at last, of his own reality, discussed the book with me, declared that the book was now complete, bade me a cordial

Jan W. Vandersande Ph.D.

farewell, and vanished in the usual manner.
If I once doubted the existence of guides, how can I do so now?

I have told my tale boldly, without any dramatizing or sentimental frills; it must surely be a pathetically warped mind, which cannot supply such omissions from its own imagination."

* Tom Harrison points out that there were some mistaken identities in this quote. Because everyone at the sitting was introduced to Roy just minutes before the sitting started, Tom's father was mistakenly remembered as one of Mrs. Shipman's parents, whereas only her mother, Mrs. Hildred, was present and her father, Sam Hildred, was a regular communicator from the spirit world. Aunt Gladys should, of course, be Aunt Agg, their main communicator. Gladys is Mrs. Shipman's first name (the sittings were at her home).

This is a long quote but it nicely describes what happens at a materialization sitting, what the materializations are like and how they disappear (very similar to descriptions given by others). I find this account by Roy of his sitting an outstanding case of survival evidence. Not one of the sitters knew Roy or knew about his wife Betty. So fraud can definitely be ruled out. Similarly, we can rule out Roy hallucinating that it was Betty who materialized, since everyone in the circle saw her. Finally, to suggest that it was a concocted story by Roy and Tom is just nonsense. For what reason would they do it?

One interesting point in Roy's account is the description of his guide's beard as being black. I have already shown two pictures of materializations with black beards and here is a third one. I have no explanation for why materializations have black breads.

Life After Death

Another very evidential case, in which information was given at a sitting and then had to be checked out to confirm that it was correct, will now be described in detail.

During a sitting on January 3, 1948 a young man spoke through the trumpet. He gave his name as Andrew, he had died in 1941 and had lived in Haverton Hill. He could not remember much else but promised to come again, which he did the following Saturday. This time he gave a lot more information through the trumpet. His name was James Andrew Fleming and he died when he was 12 on June 6, 1941. He had no brothers or sisters but did have a pet dog he liked very much. He thought he had lived in Coniston Avenue, or something like it, in Haverton Hill. He had tried to visit his home but he said there seemed to be a mist he could not get through. He asked the sitters in the circle to help him.

Tom was free the following Wednesday afternoon and told Andrew he would try to find his home. Haverton Hill was a village near Middlesbrough, where Tom lived. When in Havertion Hill Tom could not find Coniston Avenue but did find a Collinson Road. He asked around and found out where the Fleming family lived. When a man answered the door, Tom asked him three questions: "Did you have a son called James Andrew", "Was he about 12 years old when he died" and "Did he die on June 6, 1941"? The answer to all questions was yes. Tom was asked in and explained to Mr. and Mrs. Fleming about the sitting and how their son had spoken and given them the information needed to find them. There also was a dog who sat in front of Tom with his tail wagging vigorously, ears pricked and whining rather than barking. He usually wasn't friendly with strangers. Tom believed the dog wasn't looking at him but at James who was standing next to him. He had thus come home.

Jan W. Vandersande Ph.D.

This case presents good evidence for spirit survival since the spirit entity James came to the circle and gave information that no one knew or could have known. Tom went to check out the information provided and found it to be correct. Skeptics will use some kind of "super-ESP" to explain this case. They would argue that the medium some how acquired this information from the "collective subconscious" or the Akashic records and that it thus does not represent a case of survival evidence. As mentioned before, I find that explanation more far fetched than the survival hypothesis.

One thing they did in their circle was take photographs of some of the materializations. These photographs were taken for the benefit of Minnie who was always in complete trance when the spirits materialized. Initially the pictures were taken with the red light on and with long exposures (90-120 seconds). The last two pictures they took were taken with infrared film and an infrared flash. (Tom Harrison gave me permission to use any of the photographs in his book. The photographs shown here are of low quality because they were taken directly from his book but the materializations and the ectoplasm can still clearly be seen).

Photograph 6 (picture 6) shows ectoplasm coming from Minnie's mouth and covering her body. This photograph is very similar to picture 2 of the medium in Johannesburg and confirms how ectoplasm comes from the medium. Here we have two photographs of two different mediums, continents and decades apart, both clearly showing ectoplasm coming from their mouths and covering their bodies. The similarity does not prove that both are genuine but it does strongly suggest that since there is no reason at all to suspect either circle of being fraudulent.

Life After Death

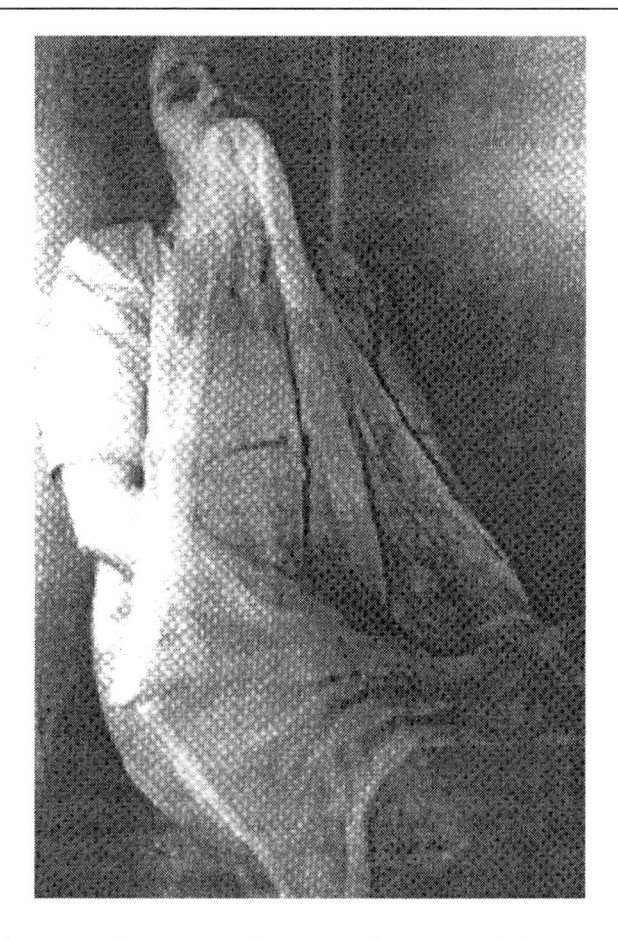

Photograph 6: Ectoplasm coming out of the mouth of Minnie Harrison and forming a sheet that covers most of the body.

This ectoplasm that came from Minnie's mouth then formed into the full materializations. The next photograph (picture 7) shows the materialization of Aunt Agg and picture 5, shown earlier, shows Tom's grandfather with the black beard. These photographs taken from Tom's book, with his permission, are not of the greatest quality. The main purpose for showing them is to show the similarity to the photographs taken of the medium in Johannesburg and the full materializations.

Photograph 7: A full materialization produced by Minnie Harrison of Aunt Agg, one of the medium's "dead" sisters.

The last photograph of Minnie (picture 8) shows how the trumpet is connected to the medium with ectoplasm, which has come from both her mouth and solar plexus. The spirit entities move the trumpet by directing or manipulating the ectoplasm. It thus does not float by itself without anything attached to it. The trumpet movement, which I have observed a large number of times and I have described happening in several circles earlier, does not itself prove survival, but it does indicate another worldly intelligence is involved. There is no way the medium, who is in trance, can somehow (using telepathy, telekinesis, etc.??) move the trumpet as I have described earlier several times. Some other intelligence clearly has to be involved.

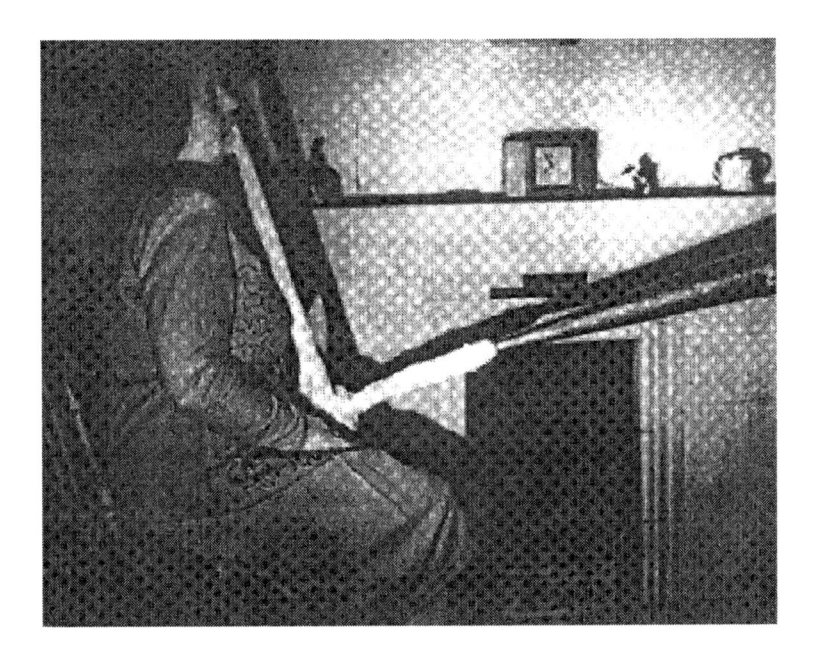

Photograph 8: Ectoplasm coming from Minnie Harrison's mouth and solar plexus and forming rods to move the trumpet.

To conclude, the book by Tom Harrison that described their home circle (the Saturday Night Club) is one of the most impressive and well-documented accounts of trumpet movements, materializations and apports. It is highly recommended.

I have no doubt that his accounts are genuine. First of all; he kept meticulous detailed accounts of each sitting, secondly; it was mainly a home circle for the benefit of the sitters, and when outsiders attended their circle there was no fee, thirdly; the independent accounts by invited sitters confirmed Tom's accounts of those sittings, fourthly; their photographs are very similar to those taken at sittings of other mediums, and lastly; what does Tom have to gain by making it all up??

Jack Webber

At this point I want to briefly discuss the physical mediumship of Jack Webber and to show some infrared photographs taken at some of his sittings. Harry Edwards, the famous spiritual healer, described Jack's mediumship in his book "The Mediumship of Jack Webber" (1940). The photographs shown here have been taken from that book.

Jack Webber was born in Wales in 1907 and died in 1940. He was introduced to Spiritualism by his wife and he discovered he had mediumistic abilities when attending a home circle. His mediumship developed very fast, finally reaching the stage of independent direct voice (like Flint and Sloan) and then materializations. He gave demonstrations in home circles and to the public. Shortly before his death he gave as many as 200 demonstrations a year. He declined the use of a cabinet and insisted on being securely tied up during a demonstration. He wanted to rule out fraud.

The first photograph (picture 9) shows ectoplasm coming out of Jack's right nostril and forming a voice box on his right shoulder. The voice box is used in independent direct voice, as described in the sections on Leslie Flint and John Sloan. The second photograph (picture 10) shows Jack in trance tied to a chair with ectoplasm coming from his mouth and attached to a trumpet. Ectoplasm also comes from his solar plexus and is connected to a second trumpet. The ectoplasmic rods move the trumpets as described earlier. I have no doubt that there is no fraud involved with Jack's mediumship because of the author's reputation, the large number of sittings that Jack gave without fraud having been discovered and because of the photographs themselves (medium tied up).

Photograph 9: Ectoplasm coming out of the right nostril of Jack Webber and forming an ectoplasmic voice box located on his right shoulder.

I wanted to show these two photographs because of the similarity between these photographs and those of Minnie and the Johannesburg medium. This similarity between the photographs of ectoplasm from three different mediums, who are definitely not fraudulent, strengthens the case for the reality of the existence of ectoplasm and materializations. Skeptics cannot counter this evidence except by arguing that it is all fraud and cheesecloth. That is such a weak argument considering the available evidence. They are just not willing to accept this evidence. There are definitely many mediums that have produced genuine ectoplasm and I have just discussed some of them. Just because there have been a lot of frauds, that does not mean that they all are frauds.

Photograph 10: Ectoplasm coming from the mouth and solar plexus of Jack Webber and forming rods attached to the two trumpets.

Life After Death

Carmine Mirabelli

Not all materialization mediums have come from Europe, the USA or South Africa. Carmine Mirabelli (1889-1950) was a Brazilian psychic who produced fantastic physical phenomena. A seventy-four page book entitled "O Medium Mirabelli" came out in Brazil in 1927. It contained accounts of phenomena produced by Mirabelli in the presence of up to sixty witnesses. I will here give some details of the phenomena he produced. I have taken the information from Victor Zammit's website and book "A Lawyer Presents the Case for the Afterlife." I have no reason to believe that that information is not correct.

Mirabelli had only a basic education and spoke only his native language of Portuguese. When in trance spirit entities spoke through him in up to twenty six different languages. Also, while in trance the spirit entities gave talks through him on subjects far beyond his own understanding.

His materializations were both in red light and in full day light (which is very rare). At a séance conducted in the morning in full daylight in the laboratory of a group of investigators including ten with the degree of Doctor of Science, some of the following materializations were observed (taken from Zammit's book):

- that of a little girl, who was confirmed by Dr. Ganymede de Souza, who was also present, to be his daughter who had died a few months before and that she was wearing the dress in which she had been buried
- another observer felt the pulse of the child and asked her several questions which she answered with understanding
- photographs of the materialization were taken and

- appended to the investigating committee's report
- after having been visible in daylight for thirty six minutes, the child floated in the air and then disappeared
- that of Bishop Jose de Camargo Barras, who had recently lost his life in a shipwreck, appeared in the full insignia of his office, conversed with those present and allowed them to examine his heart, gums, abdomen and fingers before disappearing.

At another séance in the town of Santos at three thirty in the afternoon before sixty witnesses, who attested to the report with their signatures, the following took place:

- the deceased Dr. Bezerra de Meneses, an eminent physician, materialized and spoke to all the assembled witnesses to assure them that it was indeed him
- several photographs were taken of the materialization
- two doctors, who had known him, examined him and announced that he was an anatomically normal human being
- finally he rose into the air and began to dematerialize, with his feet vanishing first followed by his legs, abdomen, chest, arms and last of all his head
- after the materialization had disappeared Mirabelli was still found to be tied securely to his chair and the seals on the doors and windows were intact
- the photographs accompanying the report show Mirabelli and the materialization on the same photographic plate.

At another séance, held under controlled conditions, Mirabelli himself dematerialized to be found in another

Life After Death

room. Yet the seals on the ropes he was tied with were intact as were the seals on the doors and windows of the séance room.

Assuming that these accounts of Mirabelli's séances are genuine (and there is no reason to believe they aren't) then Mirabelli was one of the truly great materialization mediums. I have not been able to find anyone who accused him of being a fraud. The large number of witnesses and precautions taken are impressive.

There are some interesting similarities between aspects in the above reports and some of those described earlier. Note that Mirabelli was dematerialized from one room to another room. A similar dematerialization/rematerialization was observed with Alec Harris a few times, so here we see that it has happened to at least two materialization mediums. Also, the disappearance of a materialization in a Mirabelli séance was observed in the air to go from the feet to the head, which was very similar to those observed in some of the séances described earlier in which the materializations sank into the floor with the head to disappear last.

Similarities between materialization séances continents apart and separated by decades in time, makes the case for the genuineness of materializations even stronger to me. The more well documented and photographed materializations there are, the more difficult it becomes for skeptics and critics to use the fraud card. Not everybody is a fraud or has been hoodwinked.

Current Materialization Mediums

One of the arguments used by skeptics of materialization is that there were lots of materialization mediums (all frauds according to them) in the late 1800's and early-mid

1900's but that there are few, if any, today. While there were lots of fraudulent materialization mediums in those days, there were also genuine ones who were tested over and over again as described earlier in this chapter. The question now is; are there any current (say the past two decades) materialization mediums, who have provided survival evidence, or have they died out?

There still are materialization mediums around today and I will mention two of them, but there seem to be less than there were 50-100 years ago. There are several possible reasons for this. Firstly; there are many mediums in small home circles, who never go out to demonstrate to the public (either for free or for money). The reason for that is that there is risk involved as described earlier to what happened to Alec Harris. So no one knows about these mediums unless one has been lucky enough to have been invited to their circle. Secondly; Spiritualism was very popular in the late 1800's, up to probably the mid-late 1900's. There just aren't the same number of Spiritualist churches now compared to say 50 years ago. It was at these churches that psychics demonstrated (mainly clairvoyance) and it was in development circles, usually organized by these churches, in which some mediums developed into materialization mediums.

However, there still are some excellent materialization mediums giving demonstrations today. One of them is David Thompson. I will now give two accounts by two different people that sat with him.

The first one is an account given by the well known psychic investigator Montague Keen of a sitting that took place on October 25, 2003 in Chalgrove, Oxfordshire, England. Keen witnessed the phenomena himself and described all the precautions taken. Thompson sat in a chair inside the cabinet. He was strapped to the chair by means of

Life After Death

plastic tree ties, which were permanently fixed to the legs and arms of the chair. The only way Thompson could be released was to cut the plastic ties. Also, a black gag was secured around his head and through his open mouth so that he could not talk (at least not recognizable speech).

Keen witnessed the following phenomena (all in the dark):

1. the trumpet, with luminous spots on it, was operated at great speed and with considerable precision, performing aerobic patterns in the air and occasionally touching sitters
2. his head was tapped by the trumpet several times
3. his tie was unknotted and placed on the floor next to his chair
4. he and his wife were touched by warm, soft and seemingly human hands for about 15 seconds
5. there were four very clear, loud and distinctive voices everyone heard and all the voices answered questions intelligently.

The voices belonged to entities who claimed they materialized and gave their names as: William Charles Cadwell (died 1897), Sir William Crookes (discussed earlier), a cockney youth named Timothy Booth and Louis Armstrong. All four spoke to the sitters and Louis Armstrong's characteristic voice was immediately recognized (his unique guttural pronunciation). The voices said that they had to speak through a voice box.

At one point during the sitting they were allowed to turn the red light on for a short time. The curtain in front of the cabinet was pulled aside and all the sitters could see the medium and a white substance (ectoplasm) stretching from the medium's face, across his chest to his lap. The full materializations of the spirit visitors were in the dark thus could not be seen. One of the spirit visitors (Crookes) explained that at his present stage of development, the white light or the use of an infra-red camera might do damage to the medium.

Keen summarized the sitting by stating that even though the physical phenomena were not clearly witnessed or photographed there still can be claims of evidence for the phenomena if deception on the part of the medium was impossible and could be totally ruled out. In this sitting the nature of the ties prevented the medium, no matter how strong or agile, from escaping the bonds without first managing to cut the ties. Even had he been able to do so, he could not have regained his seat and retied the knots unaided, employing a new set of uncut ties, unless he had been helped by someone able to work deftly, accurately and swiftly in the pitch dark. No-one in the séance room could have done that without being detected. Also, Keen's careful examination of the chair showed no sign of any movable join. Finally, the reversal of the medium's cardigan while he was still bonded to his seat defies normal explanation.

This is an excellent account of a direct voice, trumpet moving and materialization sitting. The precautions Keen took were superior to those taken by previous investigators. No magician, no matter how good could have gotten out of the chair David was tied to. As discussed before, even if the medium was able to release himself from the chair, it is impossible to move the trumpet around the room, touch sitters on their heads without bumping into sitters, chairs or other objects. Also, producing four distinct voices with a gag in your mouth is impossible.

I do have one concern- the materialization of famous people. I am not saying that it is not possible, but it does make me nervous. However, as long as the spirit can prop-

Life After Death

erly prove beyond any doubt (irrefutable proof) that he or she is who they claim they are, then I would have to accept it. The key is to make them provide the evidence to prove they are the person they claim to be.

David Thompson is still giving sittings and many of these have been described in detail by Victor Zammit on his website (www.victorzammit.com). Two of these sittings were in Sydney, Australia on June 30, 2006 and October 20, 2006. I have taken the following from Zammit's account of the sittings.

They took meticulous precautions to prevent fraud. The medium was strapped into a metal chair by means of secure belts and buckles firmly attached to the chair. Also used were heavy plastic one-way (self-locking) cable ties that were secured through the buckles and cut off short so that the only way they could be released was with a metal clipper. The medium had a black gag tied securely around his head through his open mouth preventing him from making any more than muffled sounds. The one window was blocked and impossible to open. The one door was locked and sealed.

The sittings were in total darkness except for a short period of time when red light was on and the sitters could see ectoplasm coming from the medium. Photographs were taken of the ectoplasm. The spirit entities that materialized in one or both of those sittings were: William, the control spirit who runs the circle, Montagne Keen, who had passed over in 2005 and actually sat with David in 2003 (see above), Arthur Conan Doyle, Louis Armstrong and a brother of a Swedish guest to the circle. These spirit entities walked in the séance room and talked to the sitters, while in some cases standing no more than half a meter away. Victor stated that he cannot validate that the materialized entities are the person they claimed they were in life. However, they all had distinctive voices. In the case of Louis Armstrong, Victor states that the voice was identical to the very characteristic voice so often heard when he was alive on earth: a deep, Southern, very resonant, uniquely friendly intonation with the same pace, rhythm, pitch and with the peculiar Louis Armstrong nuance in his communication. While Sir Arthur Conan Doyle sounded very definitive and authoritative, just like he was in life. Also, Zammit mentions in an e-mail he sent me that the content analysis of what Sir Conan Doyle said at the sitting and what he wrote while on earth shows consistency.

David Thompson is still giving weekly sittings in Australia at this writing (September 2007) and accounts of the sittings can be found on Zammit's website. He definitely appears genuine. The precautions taken by both Keen and Zammit to prevent fraud were very impressive and make fraud impossible, as far as I can ascertain.

Another British medium who has produced materialized spirits is Stewart Alexander. An account of a sitting in which he was the medium was given in the October/November 2004 issue of The Psychic Times. I will now briefly summarize the main aspects of that sitting. Two trumpets flew around the dark room without hitting anything. One of the regular communicators partly materialized and spoke to the sitters via direct voice using an ectoplasmic voice box. Other spirits also materialized, shook hands with sitters, spoke to them and gave messages. One of the sitters reported that the spirit hand he shook was very large, much larger than that of the medium Stewart. The medium was securely tied to his chair with plastic straps. Lastly, sitters reported how the ectoplasmic spirit forms sank into the floor and disappeared (as the ectoplasm returned to the medium). The description of this sitting is very similar to all the materialization sittings described above. Stewart apparently still gives regular sittings.

David Thompson and Stewart Alexander are two examples of current materialization mediums. They are not yet as advanced as mediums like Alec Harris and others who produced numerous full materializations in red light, but they do produce ectoplasm and partial/full materializations in the dark. The evidence they provide has still been very evidential to many of the sitters.

Christmas Sittings with Mickey and Sara

Mickey and Sara each year held several sittings in December called Christmas sittings. Marlene and I attended a few of them. Typically 6-10 people were invited to each sitting. Everyone was asked to bring a wrapped present, which was given to charity. The séance room was set up as usual but now small toy musical instruments had been placed on the floor in the center of the circle. The instruments were toy whistles, a drum, a trumpet and mechanical friction toys. There was also the usual trumpet with its luminous spots. As usual, Mickey and Sara sat in the corner of the room behind a black curtain.

The sitting started as usual with Brian coming through Sara to talk to each sitter. After Brian had spoken to every sitter for several minutes the trumpet started flying around the room touching each sitter on the head and/or the knees (this has been described in earlier sections in detail). This all happened in the dark. At this point, after the trumpet had returned to its position on the floor near the curtain, the real purpose of the sitting started.

All of a sudden all or just about all of the instruments started playing. It sounded like at least three to four were being played at the same time. We were told by Brian that several spirit children had materialized and were playing the instruments. It was dark so we could of course not see the spirit children materializations except when a friction toy gave off some sparks and parts of an ectoplasmic child's body could be seen for an instant. It is extremely unlikely, if not totally impossible, for Mickey and Sara to have crawled out from behind the curtain and to have started playing the instruments. The room was small and there just wasn't enough room for two (or even one) adults to crawl from behind the curtain, past sitters without touching them, finding the toys and then playing then, all in the pitch dark.

After the spirit children played the toy instruments for a while, they stopped and everything became quite. At this point some of the sitters started feeling little hands touch their hands or pull on their pants. Marlene said she felt several small fingers touch her hand. I had someone pull on my pants just below my knee. It was difficult to tell if it was a small or large hand doing the pulling, to be honest. Not one of the sitters mentioned that anyone bumped into him or her. It clearly appears that the spirit children could see in the dark.

When the touching had ended, the spirit children started unwrapping the presents that the sitters had brought and which had been placed in the center of the circle with the toy musical instruments. After several minutes all presents had been unwrapped but, those in boxes were left unopened. Then finally there was some more playing of the musical instruments and when that finished the spirit children were gone. Brian came back to talk to us and closed the sitting.

Marlene and I really enjoyed these sittings and apparently so did the spirit children. As I mentioned earlier it would have been impossible for Mickey and Sara and/or

Life After Death

other sitters to have done what we heard and experienced. To do all that in the dark, in a small circle, with the floor in the center of the circle covered with presents and musical instruments, without bumping into sitters or standing on what was on the floor and then touching sitters on their hands or pants is impossible unless you could see where everything was. The spirit children obviously could see everything.

These Christmas sittings do not prove survival after death per se, but do indicate the presence of materialized spirit forms that have intelligence and can do this in the dark that we humans cannot. I have no doubt that spirit children materialized, even though the evidence is somewhat circumstantial except for those brief instants when parts of spirit children's bodies could be seen. I definitely wanted to mention these sittings because to me they just add one more piece of evidence that there is something after death.

In this chapter on materialization I believe I have presented some of the best evidence for life after death. The cases presented are of mediums that are beyond any doubt genuine (fraud has clearly been ruled out) and the evidence provided is some of the best I could find and have experienced myself. Skeptics cannot use their usual fraud card so will have to use the "super-ESP" card to explain the phenomena, or resort to a carefully manipulated conspiracy among the medium and the sitters (which is just ludicrous and impossible). The materialization of deceased spirits is a lot more believable than some nebulous "super-ESP" explanation.

My Meeting with a Magician and Victor Zammit's Challenges

In this short chapter I want to briefly mention my meeting with a stage magician-illusionist (a well known psychic debunker) and want to mention the challenges Victor Zammit has made to all skeptics and debunkers.

I was a visiting Associate Professor in the Physics Department at Cornell University in 1982-1983. The magician, James Hamilton Zwinge Randi, visited Cornell at that time and any scientist who wanted to meet with him personally to discuss psychic phenomena had the opportunity to do so. Randi called himself an open-minded psychic investigator so I thought I would show him the pictures of the ectoplasm and materializations produced by the Johannesburg medium (pictures 1-4). I was given a time to meet with him and at the meeting I showed him the four pictures. He looked at each picture for at most one second each and immediately said: "This is fraud. I can do this". He did not ask me one thing about the pictures, such as when were they taken, how they were taken, what precautions were taken, who the medium was, etc. Those are the questions he would have asked if he were a genuine investigator, but he showed no interest at all in them. All he would say that it was fraud and he could do the same. I told him that in no way he could produce ectoplasm, but he continued to say that it was fraud and ectoplasm did not exist.

I also told him about the trumpets we observed flying around the room in sittings over a period of eight years. His reply again was that it was fraud. That was his reply to everything we discussed; "it is fraud and he can do that." As you can imagine I was very surprised and frustrated that this "psychic investigator" was not interested in hearing any facts or the details about what I had observed. He obviously was a debunker of anything psychic.

Randi now has a million dollar challenge. He will pay this amount to anyone who can provide convincing evidence of any paranormal, occult or supernormal event of any kind under proper test conditions. However, there is the small print to the challenge with numerous conditions, which make it very difficult for anyone to provide this evidence. Psychic investigator Montague Keen (mentioned earlier) wrote two articles on Randi: one on "The Ultimate Psychic Challenge" (a TV show shown in England in 2003 which Randi appeared in) and one on Randi's challenge. The articles are titled "The Ultimate Psychic Challenge - A Challenge to James Randi" and "A Further Response to James Randi". Both can be found on the website: www.survivalafterdeath.org under "articles" and under "Montague Keen". These articles are worth reading. They go to show to what ridiculous extremes skeptics and debunkers will go to try to show that all psychic phenomena are fraudulent, or miss-observation or whatever else they can come up with.

Keen points out in one of the articles that a survey of magicians specializing in psychic entertainment showed that four fifths of them believe in the existence of extrasensory perception!! He believes that is based on their close observations of those with psychic powers.

Life After Death

Victor Zammit (mentioned earlier) has an excellent website; www.victorzammit.com and has written an excellent book, "A Lawyer Presents the Case for the Afterlife". Both the book and the website are highly recommended.

Zammit has issued his own one million dollar challenge to anyone who can rebut his objective evidence (expressly stated in 23 areas) for the existence of the afterlife. The challenger must show why the evidence Zammit presents for the existence of the afterlife cannot be admissible. He expressly made the challenge to Randi, who Zammit on his website calls a debunker, materialist, closed-minded skeptic. According to Zammit, Randi confessed to scientist Dr. Dennis Rawlings "I will always have a way out" referring to his own alleged challenge to psychics. Also, according to Zammit, Randi recently stated that "all psychics are vultures". With this kind of attitude, how can he be qualified to test mediums and psychics? So far (almost nine years later) no one has taken Zammit on to win the million dollars.

Obviously, I was pleased to read the articles by Keen and the comments by Zammit because they confirmed the experience I had with Randi. It confirmed to me that he is not an unbiased investigator but someone who makes a good living by being a psychic debunker.

Zammit has also issued a sponsored half million dollar challenge to anyone, especially skeptics and debunkers, who can duplicate the materializations produced by David Thompson (discussed in the chapter on Materialization) by means of fraudulent methods or who can show that Thompson's materializations are produced by fraud. The conditions of the challenge are: neither party (Thompson and challenger) would know where the venue was until two minutes before the experiment and all the sitters and the medium would have to be tied to their chair or to each other by experts. Then if the skeptic or debunker cannot duplicate the materializations produced by Thompson by any fraudulent method or cannot show his materializations are produced by fraud, they would have to pay Thompson half a million dollars. If they can duplicate the materializations then they get the money. No one has taken up this challenge.

Well Randi, you told me you could duplicate the materializations on the photographs I showed you, so here is your chance. Take up Zammit's challenge to prove that you can do what you have claimed you can do. If you don't, then I think you should stick to your magic tricks.

The reason I mention my meeting with Randi is to show that there are skeptics who claim to be interested in investigating psychic phenomena, but in reality are nothing but debunkers. They appear on T.V. and get lots of airtime and press, but unfortunately do not present a genuinely unbiased position. That is very unfortunate because, as I have shown in this book, there are genuine and good mediums who provide evidence for the afterlife.

Conclusion

In this book I have tried to describe in considerable detail some of the best evidence that I am aware of for life after death. I have based this evidence on my own experiences which included sittings with trace mediums and channelers as well as sitting quite regularly for eight years in a circle with Mickey and Sara Wolf.

It was in those circles that we experienced flying trumpets, direct voice and ectoplasm. Those experiences changed my life in at least two ways. Firstly, it gave me the conviction that there is life after death. Secondly, it made it possible for me to be able to critically read much of the literature about psychic and paranormal phenomena.

If we had not experienced the flying trumpets in the dark ourselves, I would never have believed the accounts given by many in their books and articles, such as the accounts by Findlay, Harrison and others. Similarly, if we had not seen ectoplasm ourselves, I would never have believed the accounts by others, no matter how reputable they were. Also, our good friends Mickey and Sara Wolf and Professor Jack Allen, whose descriptions of their first hand observations of full materializations with Alec Harris and the Johannesburg medium, respectively, increased our understanding of these phenomena and convinced us that they were real. Hence, I feel that my experiences give me the credibility to report on what I experienced and to choose from the literature those psychic phenomena and cases that provide the best evidence for life after death.

I am sure that there is a lot of good evidence for life after death but I only wanted to present what are to me some of the best cases I have come across. I could have presented many more cases but felt that I have given you, the reader, enough to hopefully give you enough material that you can now seriously consider the possibility of life after death. For those of you who already believe in life after death I hope I have made your belief even stronger. I also hope I have whet your appetite about psychic phenomena and hopefully you will delve into the subject more on your own accord. I have given several references and recommendations for additional reading and research.

I have also pointed out the many pitfalls and the fraud that exists in this field of psychic phenomena so hopefully you are now much better informed. If you do have the chance to sit with a channeler or trance medium then please follow the advice I have given. If you ever have the opportunity to sit in a circle to witness flying trumpets, or direct voice or ectoplasm then grab it with both hands. They are experiences you don't ever want to miss, assuming of course it is genuine - always be on the lookout for fraud.

As I mentioned several times, even great mediums have off days, so if you ever have a bad sitting don't give up. Try again. There are good mediums out there.

I have tried in great detail to refute the criticism of the skeptics and debunkers. I believe that their theories and hypotheses such as "super-ESP" are much more far fetched than the survival hypothesis. Especially considering that nothing we have so far learned about ESP (e.g. the laboratory telepathy experiments) gives the skeptics the right to claim that "super-ESP" can do what the hypothesis requires of it, such as telepathically tapping into sitters and other

Life After Death

living people's minds (memory stores) and clairvoyantly scanning archives, records, universal subconscious, etc. in order to gather the information needed.

The other criticism of psychic phenomena the skeptics use is that of fraud. There have been a large number of fraudulent mediums, many of whom were exposed by skeptics. However, as I discussed in detail the mediums whose evidence for survival I have presented, all took precautions to eliminate fraud and some were extensively tested. None of them were ever found to be fraudulent. The precautions taken nowadays at materialization sittings such as with David Thompson make fraud impossible. No skeptic, debunker or magician has taken up the half million dollar challenge offered by Victor Zammit to duplicate the materializations produced by Thompson by any fraudulent method, or to show that Thompson's materialization are produced by fraud. That tells you that the skeptics and debunkers are all talk and no action.

I would like to end with a question Victor Zammit asked me when we met in Las Vegas in late June 2007: What did I consider the best evidence for survival after death that I witnessed myself? After giving it some thought I replied that I thought that the trumpets flying around the room in the complete dark was the best evidence I experienced. He was surprised and asked me why. I replied that the only explanation for the trumpets flying around the room, without hitting anything and gently touching the sitters on the head and other places, had to be due to an intelligence, other than that of the medium, directing the trumpet to move using ectoplasm from the medium. This directing intelligence would imply that there is another dimension where this intelligence/spirit resides and that is in the "hereafter". The subconscious of the medium cannot be responsible for the trumpet moving since the medium was

Jan W. Vandersande Ph.D.

in trance and the room was completely dark.

It is not the purpose of this book to discuss what it is that exactly survives death and what the spirit world is like. There are many books that discuss those topics and I recommend those of you who are interested to do additional reading.

Unfortunately we never saw full materializations ourselves (but we did see sheets of ectoplasm and did touch spirit children's hands) otherwise I would have answered that the best proof is a full materialization that one recognizes to be a relative or friend who then speaks to you. Unfortunately only very few people have been lucky enough to have witnessed full materializations. I hope that my descriptions and photographs of materialization sittings have given you the reader some of the best evidence for life after death.

Bibliography

Considerable information was obtained from the website: www.survivalafterdeath.org
This website has photographs of ectoplasm and full materializations:
- Florence Cook and Katie King
- Minnie Harrison
- Jack Webber
- Others

This website has the following papers that I have used as references:

Barnard, G.C. (1933) "Materializations"
Dingwall, E. and Langdon-Davis, J. (1956) "Mental Mediums and Survival"
Edwards, E. (1940) "Materialized Forms of Jack Webber"
Goldston, W. (1932) "Helen Duncan Confounds the Magicians"
Hart, H. (1959) "Dodds and Murphy versus Drayton Thomas"
Keen, M. (2002) "Super-PSI or Survival? A Response to Prof. Stephen Braude"
Keen, M (2003) "The Ultimate Psychic Challenge- A Challenge to James Randi"
Keen, M. (2003) "A Further Response to James Randi"
Orman, A. (1998) "A Discussion on the Evidence for Survival"
West, D. (1954) "Séance-Room Phenomena"

Another website that contains a lot of information is: www.victorzammit.com and some information was obtained from it.

Other books and articles that were used as references are:

Alvarado, C.S. (2003), "The Concept of Survival of Bodily Death and the Development of Parapsychology" J. of the Society for Psychical Research, Vol 67.2, number 871

Blum, D. (2006) "Ghost Hunters", Penguin Press, New York

Braude, S. (1992) "Survival or Super-PSI"? Journal for Scientific Exploration, Vol 6,

Edwards, H. (1940) "The Mediumship of Jack Webber", Rider & Co, London

Findlay, A. (1931) "On the Edge of the Etheric", Psychic Press Ltd., London

Flint, L. (1971) "Voices in the Dark", Macmillan, London

Gauld, A. (1983) "Mediumship and Survival", Paladin Books, London

Hart, H. (1959) "The Enigma of Survival", Rider, London

Harris, L. (1980) "They Walked Among Us", Psychic Press Ltd., London

Martin, J. and Romanowski, P. (1988) "We Don't Die: George Anderson's Conversations with the Other Side", Berkley Books, New York

Price, H. (1939) "Fifty Years of Psychical Research", Longmans, Green & Co.

Roach, M. (2005) "Spook", W.W. Norton & Co., New York

Schwartz, G.E. and Simon, W.L. (2002) "The Afterlife Experiments", Pocket Books, New York

Sutton, L. (2004) "Sitters Witness Spirit Fingers during Séance", The Psychic Times, October/November 2004.

Zammit, V. (1996) "A Lawyer Presents the Case for the Afterlife", Ganmell Pty., Sydney

Printed in the United Kingdom
by Lightning Source UK Ltd.
129614UK00001B/121/P